SECOND LIVES

Tim Guest

HUTCHINSON
LONDON

Published by Hutchinson in 2007

2 4 6 8 10 9 7 5 3 1

First published in Great Britain in 2007 by Hutchinson
Random House, 20 Vauxhall Bridge Road, London SW1V 2SA

www.randomhouse.co.uk

Addresses for companies within The Random House Group Limited can be found at:
www.randomhouse.co.uk/offices.htm

The Random House Group Limited Reg. No. 954009

A CIP catalogue record for this book is available
from the British Library

ISBN 9780091796570

The Random House Group Limited makes every effort to ensure that the papers used
in its books are made from trees that have been legally sourced from well-managed
and credibly certified forests. Our paper procurement policy can be found at:
www.random house.co.uk/paper.htm

Typeset in Sabon by Palimpsest Book Production Limited,
Grangemouth, Stirlingshire

Printed in the UK by CPI Mackays, Chatham ME5 8TD

CONTENTS

1

INTRODUCTION
Through the electronic looking glass

When I pulled up at the Evergreen Center – a single-floor, low-eaved building in Mattapan, on the outskirts of Boston, and daytime home for 37 men and women, all severely mentally or physically disabled – the last thing I expected was mischief.

I was already stunned from the journey. The day before, my London home had been burgled, and my laptop stolen. I had a last-minute work-visa problem, which led to careful and selective explanation at US immigration. At JFK airport, I had rented a cellphone; in the cab from JFK airport, I had lost the cellphone. I spent a sleepless night slumped at a coffee bar in New York's Penn Station. Above me, on a wall-mounted TV, a gaggle of models and actresses, who hoped to boil away their sorrows in the bright light of celebrity, shut their eyes, dreamed of a better life, and ate cockroaches by the bucket. After the 4 a.m. Boston train, I followed my directions all the way to the wrong end of Boston's Red Line subway. I called to report the loss of my cellphone, and headed back to the other end of the line. So when I slid down a bank of grey snow and into the passenger seat of June-Marie Mahay's dented silver Mercury Lynx, with all my bags in tow (there had been no time to check into a hotel), I was exhausted.

June-Marie, a freckly, frizzy-haired redhead of about 40, hunched forward over the steering wheel and cackled. 'You think you've had it bad!' she said. She told me about the last trip she'd made with 'Wilde', the group of nine men and women with severe cerebral palsy and mental retardation who were the focus of her care work at Evergreen, and who were also the reason for my visit. At the Boston Logan airport security checkpoint, each of the group in turn was lifted from their wheelchairs and thoroughly searched because, she told me, 'there are so many places they could hide something.' The searches, in full public view, took the better part of an hour. Then, on the return journey, the nine were searched again. Their humiliation was such that June-Marie swore it was the last time. 'I'm never taking them on a plane again,' she said. But the nine had found other ways to conquer distance.

At the Evergreen Center, June-Marie led me along a series of blue-walled hallways to the main playroom. There, among the Evergreen residents – busy with magazines, jigsaws or portable radios – she introduced me to the nine she called her 'posse'. Almost immediately, the mischief began. June-Marie introduced me first to a woman in a wheelchair, in a shiny red down jacket, her black Smurf hat pulled low. 'This is Johanna Goode. Johanna has severe cerebral palsy,' June-Marie said. 'She's in her sixties. Would you believe it?' I shook my head. Johanna's arms twisted, and her jaw writhed in pleasure. 'Watch out for her,' June-Marie said loudly. 'I call her Johanna Bad.' Johanna giggled. 'She does bad things. Right, Johanna? Don't go near any open closets while Johanna's near. She's liable to lock you in.' Johanna reached out to grab at my arm. June-Marie playfully batted her hand away.

A big, round black man strolled up. He wore large, thick-rimmed glasses, an oversized Super Bowl T-shirt, and a bushel of gold-plate necklaces. 'I'm Micah. Playstation, computers, and fuzzy posters,' he said, by way of introduction. Micah looked puffed-up: his chin rolled and his ankles were wide. His words were muffled, delivered half through his nose, but Micah could walk and speak. (Micah had 'mild mental retardation', June-Marie later explained. 'Although he prefers the term "special needs".')

Micah handed June-Marie a printed form. Since his last doctor visit, she read, Micah had lost 15 pounds. 'You know what? We are not our bodies,' June-Marie told him. 'We are the good stuff that's inside. But I'm happy for ya, Micah.'

There were no name-badges; the Evergreen Center made no clear distinction between residents and staff. As we walked around the playroom, I faced everyone with the same cautious smile: I wasn't sure if they were going to offer coffee, or ask for help with a jigsaw. Micah tagged along by June-Marie's side. 'Micah's always trying to take Scott into my office for a wild party,' June-Marie said. 'Eh, Micah?'

Micah nodded. He shifted his bulk from side to side. 'Yes, Mina.' (Micah calls her 'Mina', June-Marie later explained, because he likes the sound of Spanish.) 'And ... and ... I'm always trying to steal your car,' he said.

Scott Soriano, Micah's party-pal, wasn't there. Earlier that morning, June-Marie explained, Scott had spilled a drink on his cushion: he was taken into another room, and removed from his wheelchair. Because of staff shortages and spin-cycle times – there are no spare cushions – for most of the day, until the cushion is clean and dry, Scott would have to sit in another room, outside of his chair and away from his friends.

Next to greet us was a grey-haired lady, also with cerebral palsy, who looked to be in her late fifties, but who I later discovered was 69: Mary Boucher. Mary lifted her head from a Sears catalogue and greeted June-Marie with a moan. Her tongue slid out and to the side. She reached up and shook hands by mashing her fingers with June-Marie's. 'This is Mary,' June-Marie said. 'Mary likes to kick me in my butt when my back is turned.'

Mary nodded. 'Yeah,' she mouthed. Next to Mary was a man in his late sixties, wearing a grey Martha's Vineyard sweatshirt, also in a wheelchair. He spoke in a low, gravely voice, with long stretched syllables I didn't understand. June-Marie leaned in over his chair. 'Hey Danny. Will you pull me up? Is that what you're asking?' Danny nodded. 'One, two, three . . .' June-Marie said, and gave Danny a sharp tug upwards. 'Better?' Danny moaned in agreement. 'Danny has been Johanna's partner for 50 years,' June-Marie said. (I later discovered, because of their cerebral palsy, over that half-century, Danny and Johanna had never been on a romantic date alone.) June-Marie touched his shoulder. 'Hey Danny. Do you want to say something about yourself?' Danny spoke to me, and June-Marie translated.

'My name is Daniel Spinelli. I have cerebral palsy.' Danny tapped his forehead. 'I'm all here.' (Later, June-Marie told me Danny loved coffee, but his condition was so severe it was hard for him to drink fluids, even through his adaptive straw.) 'I've got a brother. I'm getting a new apartment. I like to do what I like to do. I don't like being in a group home.'

'Danny's been to Washington DC and protested for the rights of people in nursing homes,' June-Marie said. 'He won $400 in Vegas, and he brought none of it home.'

Danny grinned.

In this way, June-Marie led me around to room to meet the rest of Wilde. There was Nichole Daley, a short black woman in her early twenties. When June-Marie introduced her, Nichole smiled and rolled her head from side to side, but said nothing. June-Marie hugged her and we moved on. (Behind us, I noticed another staff member brush past, and Nichole recoiled as if from a static shock.) There was Charlene Lessonary, also a black woman in her early twenties, also with cerebral palsy. Charlene could speak, but her condition had affected her vocal cords. Her voice was high, and she warbled like a songbird. Beside Charlene was an older, white man in a wheelchair, his shirt buttoned up to the top, a black beret at a dapper angle. This was John Gray, 54. John G. had mild mental retardation, but was also mute: he couldn't sign a word, June-Marie explained, but he smiled often. June-Marie leaned in, and John G. kissed her on the cheek three times. 'John G.'s been in a work programme all his life,' she told me. (She later explained he had spent 40 years on an assembly line.) 'He likes 50s music, but he's now starting to get interested in computers.'

Finally, June-Marie introduced me to John Salkowski, a 31-year-old quadriplegic with severe cerebral palsy. 'This is John S.' He had virtually no limb control and radically limited speech, she explained. John moaned, and looked up at June-Marie with pleading eyes. She leant down close to John's face. 'Shall I talk about you, John?' John nodded. 'OK. John likes to stand up for who he is. He's sensitive, insightful, and caring. John has a ravenous hunger for knowledge. I call him hungry sponge. He wants to write more, spend longer online. His dad is in the Boston Symphonic Orchestra; it's a blessing and a curse.' (She later explained John's father's position had instilled a love of culture in John – he had the strongest education in the group, having taken college courses – but there were times when the last thing John wanted to hear was a piece of classical music.)

Then June-Marie straightened up and clapped. 'OK guys! It's time to go through to the computer room.' The eight remaining members of Wilde headed for the door. They were excited, and they wanted to let the world know: their journey to the computer room began in a hullabaloo of moans, grunts, shrieks, and whistles.

Mary threw her Sears catalogue into her lap and squawked. June-Marie understood. 'Can I come too? Is that what you're asking? No, Mary, of course you can't. You're never welcome!' Mary's mouth formed a crooked oval; she croaked with laughter. (I later discovered that June-Marie's question, and Mary's answer, had been the same for years.)

Mary's hands jerked involuntarily, and her electronic wheelchair rammed into the doorframe. 'OK Mary, I'll help you get through,' June-Marie said. One by one, the others began to walk, or push the joysticks of their wheelchairs, toward the playroom door. Danny wheeled by with a grin; a thin line of dribble ran down onto his sweatshirt. As her 'clients', as she called them, passed her in the doorway, June-Marie touched each one: her hand on an arm, her waist against a shoulder. Her biggest embrace today was for John S.: she leaned in and pressed her body against his. His face writhed in pleasure.

The eight filed down the blue-walled corridors of the Evergreen Center, past doors marked 'Art Room' and 'Exercise Room'. 'Basketball!' Micah said, pointing to the latter.

'It's computer time,' June-Marie told him. 'You can shoot a few hoops later, OK Micah?'

Micah shuffled from side to side: 'Mmm-kay'. As the group filed into the computer room, another care worker, Ruby – a thin black woman with a blue wool hat and dreadlocks – smiled at the group. 'Where's Scotty?' she asked. June-Marie shrugged and pointed down the corridor. Ruby tutted, and strode away.

Micah tugged again at June-Marie's arm. 'Mina? Can I borrow your car?' he asked.

'Where are you taking it?' June-Marie asked.

'California!'

In retrospect, I should have guessed the group would be so

mischievous. Like all comedy, their mischief was a trick, a sleight of hand through which the group could retrieve some of the power and agency they had lacked all their lives. Their unruly impulses were a celebration of triumph over sorrow, and the reason I came to visit Evergreen was because Wilde had discovered a different, technological means to transcend their daily struggle.

The computer room, twelve feet by ten, was just big enough. Everybody jostled into place, until a jumble of wheelchairs faced the blank far wall. June-Marie squeezed round behind the door to boot up the computer. After a moment a projector, balanced on the edge of the one rickety table, flickered on. A scene appeared, stretched five feet square across the wall. It was pastoral view: green grass, trees, a grey-brick church spire, all drawn in the clear, perfect lines and shades of computer graphics. Next to the church, piece-by-piece, a man appeared. First came his broad torso, then thick, spiky hair and long pointy ears. His skin, oddly grey, suddenly turned orange. His spiky hair bled with colour, from grey into bright red. The group cheered. After a few seconds, the man's clothes – baggy blue pants and a Boston Red Sox T-shirt emblazoned with 'Who's Your Pap?' – materialised. The group cheered again. The computer-generated man projected on the wall was Wilde Cunningham, the groups' alter ego. According to the group, Wilde Cunningham was the reason their time with the computer was the most important time of their lives.

The image on the wall was a window into a virtual world called 'Second Life'. In the real world, Second Life existed only as ones and zeros on the hard drives of 700 Debian Linux servers in a San Francisco data warehouse. The Second Life computers functioned like web servers, only, instead of serving up web pages, they served up a whole world. All the buildings, objects and terrain the group could see were computer-generated; the other people, who also paid to inhabit this virtual world, looked digital, but were controlled by real people from all across the real world. Second Life was launched in June 2003, with 500 'residents'. When I visited Wilde, Second Life was home to 25,000 people from more than 70 real-world countries who logged on to share this new, idealised place.

Twice a week, for an hour at a time, the nine entered the world of Wilde, as a cinema audience enters the world of a film. Unlike with film, though, when the Evergreen residents sat in front of this screen, they weren't just witnesses. They journeyed further: through the electronic looking glass of their computer screen, and into the ideal world we could see on the other side. Just like the cinema screen, virtual worlds like Second Life have the capacity to entrance us, to make us forget ourselves. In their time with the computer, the group didn't just watch Wilde: they *became* him.

As Wilde, they were liberated from their daily plight. As Wilde, they could walk. As Wilde, they could dress themselves. As Wilde, they could pilot an airplane, walk the sea floor, live on a tropical island, visit hell. As Wilde, they were eloquent, funny, and they could fly.

'Look at me!' Mary squealed. She pointed a crooked arm at her shared alternate self on the wall. 'I'm so beautiful!'

2

EXODUS

Leaving the real world behind

I remember the first time I, too, felt alive in a virtual world. It was when I first met the digital version of June-Marie, a month before my visit in person. Then, I didn't have to travel for two sleepless nights. I didn't have to lose a cellphone, risk deportation, or carry my bags both ways across town. Then, I used a computer to conquer the distance. Meeting Wilde in the real world took two days; meeting Wilde Cunningham online took two seconds. I leaned forward at my desk, and clicked my mouse button.

My trajectory towards that moment, though – my own journey through the electronic looking glass – took years. When I was nine years old, my favourite thing in the world was to go with my father to the video arcades. We travelled through air-conditioned malls to the rooms full of blinking game cabinets, where we entered simple, line-drawn science fiction and fantasy worlds – Gauntlet, Indiana Jones and the Temple of Doom, Marble Madness – paying our way a quarter at a time. We yanked on the joysticks and bashed the plastic buttons as fast as we could, and we became other people, and other things: a wizard battling ghosts and thieves; Indiana Jones, garrotting thuggee guards; a marble, lost in a crazy chequerboard maze. For me, these games were my ecstasy, our time in those air-conditioned arcades a kind of rapture. I was transported. I could become someone else, but remain myself. I could kill, but go unpunished. I could die, but live.

In later years, I persuaded my father to buy a home games console, and we played the same games at home; after my real-world martial arts class, I plugged in our Atari console to practise kung fu on the living room television. I preferred the ease of my virtual kicks to the hard work of stretches and push-ups in the real-world community hall. (I wasn't alone – our console, the Atari 2600, eventually sold 40 million units.) I wouldn't have been able to articulate it then, but the thrill I felt was from my first shaky steps through the glass. I had dipped my toe into that perfect world. There I was – look, that was me – *inside the TV*.

In later years, my father and I lived mostly apart, but when we were together, we played computer games again. By then, the games were more complex: 3D worlds instead of 2D side-on views. We explored dungeons; I took control of our computer-generated self while he traced our steps on graph paper. To find our way together, we drew careful maps of non-existent places. Later, for years, I left computer games alone.

Then, in the mid-nineties – in my mid-twenties – I began to play games again. I had a boring job, I was broke, and my relationship was a struggle, so, as an experiment and a distraction, I bought a PlayStation console. Most games, though, seemed to transport me into a world as dull as my own. I gave them a chance: I mowed down demons with machine guns, but turned down the death-metal soundtrack. Most of the games I bought•felt like spending time in the company of a teenage metal-head. But here and there, within these budding virtual spaces, I caught glimpses of something more perceptive and revealing. Games offered us the experience we desired – adventure, importance, ease of motion – without any physical challenge or change. It seemed a world both full and hollow. 'Nought's had, all's spent / Where our desire is got without content,' wrote Shakespeare in *Macbeth* – a quote repeated by the agent handler Colonel Campbell, as advice to the bandana-wearing black-ops mercenary Solid Snake, as he guided him to destroy a top-secret undersea robot, in Metal Gear Solid 2, a 2001 PlayStation 2 game. When, after destroying a power plant that had been commandeered by operatives from the renegade terrorist group Dead Cell, I read this quote – delivered to your in-game character through an in-ear microphone – I was intrigued. It seemed to show a new kind of self-consciousness about video games: their gift (experience without risk), and their curse (experience without risk).

Soon, though, I gave up on the PlayStation. Games left my life again. Then, as I approached thirty, the pressures of life seemed to increase exponentially. I looked for distraction again inside another game: EverQuest, an online fantasy game, where you sat in front of your PC, logged as a gnome, dwarf, or human, and hunted animals and the un-dead. I knew EverQuest was an online game, and that up to half a million players logged in to share the game world. I knew, too, that many players found their online life so compelling the game was soon dubbed 'EverCrack' – but I assumed EverQuest would be much the same as the games I already knew. Instead, I entered what seemed like an entire new world. I discovered that players gathered in tunnels to create their own bazaars, trading gold and armour for magical items and pieces of information about the game. I discovered some players identified so much with their EverQuest characters that they held marriage ceremonies, traded virtual rings and shared virtual bank accounts – with people they'd only ever met in the game. (This last part worried my then-girlfriend, who insisted I play as an ugly gnome; to make the point clear, she christened my new, squat self 'Funnyface'.) Without thinking, I assumed most of these players were the kind of people who pitched tents to see science fiction film premieres, and who spoke invented languages. Still, there I was again, inside the TV; and this time other people were there with me.

I played Funnyface for months, hunting rats then lions then bears, until I trekked across the world – it took hours – to the desert, where I hunted crocodiles. The world was repetitive – more repetitive, in fact, then the world I was trying to leave behind – but compulsive, too. Somehow, being liberated from my particular anxieties made the smaller, safer anxieties of the online world infinitely more appealing. I began to play other online games, too. For a few months I logged on to Star Wars Galaxies, another multi-player world, billed as a chance to live inside the Star Wars universe. I rode land-speeders across deserts and seas, met Jedi Knights, and bought my own droid, which beeped and followed me around.

I had no idea of the scope of these worlds: the number of people who inhabited them; that Marshall McLuhan's global village was now a real place, although it was more of a global universe, populated by millions. But, in these new virtual spaces, free from many of the pressures of the modern world, I could see something was being born. Then, I met Wilde.

I first read about Wilde online, in a journal written by Wagner James Au, then employed by Linden Lab, the producers of Second Life. In his blog, James Au interviewed Wilde and June-Marie Mahay. I emailed June-Marie. For days, we missed each other's calls, until finally she suggested we meet online, 'at her place': her own plot of land inside Second Life.

I had heard about Second Life, a more free-form virtual world, some time before, and had created an account – named Errol

12

O'Flynn, after the dapper self I planned to create – but I'd never actually logged on. Then, when it came time to meet June-Marie, my previous virtual self seemed to have expired. I couldn't log on. I emailed Linden Lab to see if I could reactivate the account; they mailed back. The account could be reactivated, but my virtual surname – O'Flynn – had expired. They'd given me a new name: I was now Errol Mysterio. To prepare for my meeting with June-Marie, I logged into Second Life, and I built myself anew.

When you first log into a virtual world, you sculpt your own virtual self to define how others will see you. In some worlds the process is basic: you choose from a set of pre-made characters, then you choose from a range of pre-selected paunches, chins and haircuts. It's a kind of virtual Mr Potato Head, which can lead to world full of oddly similar people. In some worlds, like Second Life, the process is more complex. In these places, you can customise hundreds of details – eye colour, face shape, height, even pot-belly width – to suit your ideal self-image. When I joined Second Life for the second time, I tried to recreate my offline self as accurately as possible. I stretched my character up to be tall and skinny, and pulled the virtual muscles of my new face until they resembled my real self. Then I added muscle tone (perhaps just a little more than my actual body).

Before I met June-Marie I had a few hours to kill, so I spent some time inhabiting my new virtual shoes. First, though, I had to choose them. In most virtual worlds, including Second Life, you can choose your clothes as well as your self. Each new Second Life character comes equipped with a range of basic clothes, free to every new user. I donned a grey T-shirt and blue tennis shoes, and placed a virtual flat-cap on my virtual head. After a few adjustments to the T-shirt size, I moved my virtual viewpoint back to check out my new self: then I quickly clicked back to change the size of my love-handles. Then I took a look around.

13

In virtual worlds, you are born fully grown: each new character is an adult, albeit one who doesn't yet know how to 'be'. In every virtual world, you can walk, talk and move things around using your keyboard and mouse – but in each world these controls are different, and have to be learned anew. Second Life's solution to this problem is for each character to appear first in 'Orientation Island', a jumble of tropical hills and beaches where, like rehabilitation in fast forward, you learn how to operate your self and inhabit the world. Under the virtual sky – perfect shades from blue to white, like the sky seen from a 747 – I wandered the island. Here and there placards – which I clicked on to read, and which appeared as text on my screen – taught me how to walk, how to talk, how to move objects at a distance, how to fly. (If the first part felt like rehabilitation, the second part felt like superhero school.) At the end of the final lesson, a teleport button transmitted my virtual self into the wider virtual world.

After Orientation Island, my character first appeared next to the 'Linden tour balloon', which had a virtual out-of-order sign. By the launch platform were two motorcycles with directions to 'Honest John's Car Lot'. I clicked on the note. It offered to teleport me; I accepted, and there I was in a virtual car lot.

Honest John wasn't around, but I browsed the vehicles. I seemed to have started with some pocket money in the form of 2,500 'Linden Dollars' – the currency of this virtual world. With two clicks, I paid 50 Linden Dollars (about 10 pence) for my first virtual purchase: a moped. I clicked to jump on, but when I did, I could only see the side of my virtual head, which filled the screen. I got off the moped again, pushed another key, and, without a vehicle – in Second Life, the animation for flying was carefully modelled on the way people fly in dreams – I set off into the air. In London, it was 11 a.m. In the US, where the majority of Second Life players lived, it was between 2 and

5 a.m. The world seemed sparsely populated. When I made my second self, I had tried to recreate my real body, but I quickly saw, from the scattered people I did pass, that most virtual residents were eager to liberate themselves from their real-world limitations. There were robot-headed monsters, cartoon-faced clowns, spiky-haired punks, leather-clad dominatrices. There were flying figures, with fairy wings instead of arms.

The landscape, too, was as varied as a dream. I flew over cartoonish architecture – fairy-tale castles, blocks of primary colours, upside-down houses in the air – interspersed with some pieces of meticulous realism: office blocks, malls, more than one seaside home of cantilevered steel and glass. I flew over what looked to be a flying Scrabble board, each square as large as the virtual me. I landed near a sign that said 'Skydiving'. I sat in a seat, travelled up until the sky grew dark and the virtual earth below turned blue. I jumped and fell for long seconds, until I realised I didn't have a 'chute. Still, this was the virtual world, and my worries were unfounded. I hit the ground flat, stood up, and brushed myself off.

I had landed in someone's garden, complete with swimming pool. I slid down a slide into the water, then clicked on a ball above the pool labeled '50-person dance animator'. It asked me for permission to make my online self dance. I agreed, and started to wiggle and shake – except, I didn't know how to stop. For 20 minutes or so, until I plucked up the courage to ask someone how to make it stop, I shimmied my way through Second Life.

Even from the sparsely inhabited scenery, I could see that, in virtual worlds, people felt freer to experiment in all areas of experience. Near to the pool, what looked like a French chateau offered 'sub/slave collars'. Opposite, a floating golden cube advertised 'Ayesha's Antiques Heaven Yard Sale'. Under the sign was a virtual furniture store, where, among antique-style Louis XV chairs and vintage crossbows to mount on your virtual wall, you could buy a series of sex positions (including 'BJ Push-up') for your virtual self.

Near Antiques Heaven was a fairy-tale castle. The portcullis was down, so I strolled in. Inside was 'Mistress Tala Fate', decked out in full virtual dominatrix gear. Tala graciously showed me around her new mansion – it took her three 'pets' (subservient players) two days to make it, she said – including a medieval banqueting hall, a waterfall, and a fully equipped torture dungeon. ('I don't know how much you know about "the lifestyle",' she said. 'Not a whole lot,' I replied.) She insisted I stick around for the longer tour; unwilling to appear rude – and I had the sense someone named Mistress Tala would know how to be persistent – I logged off, waited five minutes, then logged on again somewhere else.

I strolled a little and found myself next to a kind of psyche-delic airport, where biplanes were lined up on the runway next to a jet fighter, a UFO, and some tie-dye 'hoverpods' – half-way between a scooter and a Frisbee. As I watched, a virtual hipster with flamed trousers and a 'Moon-age Daydream' T-shirt flew down and bought a pod to match his trousers. He got on board and zipped up into the sky. I thought about paying for an auto-mated balloon tour (80 Linden Dollars) when another balloon flew past above. I flew up alongside. Hank Ramos, the balloon pilot – a man with a beard, long hair at the back, black wool vest, white T-shirt, jeans and sneakers, who looked a lot like cartoonists do when they draw themselves – invited me to join him. In most virtual worlds, residents talk to each other via typed text. In Second Life, I saw when each virtual self talked they held out their hands and mimed typing into the air. 'Hop on,' Hank said. 'I'm giving tours while the Linden Balloon is down.'

I took my place in the basket, alongside a shock-haired robo-man with gravity boots and missiles on his back. This was Kai

Rubio (in Second Life, there are no introductions; people's names hang above their heads). Judging by his virtual costume, Kai obviously liked Japanese Manga cartoons. Kai didn't talk much.

We began to move. Below us, Hank pointed out a meticulously recreated Wild West town, like the studio streets where they film westerns. You could get shot here, Hank explained. 'It's damage-enabled.' (This wasn't as sinister as it sounded. In virtual worlds, we have conquered death, and the question of reincarnation has been resolved. If you 'die' from a virtual sword or bullet, you simply reappear, perfect and whole, somewhere nearby.) The balloon moved on. 'Hop on Wednesday,' Hank says. I look around; a skeleton with a scythe drifted past. 'Thanks, but I've got to work,' Wednesday the skeleton said, and flew on by.

We flew over a huge office complex, with a virtual neon sign: 'Nexus Prime'. Hank pointed out a virtual Venice, complete with Palazzos and gondolas. We drifted over a long highway, with huge concrete gateways. On each pillar, flags flew in the virtual breeze we couldn't feel. Occasionally words appeared on-screen ('Drift 100, pressure down 2') – it was the balloon talking. Hank pointed out a huge virtual amusement park below, complete with roller coaster rides and a virtual Ferris wheel. 'Linden World' was closed now, Hank explained. Half the rides were permanent, he said, and the other half were rides and attractions designed by 'Lifers', as Hank called Second Life residents. Like a real-world funfair, the Lindens were currently dismantling Linden World to move it to another area. 'There are whole rows of virtual shops,' Hank told us, 'which in this prime location so near the fair, are much in demand.' The shops worked on two-month leases from the Lindens, he said. The owners paid their virtual rent in virtual money, and their income from selling virtual clothes, jewellery, furniture, and more esoteric items like new animations (a dance, a sex-move), was in Linden Dollars too. That income, though, Hank explained, could be converted into other currencies at a whole range of third-party websites. Some residents made a real income from their virtual jobs, he explained. They traded enough Linden Dollars to pay their real-world rent.

A colossal complex of pagodas and bamboo gardens appeared. 'That's Shangri-La,' Hank said. 'That was made by a builder in Beta. He's no longer with us. Lifers campaigned to keep it.' Next to me, Kai Ramos, the robo-man, finally piped up. 'It's soooo beautiful,' he said.

Hank showed us the Globe theatre, a full-scale recreation of Shakespeare's original. Next to the Globe, a chessboard loomed out of the mist. 'Someone's working on a Scrabble board,' Hank told us. I told him, proudly, that I had already seen it and it was complete. Hank told us about the time he played full-size 'Seond-Life-opoly'; his own virtual self took the place of the top hat.

We drifted over a volcano, over a tree house, over a boat yard, over a towering billboard of a woman I didn't recognise. For a while, it looked like we were coming in to land over a virtual LA: suburban homes in rows, each with their own glittering backyard pool. If the story of Brezhnev's first doubt about the outcome of the cold war is true – from a plane over LA he saw the fields of glittering swimming pools, and he realised the West would win – then virtual worlds have the edge even over the real; in Second Life, to buy your own pool is a cinch. I asked Hank how to buy some land. He explained virtual property was sold off in parcels via auction or lottery, for prices in Linden Dollars at the equivalent of around $100 an acre. I wondered aloud about how to get my own virtual seafront home. 'Seaside property is much in demand, here as in First Life,' Hank said. I'd have to pay over the odds for a view of the virtual sea.

The balloon spoke its mysteries, and we rose over a cliff to pass a fairy-tale castle, a flag billowing from each spire. Everything we could see had been built by the residents, Hank explained. Linden Lab made only the terrain; everything else was built by what Hank called 'the community', out of basic virtual shapes called 'prims'. Hank explained how in his spare time he taught residents how to build virtual buildings. (They paid him in virtual money.) In 'First Life', he said, he was a programmer.

The terrain became even more dreamlike. We drifted over platonic solids: a lone torus, a flock of dodecahedrons. Kai piped up again, and he and Hank discussed the iTunes music store.

Then we were back over more realistic virtual ground. We passed a V-2-shaped, Tintin-goes-to-the-moon rocket ship. Nearby blatted a helicopter. On the roofs of some apartment buildings, jetpacks were parked. I began to set my heart on a property of my own, something modest, maybe a yacht moored in the bay . . .

'Look, there's John Linden,' Hank said. Every member of the Second Life production team has the surname 'Linden'; John's surname meant he worked for the people who made this world. I told Hank I would catch up with the balloon, and then I flung my virtual self from the side. I fell, my virtual arms flailing, into the virtual sea.

That day, John Linden had spiky red hair and deep black skin. He looked like the Silver Surfer after too long on a sunbed. I asked John about his job. He helped shape the worlds, he told me. He asked me to follow, and he lead me over the terrain, deep into the ocean – in Second Life you can breathe under-water – then high over a range of newly sculpted hills. As he showed me around, John Linden exhibited the same careful courtesy as had Hank Ramos; in virtual worlds, with many fewer physical cues, it is easy to be misunderstood, and most people seemed to bend over backwards to be civil.

I asked John Linden about the virtual money. Could people cheat in Second Life? In earlier versions of Second Life, he explained, during a limited test before it was released, people did find ways to create money. But Linden Lab could tell immediately; they monitored the economy closely, he said, and they could spot the appearance of large amounts of money. 'That sounds like total surveillance,' I remarked. John insisted they didn't monitor everything. 'Only in cases of dispute, where it's absolutely necessary.'

'That makes me laugh,' I said. 'That's exactly how everyone everywhere who uses surveillance feels.'

In most virtual worlds, the residents communicate with more than just words. Each virtual self has a range of animations for everything they do. In Second Life, you can dance, wave, gesticulate, hug another virtual self, do a back-flip. The animation for flying is Superman-style, fists in the air. As I spoke with John Linden, I noticed that certain phrases triggered animations in my virtual self, so that when I typed 'That makes me laugh', Errol Mysterio bent forward double and clutched his belly with laughter. John Linden wrote 'lol' – short for 'laugh out loud'. He too clutched his belly and dipped low. For a moment our laughter was identical, our two virtual bodies perfectly synchronised.

Then, high up on the hills, talking with the man who made them, I received a message from June-Marie. Her virtual self, Lilone Sandgrain, was online. She offered to teleport me to her location. I clicked 'Accept' and seconds later I was by her side.

Lilone Sandgrain, it turned out, was a voluptuous virtual redhead, wearing a skimpy dress made from what looked like virtual crepe paper. 'Have a seat!' she said, smiling. She patted the sofa next to her. I chose a more cautious spot, on a nearby rainforest-print virtual armchair. Lilone smiled. 'Welcome to my place!'

Around us fluttered a cloud of virtual butterflies, in every colour of the rainbow. There were rainbows too – three of them

– as well as a multicoloured fire, a waterfall, and a row of glittering fir trees. The air was thick with virtual dandelion seeds. 'Peace to your soul,' Lilone's scarlet and indigo 'elven fire' told us automatically. 'You are more than you think you are.' In virtual worlds like Second Life, it's not just your virtual body but also your sculpted virtual landscape which broadcasts your intended self. Here, in Lilone's hand-sculpted garden of new-age delights, I got the impression she liked to look on the bright, multi-coloured, fairy-lit side of life.

Among the butterflies, we began to talk about Lilone's work. In her real life, she explained, as June-Marie Mahay, she helped out in a Boston, Massachusetts, day-care centre for the physically disabled. Much of her time with her posse was spent handling and discussing the challenges of disabled life. (On one occasion, she told me, it took an hour and a half to determine that John, a man in her care with spina bifida – who could only nod to her questions – needed a drink of water.) One afternoon, chatting with her posse, she mentioned her online hobby, playing Second Life. They all clamoured for a try. The group created a character by consensus, voting on each element of appearance: spiky red hair, because they'd always wanted to show off; orange skin, because there were both black and white people in the group and they knew 'neither was better'. They called the character 'Wilde', after the rambunctious group's nickname among staff and residents at Evergreen. ('They wanted to express they were full of life and not predictable,' June-Marie told me.) Wilde loved their new online life. They met people, made friends, and built an online gift shop, which, through exchanging virtual money for real money at exchange websites, brought them real-world income. With Lilone's help, they began to spend as much time in Second Life as the day-care centre bureaucracy and their ailing computer network would allow. They were nine real souls inhabiting one virtual body; multiple personality disorder in reverse.

Lilone told me she was amazed, even after only six months of Second Life, how much the group had changed. 'They're so much more confident now, even in the real world,' she said. In the three years she had worked with the Wilde posse, Lilone told me, she'd never seen anything enrich their lives as much as the virtual world.

Then, as Lilone and I talked about Wilde, I realised something had happened. I had forgotten myself. Like a moviegoer entranced by the screen, I had become what I saw. I was no longer sitting at my desk, tapping on my laptop. I was sitting on an armchair, surrounded by rainbows, talking to Lilone Sandgrain. I was Errol Mysterio. I had entered the virtual world.

For two hours, we talked about Wilde's real-world lives, and how Second Life allowed them to experience a completely different and liberated existence. When I logged off – because of the time difference, it was 2 a.m. – I couldn't sleep. I knew I wanted to travel to meet the real nine souls of Wilde, and June-Marie Mahay. I also wanted to spend time with them online, and meet others like them: people living new kinds of lives outside their bodies, in entirely re-imagined selves.

That night, I read up about Second Life, and other online worlds. I discovered Second Life and EverQuest were part of a much larger story. In the real world, June-Marie had told me, Wilde often felt alone; online, Wilde was part of a vast new virtual community. I found that the very same illusion I had experienced – of leaving my body and the real world behind, to inhabit an entirely virtual self – was colonising the imagination of millions.

At the time of writing, between 25 and 30 million people worldwide – more than passed through US immigration at Ellis Island throughout the whole of the twentieth century – regularly log on to virtual worlds, to abandon our reality in search of a better place. This time, though, our new lands have no indigenous inhabitants to dispute our claim to the territory. Virtual worlds are empty except for us, and shaped entirely to our desires.

In the past, mankind could only dream of such magical kingdoms, places where the self could rest and be refurbished. Heaven, Eden, Oz . . . lands somewhere over the rainbow, where life could be renewed, and all loss made good. Now, through computer technology, we have built ourselves a new kind of heaven: perfected virtual worlds, where we can finally move in and take up residence. Through computer screens at home, in offices, in libraries, in cyber-cafes, in military bases, in colleges and schools, more people than inhabit Australia have stepped through the electronic looking glass to inhabit their second lives. In virtual worlds, it seems, we can finally break free of the forces of nature: we can shed gravity, because in most games, you can fly; and we can rid our lives of friction, because in online worlds, nothing takes any physical effort at all.

For the most part, these millions leave the real world behind to inhabit massive multiplayer games: playful but constrained virtual spaces like Sony Online Entertainment's Dungeons & Dragons-style world, EverQuest – the planet's fifth-largest virtual world (half a million players) – or Blizzard Entertainment's World of Warcraft (at the time of writing, 5.5 million players and rising). In South East Asia, I discovered, the numbers rise sharply. In 2005, one South Korean game series, Lineage and Lineage II, boasted 4 million active accounts. At the time of writing, more people reside in Lineage and Lineage II than reside in Ireland – and the numbers are rising exponentially. The population of virtual worlds seems to double every year. 'I expect there will be 2 to 3 million more people in the US that come on board in the next two years,' David Cole, president of the multimedia research firm DFC Intelligence, told *Salon* magazine in July 2002. The actual figures were in the top range of his guess – and 8 million more residents have joined since then, attracted by a freedom of movement and expression that is harder to find in the real world. (And that's not even counting the millions in South East Asia.) In 2002, game designer Brad McQuaid, then a creative force behind EverQuest, predicted virtual worlds 'will rival the movie industry in the next five to 10 years.' We're well on the way. In 2005, Hollywood took $9.2 billion in US box office receipts (worldwide, that figure rose to $23 billion). In the same period, the combined annual revenues from these new virtual worlds were estimated at $3.7 billion, a figure predicted to rise to $19.3 billion by 2009. By then, if current trends continue, virtual worlds will make more money than American football, baseball, and basketball combined, and, each year, more people worldwide will visit a virtual world than will visit a McDonald's restaurant.

The economies of virtual worlds, I discovered, ran far beyond the income of the people who made the worlds. In each world, there were virtual currencies, and the mass exodus from the real world had brought with it such a mania for virtual items that people were now willing to pay real money to acquire them. People who dwell within virtual worlds, entranced by the possibilities of reinvention in an entirely risk-free second life, will happily pay real money for virtual objects or property to expand their online lives. People who want, say, a more powerful sword, or their own virtual Frank Lloyd Wright-style cantilevered home by the virtual seaside, but don't have time to construct it themselves, will pay substantial sums of real-world money instead. The money is paid via credit card, on websites in the real world, and the goods are delivered virtually, inside the game. I knew virtual worlds had their own currencies (in EverQuest, I'd killed rats for a week to scrape together a single gold piece), but I'd had no idea how my money was connected to a whole series of economies inside virtual worlds, which had begun to affect our own real-world currencies. On a single day in June, the largest virtual items broker, Internet Gaming Entertainment – like hedge-fund managers, with a collateral of virtual swords and property instead of stocks and bonds – would have sold you virtual currency from one of 14 non-existent places, for real-world cash.

The income has become so reliable, I discovered, and the exchange rates between virtual currencies so stable, that enterprising businessmen in poorer areas of the world – Mexico or China, for example – had set up 'virtual sweatshops': offices where employees worked (and sometimes slept) at their PCs, working in virtual worlds to make gold and other items to sell for a real-world salary.

In 2001, economist Edward Castronova, a professor at California State University, studied welfare research. His wife worked in a different city; for comfort, he spent many evenings online, inside the virtual world of EverQuest. Then, he noticed players were selling virtual items for real money on eBay – the game had an economy, which intersected with the real. In his 2002 study, *On Virtual Economies* (which turned his career around) he examined the economy of EverQuest, then the planet's second-largest virtual world, with just under half a million residents. He found that EverQuest had a real, consistent US dollar exchange rate, which put the average wage of each player – the virtual money they earned while playing the game, hunting for virtual booty and creating new virtual items – at the equivalent of $3.42 per hour. One EverQuest platinum piece, he found, was worth about one cent: more than one yen or one lira. From that, Castronova calculated the virtual world's gross national product: $135 million. EverQuest, he concluded, had a per-capita GNP of $2,266 – richer than India, Bulgaria, or China, and almost on a par with Russia. By these measures, the world's 77th largest economy was a sub-continent that only *nearly* existed. Since Castronova's study, virtual business has boomed. In 2002, virtual game items – non-existent things – were sold on eBay alone for more than £10 million (despite a ban, instigated by eBay in April 2000, at Sony's request, on sales of EverQuest items). In October 2004, Edward Castronova, now an economist at the University of Indiana, estimated the global market in virtual goods at £50 million. By 2005, a company which specialised in trading virtual goods put the market at £400 million. (By then, Castronova was hedging his bets; he placed the market at between £113 million and £565 million.)

These online worlds offer a powerful enchantment: an entire alternative life. To some, the liberation afforded by these second lives is seductive to the point of obsession. At the time I visited Wilde, one in ten Second Life players spent 80 hours or more per week logged into their online alter egos. When I spoke with the EverQuest design team, in 2002, they told me EverQuest residents inhabited their virtual selves for an average of 20 hours per week. In another Castronova study, from 2001, a third of EverQuest residents claimed to spend more time in their virtual world than at their real jobs – a figure that has been shown to remain true across other virtual worlds. In interviews with Castronova, one in five players claimed they thought of EverQuest – not their apartment – as their actual home. For these people, the real world was where they worked in order to buy time to live other lives online.

The night I first met June-Marie online, I read about the mania that was emerging around virtual worlds. The word 'virtual' has roots in the power of certain qualities – virtues – and has come to mean possessing essence and effect without possessing form; something not quite physical, but with a measurable impact on the real. True to their name, virtual worlds had begun to have an effect on the real. I read about online weddings, where

26

people swore devotion to partners other than their offline spouses. I read that, in the summer of 2005, Sony, as makers of the sequel EverQuest II, had launched a competition to find a real-world lookalike for the queen of that virtual world, Firiona Vie. But they were too late; Firiona already had a real-world incarnation. In January 2005, Tabitha Ayers, an American virtual world resident and committed EverQuest player, named her real-world daughter after the virtual Elf-Queen. I discovered, too, that the devotion to virtual selves wasn't always harmless. In June that same year, two 29-year-old South Korean parents were so enchanted by their favourite virtual world, World of Warcraft, they left their four-month-old baby alone to sneak off to the local Internet cafe. When they returned five hours later, their baby had suffocated. I read about the runaway boy who supported himself by stealing entirely virtual objects and selling them for real money. I read about the husband who hacked into his wife's game account and staged her virtual suicide, in order to make her seem unbalanced and influence a real-world custody case in his favour. I read that in Korea, where game scores are read out on television news, there is an entire police division dedicated to cyber-crimes, almost entirely around a single virtual world – called Lineage: The Blood Pledge – which has 4 million Korean residents. I read, too, that others were using virtual worlds to plan their dominance over the real world: the US Army had commissioned one virtual world company to build a model of the entire real world, built to half scale, where thousands of virtual soldiers could rehearse conflict anywhere on the globe at a moment's notice.

In the affluent West, we sometimes forget how much of our experience is virtual already. The radio we listen to in the car, the music we listen to on our headphones, the TV we turn on when we get home – even the print we read in books and newspapers – are all means to simulate company that we don't have in the flesh. We play recorded music instead of hearing it played live. We watch recorded people instead of seeing them in person. And the horizon of our virtual experience is expanding fast. We can buy and download movies, music, books; we can watch TV online; we can listen to radio through our mobile phone. Through technology, we have extended our selves; through technology, we have overruled each other, placed ourselves at the centre of a kingdom of choice and self. Our mass media age exposes us with ease to extremes of personality, where beauty and success are the norm. We choose our company from remarkable people, spread across the world – the celebrity world David Mamet calls 'society's prize hogs' – instead of suffering the company of the normal people nearby. In our 'reality' TV shows, through, say, voting for band members, the audience is given the illusion they are involved in the creative process, for the price of a telephone call – we want creativity without sacrifice. Through marketing, we enflame our desires, but we can't contain them; we project our desires out into the world, and call them market forces. At the same time, we are snared in a barely visible web of concepts, brands, advertising, and persuasion, all carefully crafted to enchant us into material acquisition. We've seen too much, but not done enough. We are prisoners of our expectations, caught in the lethal trap of experience without risk.

That night, as I looked into virtual worlds, I could see virtual worlds offered the same kind of addictive enchantment. Somewhere, it seemed, I would find people so entranced by the possibilities of the world through the screen, they would become reluctant to come home to their flesh.

The morning after I met June-Marie, I went to my local Blockbuster video store and took a walk along the shelves. There, among the DVDs, were rows of these interactive shared fantasies: boxes of software, which allow you to log into virtual worlds and abandon your self. There were dozens of worlds, each ripe with a different possibility of re-invention. The advertising slogans all encouraged me to move to a better place. In City of Heroes ('There is a place we can all be heroes!'), you can shed your own clothes for the cape of an aspiring superhero, free yourself from gravity, and leap across the tall buildings of a Metropolis-like city to save old ladies and fight crime. 'You're in our world now,' the EverQuest box's sales pitch declared. There was an online version of the Sims (previous versions of which, offline, had become the best-ever selling computer game), where you could join thousands of others to buy furniture, date, or even, by mistake, set your virtual house on fire. If you wanted to fight, you could log onto worlds with names like Battlefield, Counterstrike and Planetside, where pitched battles of various sizes were played out over and over, forever. In these eternal struggles, over the same patches of virtual ground, death and victory and death were repeated over and over again – all at no real cost, except the pocket-change you paid to play.

If you were disappointed with NASA's fading space programme, you might choose to journey not to Mars, but to a more interesting place entirely: another universe, like Star Wars Galaxies ('Visit a Galaxy far away – right now!'), modelled scrupulously on the films of George Lucas. In this patented galaxy, like a colossal residential theme park, you could become an alien, fly between the stars, meet Darth Vader or Jabba the Hut, and – after years of practice – become a Jedi Knight.

In many virtual worlds, the world's makers decree the purpose of your new virtual self. These worlds offer a specific, restricted path: you fight monsters, make deals, and practise your skills in order to become a more powerful wizard, warrior, or Jedi Master. In these worlds, like Star Wars Galaxies or EverQuest, the purpose is to advance up a series of levels; to become a more powerful character by hunting animals, and other computer-generated characters – bandits, evil wizards – controlled by the game. Essentially, you track down, attack and kill stronger foes, a repetitive and lengthy process players have christened 'grinding', because of the time and effort involved. (One resident of another fantasy virtual world, World of Warcraft, set his sights on a single suit of rare 'Enchanted Thorium' virtual armour. He timed the quest: it took 95 hours.) The developers fine-tune the games into a kind of virtual Skinner-box: they deliver just enough reward to keep you playing. My own time in EverQuest had mostly consisted of working in this way, as a computer-generated Rentokil operative, hunting virtual rats until my wrist was sore. But I also discovered other, newer worlds – including Second Life – where the purpose was less defined. There were no foes to defeat, no levels to progress through.

In these brave new online worlds, the players themselves make the universe and dwell within it. There is often no goal, except simply to live a virtual life. You build an 'avatar' – a virtual you – which you can dress like a doll and inhabit as a second self. You can act out your original self, or a build a whole new one, online. In real life you might be a taxi driver, but in your second life you can be an architect, a fashion designer, a superhero, a wizard or a king. Through these worlds, almost anything is possible. You can set up a spaceport, be crucified, become Conan the Barbarian. Through your second self, in accelerated time and with accelerated ease, you can build houses, make and sell things, work, get married, divorce, and die. People wear virtual clothes, drive virtual cars, construct virtual flat-pack furniture. There are virtual garages, virtual tax collectors, virtual art shows, virtual war memorials, virtual courthouses, virtual strip-clubs (because virtual doesn't necessarily mean virtuous). If you haven't got the money or contacts to buy virtual land, you can rent rooms in virtual apartment complexes, to shelter your virtual self from the virtual rain. The writer J. G. Ballard, the notorious doomsayer of the dark-side of urban sprawl, has envisioned a future where people abandon reality for virtual worlds, like they once abandoned old Europe. That morning, I discovered they already were.

There was room for everybody. The only limit to the geographical size of virtual worlds is the number of Internet servers used to store them. By 2000, the landmass of EverQuest, to scale with the size of each player's online self, was roughly three times the size of Manhattan. In Star Wars Galaxies, there were nine planets, each with more surface area than all the land in EverQuest. To walk the equator of each Star Wars planet, one after the other, would take a week.

Over the next few weeks, I spent more time online with June-Marie – more accurately, I spent time with Lilone Sandgrain. Lilone showed me around Second Life, and told me more about her work with Wilde. She showed me the virtual tropical island, 16 acres owned and maintained by Wilde, which they had christened 'Live2Give'. Another time, we met at a pair of virtual swings hung over a tropical creek. In the background, as we talked, a group gathered to practise their virtual construction skills on some abstract shapes. Huge flashing cubes, filled with bright blue spirals, billowed up behind us, as she explained how hard it was to give Wilde as much time online as they'd like. Hanging out with Lilone on the swings – a curvy redhead, her legs crossed, with me splashing in the water below – felt weirdly like a date.

On our final meeting before my trip to Evergreen, Lilone and I met at the top of a tall white tower on Wilde's island. (Wilde liked to teleport to the top of the tower and then jump off, she explained.) We sat and sipped virtual Turkish coffee. Or at least, I tried to. In virtual worlds, it takes time to learn how to control your virtual self. In Second Life, for example, your virtual head turns to gaze wherever your mouse is pointing. If you do nothing

31

for long enough, your avatar's head slumps forward to let other people know you're not paying attention. I spent much of this particular meeting apologising to Lilone for staring at her feet, or gazing off to the horizon with my head at 90 degrees, pouring virtual coffee down the side of my neck.

This time, Lilone had a surprise for me. 'Hold on,' she said. There was a pop, and, on the stool next to her, someone appeared. It was Wilde's virtual self. The word 'avatar' comes from the Sanskrit 'Avatāra', meaning an incarnation, usually of a god in our mortal world. This was Wilde's avatar, their incarnation in the virtual world, with spiky red hair and orange skin.

'Wilde! Great to finally meet you,' I said. I half-expected a chorus, but of course, the reply came back as a single line of text.

'The room has filled with smiles,' June-Marie typed back at Evergreen, for Wilde. 'They are glad to see you too.'

'You look a bit different to how I expected,' I told Wilde. 'You're a woman today.'

Wilde laughed. 'It's a bit tough for the men, but we alternate playing two months male and two months female. February is our last month as a woman.' ('The guys feel funny dressing in dresses,' June-Marie later told me. 'Perhaps because we girls tease them; the girls don't have any problem being a man.')

Wilde was full of questions for me, about the life of a writer. When I'd answered as many as I could, I asked them about Second Life. June-Marie reported the different voices clamouring to be heard through Wilde's single voice. 'Scott says it's like opening a whole new world. He says it allows him to have a voice and to say things important to him – things he's always wanted to say. The whole room agrees – it's so much easier to talk this way than in real life. In person people would have a hard time understanding us, and it would take soooooo, soooooo long.' (In the real world, the group's lack of language can cripple their interactions; online, with June-Marie as typist and interpreter, they can hold real-time conversations, without all the confusion and anxiety of being misunderstood, or dismissed because of their appearance.)

Since my last online meeting with Lilone, I had shopped for virtual outfits. That evening, on Wilde's rooftop hideaway, I wore my first attempt at a virtual suit – a white tux and bow tie. I joked that I thought I should be serving the Turkish coffee, not drinking it. Wilde laughed, and I saw it happen. Wilde's avatar doubled over with her hand on her stomach, in exactly the same way Hank Ramos and I had laughed two weeks before.

In virtual worlds, where landscape is an extension of self, every man can choose to be an island; I asked Wilde how they felt about owning their own. 'The room all agrees they love having the island. They love to have a single place to reach out from. The island becomes in a way like a voice for us. We hope in the future to have other people come and also build here. To make it like open arms.' A new member had asked to join their island, Wilde told me. Their new virtual neighbour was a UK resident, who wanted to remain anonymous; he had cerebral palsy, but could operate Second Life with his toes.

I asked the eight who were present that day if they enjoyed sharing the same virtual self. 'Everyone enjoys playing together,' Wilde said, after a pause. 'At least those here today. The others we can't ask. Mary would love to be here today, but her elevator was broken.' And how important was Second Life to them? 'John S. says it's very, very important to him.' Wilde said. 'He says it is his favourite activity. He also enthusiastically says it has changed his life. Scott gives the same answers as John – using the scale to 10, he gives them all tens. Nichole says the computer is important to her; it makes her life happier. Dan says without question

33

that the experience has changed, and is changing, his life. It frees him up to be who he is inside.'

There was a long pause. 'We feel the most like the rest of the world that we've ever felt,' Wilde said.

Had I not known in advance, from our conversation that night I would perhaps have guessed Wilde Cunningham's peculiar composition. Her ambitions were enthusiastically wide-ranging. She wanted to build a house. She wanted to build a castle. She wanted to build a waterfall. She wanted to run a store. She wanted to pilot a helicopter. She wanted to influence the world positively. She wanted to buy some guns. She wanted to publish her life story. She wanted to be a man. She wanted to remain a woman. Wilde seemed full of voices and ambitions, and as playful as a dolphin.

I asked what the group had been up to in Second Life. 'We went to hell yesterday.' Wilde bent forward in laughter. 'It was so fun. For our very first exploration day on the new computer, we teleported there. But we couldn't find it! We looked everywhere for hell. Its much harder to get into hell than people lead you to believe!'

I asked if they had tried virtual sinning. Wilde laughed again. 'No, we didn't think of that! It was a hoot. By the time we found it and had a chance to be stabbed and have blood gush from everywhere it was time to leave.'

Then someone outside Wilde's computer room needed help, and they had to log off. Our brief time together was at an end.

That day, after I logged off and re-entered my physical self, I decided I wanted to venture further into these worlds, to see what I could discover. Our new virtual worlds seem at first to be a perfectly imagined heaven: full of abundance and ease; the best of all possible worlds, outside of gravity and beyond scarcity and loss. In virtual worlds, even death was conquered: if you died, you could simply click the mouse to be reborn. It was a new version of an old dream – the desire to create a new world, unfettered by the old, in which pain and loss are solved, responsibilities neutralised, and the self set free. I wanted to travel through the electronic looking glass, along with the millions who had already made the journey. For centuries we have enacted ourselves in art and literature, more recently in cinema. In those cases, though, the majority acted as witnesses to the acted dreams of a central few – the film-makers, novelists, and musicians. I wanted to explore how we had begun to enact ourselves more personally in virtual worlds, to examine why so many people yearned to be elsewhere, and to discover what that said about the actual world in which we live. There would be a dark side, too, to the exodus. What was wrong with the real world, for so many people to leave it behind?

There was also a personal motivation to my journey. It was a time when the daily tasks of the Western world threatened to drag me under. Tax, car insurance, parking fines, finances, deadlines: no amount of personal organisers (I went through five) or time-management plans seemed to stem the tide of paper and fines. Emails went unanswered, parking tickets went missing, bills went unpaid. I couldn't remember the last time I'd seen the end of my to-do list. I began to suspect there was no end. At any given time of day, it seemed, the odds were even that I would be on hold to a utility company. Even without a mortgage, I was tens of thousands of pounds in debt. (Much of my income went to service this debt, leaving little spare; for at least two weeks, my main source of nutrition seemed to be leftover olive oil.) The modern world was overwhelming me. At times, it seemed as if my room was snowing paper – and, if my paperwork was snow, then I was lost in a blizzard. The real world in which I lived offered me the freedom to do as I pleased, but it also forced me, I felt, to manage every aspect of my life without assistance.

35

Underneath the endless tasks of real life, I felt something else too: a kind of sorrow, never far away. For years, I had struggled with my own difficult history, with the sorrow my past had planted in my chest, like an old bruise. It arose almost every day, lodged in me, and it refused to be disgorged. I could distract myself for a moment from this sorrow: by smoking, or listening to music, or watching films. All these activities surrounded me with ghosts, gave me the impression I was warm and belonged, instead of out here alone. But always, when the cigarette was out, the song over, or the movie finished, the sorrow returned. It felt like a flaw that couldn't be removed, a grain of sand that no amount of advertising or distracting entertainment or imagined perfection could rinse from my self.

I couldn't work out where the sorrow came from. Was it mine? Or did it belong to the world? Did I somehow have implanted in me, because of my idealistic childhood, the idea that life could be easy? Or did we all, somehow, feel this way? Did we all want, as these virtual worlds seemed to offer, to reach up, to let go of our skins and find a new place – a heaven – without sorrow and loss?

I knew I'd had an isolated childhood. I knew I had inherited various breeds of sorrow and struggle from the tangled roots of my family. I knew I had chosen a solitary career. A writer's life is perhaps more virtual than most; my contacts with agents, editors, often even friends, took place mostly on the computer monitor. Most days, I sat at my desk and hoped if I pressed computer keys in the right order cheques might come through the letterbox. It was hard to discern how much of this struggle was a reflection of me – my personal history, my own particular losses – and how much was a reflection of our society: isolated, set apart, in doubt about our feelings. It seemed to me that the sorrow wasn't just inside. It also surrounded me. I waded through it, and other people around me seemed to wade through it too.

People in the streets, on buses and underground trains seemed hedged against some loss: hunched into newspapers and books, but now also blocking out the world with iPods and mobile telephones (and even more direct medication: in the 10 years to 2002, UK prescriptions for antidepressants had more than doubled). We were unhappy, but we weren't supposed to be. Immersed in a constructed world, we sought comfort in record stores, in the mall, in the cinema. Email and mobile telephones meant you could no longer lose yourself anywhere on the globe, but, I read, since the seventies the number of Europeans living alone had doubled. We were all more connected, and all more separate. All our media are a way of projecting company, virtual worlds most of all – and, it seemed, we needed each other's company more than ever.

We conjured up ghosts to keep us company, but our bodies still existed in isolation. Without those stimulations, the compensation for our isolated Western lives, we were thrown back on what Jean Baudrillard called 'the desert of the real': the absence of others from our lives. It was this desert that I, it seemed, along with millions of others, was trying to avoid. Our constructed world was a boon – all those spirits kept us company – but also our curse. After all, to recover from loss, first you must remember what went missing. It seemed to me we had all forgotten what was gone.

For years, I spent late nights on the Internet, finding a way to transcend my own bodily absences through an electronic connection. At night, when the calls stopped and the call centres closed, I could relax, log on to virtual worlds and spend some time elsewhere, away from my struggles, in a safer world where death, and therefore anxiety, was gone. In Second Life, there was no tax, and so no tax returns to be late with. In World of Warcraft, you didn't even have a home to care for, much less – as I had in the real world – a landlord who held your belongings hostage against four months' missed rent.

And, I discovered, I wasn't alone. Millions of others were joining me. (Recent research showed UK residents spent on average 23 hours a week online: four more hours than they spent watching TV.) Isolated at home, these people came together online. Were these new virtual émigrés, like me, escaping the suffering of the world? Or were they forging new worlds, building a new perspective on our plight?

There was something else, too. Linden Lab had named my virtual self 'Errol Mysterio', but it wasn't the first time I'd been given a new name. The dream of a perfect world was a dream that I knew intimately, from a childhood spent living in communes in India and Oregon, under the feet of my mother, her guru and her friends, as they dyed their clothes orange and hunted heaven. They, too, left the world behind to find something better; what they found was a kind of heaven, and also a kind of hell. When my mother was 29, she decided to leave our family home, and enter into a commune headed by the Indian guru, Bhagwan Shree Rajneesh. Then, I followed my mother into a series of communes because I wanted to be with her: I had no role in her decision, nor, as a child, did I have any sense of the pressures that led her to leave our family life behind. Now, at the same age myself as she was when she decided to leave the world behind, I felt all same pressures. Only now, perhaps, they were worse. Twice as many people lived alone, and in the same period – since the seventies – bankruptcy filings had doubled. People were folding under the pressure. The system my mother tried to create an alternative to – global free market capitalism – was now the dominant global dream. She and her friends had lost their war against the advancing front. For better and for worse, we were living under the occupation.

I was the same age now, and I, in turn, felt drawn to build

an ideal place. Something else about the spirit of virtual worlds reminded me of the idealised and troubled communes of my childhood. My first few excursions into virtual worlds had uncovered a new kind of experimental attitude, which reminded me of the freedom sought by my mother and her friends. Even the sexual experimentation – the BDSM gear, the online strip clubs and escorts – seemed to offer parallels with the sexual experimentation of communal living of that time. My mother and her friends once sought freedom in communes, to dramatise their selves away from the prying eyes of the outside world. In virtual worlds, it seemed, a new wave of people were finding similar kinds of freedom – of space, of creativity, of motion. Back in the seventies, they called their communes places 'beyond the frontiers of the mind'. The virtual world émigrés were travelling beyond a new kind of frontier, and virtual worlds seemed to attract the same kind of pioneer spirit.

I decided to finish what I couldn't complete when I was nine; to journey into these perfect worlds, and see what consolation and what trouble I could find there. My journey would take me to Naboo, to fight Jedi; it would take me to ancient Rome, to speak with the first barbarian to be crucified on the virtual cross. The short conversation with John Linden about people cheating to make money would later lead me into an entire virtual underworld, where hackers and even virtual mafia hit-men used computer skills and intimidation to make small fortunes. I would work as a virtual mafia foot soldier, and nearly get banned from virtual worlds for my crimes. The journey would take me as far as Korea, to meet the king of the largest virtual world, who in the real world looked over his shoulder each morning, in fear of his online foes.

The word 'utopia' contains within itself its own impossibility. The word, coined by the fifteenth century writer Thomas More, means both 'perfect place' and 'no place'. When we try to override that impossibility, when we try to create heaven, we can't help but also create hell. Oz had its wicked witch; Eden had the snake. My mother's guru ended up in jail, after a group of his disciples poisoned 800 people and plotted to murder an Oregon District Attorney. I knew that the journey into virtual worlds, too, would take me to both the dark and light sides of the story. (I knew, from my childhood, that wherever people travelled to extremes of experience, others would be quick to judge.) I wanted to begin my journey, though, on a small scale. I wanted to start with a small world, Second Life, and I wanted to visit a group of people for whom virtual worlds were unequivocally a good thing.

We all want ease, and we all dream of a better life. Television divorced experience from risk, a glamorous and lethal liberation. Now, it seemed, virtual worlds had liberated travel from struggle. This didn't seem to me necessarily a good thing – without struggle, we don't build muscle – but it felt fitting that I was about to begin my journey into virtual worlds with a group for whom that liberation was a long-awaited release. For some, virtual worlds offered shelter from their real-world struggles. The nine souls of Wilde Cunningham had been disabled from birth; they had spent their entire lives struggling for freedom from their restricted real-world selves. They wanted anything but shelter. For Wilde, virtual worlds turned a negative into a positive. June-Marie was convinced virtual worlds did more than just liberate Wilde from their disabled bodies; they liberated us from our prejudices, too. 'It is you who will feel disabled,' she wrote to me, 'from all they will share with you.'

I got on a plane to see Wilde.

3

WILDE CUNNINGHAM
Multiple personality disorder in reverse

And here I was, at the Evergreen Center, on the other side of
the screen – in the real world, this time – watching Wilde, piece-
by-piece, become their other self.

On the computer room wall, Wilde Cunningham was still
appearing. Like some virtual worlds, Second Life stores all its
virtual objects and people as data on the servers – in this case
those of Linden Lab, the world's San Francisco-based developers. As every object, including every player's virtual self, is
custom made, it can take a little while after you connect to
Second Life for your character and your surroundings to download. In front of us, a pair of shoes materialised; Wilde
Cunningham was now fully clothed. The group cheered.

Wilde's joy was a momentary triumph over their real-world
lack of control. Later that day, the Evergreen Center Director,
Kathleen Flatley, a tough, no-nonsense woman with a marked
Boston accent, drew my attention to Scott's jacket: a shiny black
bomber that seemed far too small. 'Look at Scotty,' she said.
'They sent him in with someone else's coat. I have 12 years of
experience in residential care, and I tell you, you get them up
in the morning and you get their brown corduroys out with their

chequered shirt, and that's what you put on them. There's no choice for them. How can you be an individual if you can't choose your own clothes?' In the physical world, Wilde can't easily control how they appear. In Second Life, from the various fashion boutiques in virtual malls and marketplaces scattered across the world, Wilde can, with a click of a button, outfit themselves in any imaginable fashion.

In Second Life, some nearby objects can take longer than others to download, and one of Wilde's favourite virtual possessions had yet to materialise. Mary groaned. 'Yeah, Mary, where'd Baby Ruby go?' June-Marie asked. She meant the virtual baby Wilde carried strapped to their back, which they had named after their second-favourite staff member. ('We named her baby Ruby because Ruby takes care of us in real life,' Wilde had told me when we met online, 'so in Second Life we take care of her.') Baby Ruby had so far failed to materialise. 'Did we have a kidnapping?' June-Marie said. The group groaned and laughed. 'Maybe it was . . . Nichole? Nope. It was Mary. Mary! You kidnapper!' The virtual Ruby appeared; they cheered again.

At that moment, the real Ruby walked backwards into the room. Behind her she wheeled another man, in a yellow and blue Old Navy sweater, with short black hair and bright, shining eyes.

'Scotty! Did you miss us?' June-Marie asked. Scott, 38, had extreme cerebral palsy. His movements were smoother and slower than the rest of the group. 'Did you miss us, Scott?' June-Marie asked again. Scott's reply was a roll of the eyes and a low moan like a sea mammal. June-Marie understood. Scott had missed them. 'Oh, Scott,' June-Marie said, and smiled. 'Scotty. I don't like you. You can't come in here.' Scott moaned again, mournful as a Wookie. Then his mouth twisted into a smile.

While June-Marie re-arranged the wheelchairs to make room for Scott, I asked about their favourite memories from Second

Life. June-Marie translated. They had all enjoyed their dance with Baccara Rhodes on their last visit, they said. In Second Life, when you log on, you re-appear in the virtual world wherever you were last time you visited. The week before, when Wilde had last logged on, they had come to the virtual church we could see on the screen to meet the bride of a virtual wedding. A well-known Second Life resident, Baccara – who worked full-time as a virtual event manager, arranging celebrations inside Second Life – had wedded another resident, Mash Mandala. (The virtual bride and groom had never met outside Second Life.) Wilde had been invited, but the group couldn't make the date. So, the night before, Baccara dressed up in her wedding gown – which no one else had yet seen – and she danced with Wilde up the aisle.

The week before, another friend had taken them flying; they rode in his virtual airplane, then, cheekily, Wilde had jumped out the cockpit to fall into the sea.

On the projected image, below the figure of Wilde Cunningham, some text appeared. It was an instant message from 'Gobbit Grasshopper', another Second Life resident. June-Marie read it aloud: 'Hello, I would like to join Brigadoon please.'

'What shall we do?' June-Marie asked the group. 'Shall we tell him to ask John?' The group shouted their agreement, and June-Marie typed her reply. 'Ask John Prototype.'

Very soon after Wilde joined Second Life, they began to receive instant messages from other Second Life residents. They wanted to meet Wilde. 'The response from the community was amazing,' June-Marie told me. One of those who came forward was 'John Prototype', né John Lester, who ran a massive online community, BrainTalk, for people with neurological conditions and their carers. He was looking for ways to support therapeutic uses for

Second Life. He had come across a virtual kiosk with some of Wilde's writing. How would Wilde feel if he gave them an island?

A new visitor entered the Evergreen computer room. John S.'s dad had taken a break from the Boston Philharmonic to visit, and to discover first-hand his son's virtual life. To show him what they'd built, June-Marie pressed a few keys and teleported Wilde back home to their own virtual island. Around them tropical sand began to appear, stretching out beneath a perfect blue. 'Do these guys live here, or are they just visiting?' John's dad asked.

'I don't know if *live* is the right word,' June-Marie replied. 'This is their island.' Wilde walked up the beach, over a stretch of wooden decking, and onto the grass. Over the months they had spent inside Second Life, Wilde and June-Marie had sculpted their island to their desires. Above Wilde swooped a virtual dove; in between meticulously tended virtual trees grazed virtual deer. Higher up, a virtual rocket ship streaked across the sky. Wilde had littered their virtual island with emblems of their lives, a celebration of their real-world selves: pictures of themselves, their families, their favourite baseball team. After John Lester's gift of the island, Wilde christened their new home 'Live2Give'; above them, on the island's central ridge, a row of billboards emblazoned the nine's message of inclusion: 'Welcome to the family of the world!'.

Wilde showed John's dad their welcome area, where, on a crystal-encrusted bookcase – John S. loved crystals, June Marie explained – they'd placed a looped slideshow with pictures of their real-world selves. Close-up, the meticulous care Wilde and June-Marie had put into their island became apparent; in the welcome area's glass tables, tiny digital angelfish swam in lazy circles.

Next door were their note-card dispensers, revolving billboards where people could read Wilde's writings: Mary's mission statements, Johanna and Micah's jokes. ('Why do people go

crazy around Christmas? Because they get Santa-mental.')
Charlene wrote a poem for the island, called 'The Pits':

> being in a wheelchair is the pits i tell you all
> even if your wonderful it will make you feel quite small
> the normal lil things you would simply like to do
> never come as easy for me as for you~
>
> i'm the same as you i know this inside
> yet never i feel it no matter how hard i've tried
> i'm happy dont misread me, i laugh often, i'm smart
> but i feel small if you peek inside of my heart

On the virtual billboard, alongside Wilde's writings, visitors could post messages in return.

Over the weekend, June-Marie had made some changes to the island (on the group's instructions, she'd added more trees by the 'charmed circle' of drums and dream-catchers) so the tour was for Wilde too. As Wilde strolled past the lagoon, June-Marie ran some new ideas by the group. She could plant reeds, add fish, or put a floating baby-Moses basket on the water. The group cheered for the baby in the basket, and the decision was made. 'Anything else you guys want right here?' June-Marie asked. 'I have a box of bees. You guys want some bees flying around here?' The group made various noises and shook their heads. The consensus seemed to be no, thank you. 'What's that, Micah?' June-Marie asked. 'Oh, Bees sting. Butterflies would be better?'

Under June-Marie's direction, Wilde walked down the beach and into the sea. The water closed over their avatar's head. (Some virtual worlds artificially restrict the amount of time you can spend underwater, to simulate a held breath; In Second Life, you can breathe anywhere.) Wilde walked through a cloud of tropical fish, each named after someone at Evergreen, down a dip in the sand to Charlene's mermaid-pool – a series of mermaid pictures June-Marie had downloaded from the Internet and pasted on the sea floor. Wilde strolled up to what looked like an underwater cliff. June-Marie looked at John's dad. 'One of the cool things about this world is you can walk through . . . what?' she shouted across the room.

'Walls!' the group shouted back.

Wilde walked right through the cliff wall. They passed through the fronds of a tiny undersea jungle, into a secret undersea cavern: a marble-floored ballroom with giant crystal chandeliers. Along one wall, granite cases displayed their collection of virtual illuminated scrolls. In another corner stood John's collection of virtual statues, copied from throughout history.

'Oh, guys, the weekend is upon us and I don't have any home-work,' June-Marie said. 'I'm going to have a very boring weekend without any homework.' She made a few suggestions for weekend improvements – a kick-ball circle, some further work to the play area. The group voted to build a circle of soft sofas, with pillows, for visitors to sit and chat.

Then, for the benefit of John's dad, Wilde headed down to John's private treasure room. They walked through the 'curtain of mystery', past the 'orb of insight' and down through an obsidian-black whirlpool. An occluded marine trench led into a smaller chamber, hollowed out by June-Marie, in the virtual rock. On the floor was a treasure chest; pearls and gold spilling onto the floor. 'John designed all of this,' June-Marie explained to John's dad. She clicked on the treasure chest. 'Friendship is life's gold,' the chest said. 'May you collect many coins and know true wealth!'

'Oh, John,' June-Marie said. 'Someone left a gift for you here, hoping you would like it.' In the night, a visitor to their island had left an extra piece of treasure on the wall: a Roman-style bas-relief of a mermaid riding a dolphin. John liked it, and he agreed it should stay. Around Wilde's head floated a giant seahorse. 'Let's see if we can blow your dad away,' June-Marie said. She clicked on the seahorse, and Wilde jumped up to ride it like a bronco. John's dad smiled, and the group cheered.

It was time to wind up today's computer session. June-Marie logged out, then opened up Wilde's website. A woman called Pam, a regular contributor to their website, who planned to visit Evergreen for the first time within a few weeks, had left a new comment. June-Marie read it to John's dad: 'Hi amazing souls! We are listening. Your strength and spirit shine through your writing. Please continue to share so that we may begin to learn your many talents and dreams. Thank you for your generous hearts and minds. A big hug to you. You are making a difference.'

After buying Live2Give, John Lester helped June-Marie set up a blog for Wilde. Wilde had spent much of their lives on the receiving end of information. Now, they could announce themselves to the world. 'I have listened to much over my life,' Scott wrote on the group's blog. 'In many many settings, situations.' The blog was their first chance for them to speak, and for strangers to listen.

They posted regularly to the blog, in articles like 'My Perfect Day'. In this piece, Johanna dreamed of flying in a private jet to Disneyworld, then a date alone with Danny, perhaps dinner with musicians, then a Whoopi Goldberg movie. Scott wanted to go to the 'hottest most fun happenin club in all of second life!', then visit the virtual casinos, where every slot would pay out. Danny wanted to tour the White House, persuade George W. Bush to change his policies on the disabled, and have all the Dunkin' Donuts coffee he could drink. On their blog, Scott published his first poem, an ode to June-Marie, whom he calls his 'shade tree':

oh shadetree fair how can you know
the comfort in your shade
sitting next to you my friend
all the worries quickly fade

Later, on the phone from the Evergreen Center office, I spoke with Scott's mother. She was direct but honest about Scott's difficulties, and how Second Life had helped. ('She doesn't pull any punches,' Kathleen had told me.) Scott's mother was a technophobe who, she confessed, didn't want to do anything on her computer unless her son-in-law could come and help her. Still, she was supportive of her son's virtual life, even if she didn't fully understand it. (She called her son's new virtual home 'Second World'.) 'It's what they could be if they didn't have the handicaps,' she told me. 'He's walking around doing what they wish they could do. He loves it. I bet he would spend most of the day on it if he could.

'He can't reach out to other people and he can't communicate.' (To indicate he had something to say, June-Marie later explained, Scott could only screw up his face.) 'It does take people a long time to meet him, and to know him. A lot of people don't take the time. If Second World allows you to communicate, and meet and reach other people, I think that's a good thing. It just adds another dimension to Scott's life, and it's another dimension that makes him happy.'

I mentioned a poem Scott had published on their virtual island, called 'because of you', which read, 'thank you mom for all youve done / and all youve given me / another would have never done / your love has set me free.'

The depth of feeling in the poem, she told me, was a first in their relationship. 'He should have figured out I would be crying when I read that,' she said. 'Any mother would be. Never mind a mother who has a child who can't verbalise what he thinks and feels, and with June-Marie's help he is able to. How could a mom not cry?'

The response to Wilde's blog from the community was immediate. 'Instead of yessing them to death, strangers cared about what they had to say,' June-Marie told me. People emailed, visited their island, left comments on the blog. One Second Life resident, a real-world musician, asked permission to set Wilde's words to music. For the first time in their lives, the group felt, their disabilities were working for and not against them.

Wilde's blog was another way to share themselves with the world; but when writing for the blog, painstaking care had to be taken to get each word right. I witnessed a short, one-hour composition session, which resulted in three complete sentences. After a few drafts, June-Marie asked the group to rate the piece from 1 to 10; if anyone voted less than a ten (and, when I watched, they did), the group went back to he drawing board. Later, June-Marie gave me a single hand-written page, the result of 10 hours of group writing and editing, which they later posted on their blog as 'My dreams for the future'. 'So much to give, feel like it's bursting to get out, like too much popcorn in a microwave popcorn bag,' Wilde wrote. 'Second Life gives us the voice we've always wanted to have.' The piece concluded with a list of how they felt playing Second Life. 'It's like being rescued after drifting what seemed like a lifetime at sea. Like a door I've been banging on was finally opened, or like being born for the first time. It feels how I imagine an innocent man who has been locked up wrongly feels when he's finally set free.'

Even before their virtual rebirth, Wilde had been eager to give back to the world that supported them. They had sealed envelopes for telethons, written letters to Iraq war veterans and Iraqis alike, and held fetes (one bake sale raised $100 for Haitian hurricane victims). Now, through Second Life, they'd found a way to give more directly of themselves – not just through their writing, but also through their new virtual earning power. After the 2004 Indonesian tsunami, Wilde converted a large percentage of their online profits into US dollars, and sent it to the relief fund. (This kind of charitable instinct has spread elsewhere. After Hurricane Katrina, Sony introduced a new EverQuest II command – 'Donate' – which would contribute money to Red Cross relief efforts.) 'They play for a mission,' June-Marie told me, of Wilde. 'Not just for fun, but for other people to learn about them, and so reach more people in care.'

Kathleen Flaherty wasn't initially enthusiastic about the group spending time on the computer – she was worried they would be disappointed. By the time of my visit, though, her opinion had changed. 'I thought it was a little ambitious. I actually really underestimated the individuals. I thought they wouldn't be able to follow this. And I think that was just my own inability to follow it all. They've actually surpassed anything that I ever thought. They've solved more problems than I ever thought they would.

'You and me, when we go to a party, we shake hands, and one of the first things we talk about is what we do for work. Danny will meet you and the first thing he'll say is my name is Danny, I've got cerebral palsy. And for Danny, it defines him. Now, when I come in the morning, I see Scott and I see Danny and I see Mary – and they're just more alive. Second Life defines them.'

Kathleen told me how hard it was for the Evergreen residents to achieve even the basic goals. 'I remember a couple of years ago, Mary wanted to get a haircut,' Kathleen told me. 'She came in on a Monday, and her hair was not cut. She said the staff at the house called in sick on Saturday so she couldn't go, so they set it up for the following Saturday. She came in the following

Monday: no haircut. The van that they booked broke down so they couldn't go. They booked it for two weeks later. By that time she'd been five weeks without a haircut. The next appointment, her staff called in sick.

'There's a Super Cuts just a block away,' Kathleen told me. 'With five dollars and a half hour I can get my hair cut. For them, it's completely different. To get a haircut took Mary six weeks.'

That lunchtime, June-Marie took me to a drive through McDonald's. On the journey, we talked about how she and Wilde got involved in Second Life. She had been working at the Evergreen Center for three and a half years, she told me. Before that, she'd worked at a high-pressure managerial position until, hassled by her boss about a cigarette break, she finally quit to help out at Evergreen. She's never looked back. 'No regrets, even when the rent's due,' she told me. From the start, she was determined to put the Evergreen residents first. Even in the face of some objections from other staff, she was always physical with her clients. 'The more non-verbal they are, the more they respond to touch,' she told me. 'John and Scott can't reach out . . . If they need comfort, I will reach right into their personal space. It taps into them and brings them out.'

Back then, in her spare time, June-Marie played in The Sims Online. She used her other self inside the Sims Online to dramatise her real-life self, to act out rituals – like the one she held in a virtual fairy forest, a ritual rebirth of her relationship with her boyfriend, Rob. This particular virtual world never fully realised its potential, though. The Sims Online peaked around 100,000 residents in July 2003, and declined to below 50,000 by January 2005.

In March 2004, June-Marie left the Sims Online to become a resident of Second Life. The following January – four months before my visit – in conversation at Evergreen, her hobby came up, and the residents all begged to try. The management was reluctant, but after months of 'pulling and tugging, lots of red tape and circles,' June-Marie said, the centre agreed to allow access to Second Life.

The management decreed the group could only access Second Life for four hours each week. Still, June-Marie told me with a burger in her hand, they weren't getting as much time at the computer as they wanted. Everything at Evergreen took time, she told me, and the computer was no exception. With all the problems that could intervene, the group was lucky to get two hour-long sessions per week. They all yearned for more, she said. June-Marie had arranged a special dispensation to allow them more computer time during my visit, but even then, over three days, they spent a total of two hours online.

Cerebral palsy, which in Western countries affects around one in 500, arises from developmental disturbances in the foetal brain, which usually results in some mix of motor disorder and mental retardation. There is no cure. One particular agony of cerebral palsy is that it can affect the body but leave the mind intact. ('I live right here,' Danny told me a number of times during my visit, as he tapped his forehead with a bent wrist.) The members of Wilde can't go for a walk, they can't go out to the store, they can't hang out with other people without the attention of a personal carer. They're talkative, but their tongues can't talk. They're playful, but their bodies can't play. There is no effective treatment. 'If they drop a spoon, they can't pick it up,' Kathleen Flaherty told me. They socialise with few people except family and each other. Those who don't live in communal care homes live alone. Danny's elevator sometimes broke down, June-Marie told me, and each time he would be stranded in his apartment for a week or more. But she said he liked to live alone.

Every one of them has been physically hurt, stolen from, or abused, in one way or another, June-Marie told me, on another lunchtime trip to the McDonald's drive through. She explained other ways neglect could take its toll on her clients. One had spent a whole day and night in bed, after her care worker failed to show up. Another had waited six weeks for a wheelchair repair. Sometimes, June-Marie said, her clients arrived at Evergreen obviously sick, or hurt; rather than extend their already long night-shift with a morning trip to the hospital, their home caregivers would rather pass on the problem to Evergreen.

It was such a struggle to take care of their basic physical needs, June-Marie told me, that many care-workers didn't look much beyond that, to think about what they needed as a person. It rarely rose above getting them to the toilet, to meals, showered, dressed, and at the right place at the right time. (Most of the Evergreen Center care workers, Kathleen Flaherty later told me, worked at least two jobs.)

'I saw one care-worker who had decided to cut corners at lunchtime by mixing everything – rice, peas, chicken – into a blender and serving lunch as a puree. Can you imagine eating that?' June-Marie said.

'Perhaps the greatest pain is when our dignity is taken, our humanity, feelings, kicked around and abused,' the nine wrote together, then published as a postcard on their gift stall, which stood by the beach on their virtual island. (On the first day of my real-world visit, Scott had a red mark on his nose, which looked like a bad shaving cut. Scott was supposed to be shaved with an electric razor, but later that morning one of the Evergreen care-workers found a razor blade behind the cushion of his chair.)

'A lot of times we're caught up in the basics: "How's your wheel chair?", "Did so-and-so show up?"' Kathleen Flaherty told me. 'It becomes very custodial. We lose the individual. Some of the most important questions to ask this population are, "What's your favourite colour?", "What do you like to eat?". But, even more than that, "What are your hopes?", "What do you dream of?". Second Life takes them out of themselves and it connects them with other people. It's totally changed them.'

Wilde's step through the electronic looking glass had turned a negative into a positive. For the nine, mired in their respective physical limitations, leaving the world behind – if only for a while – was the most exciting thing in the world. For us, the liberation from gravity and friction, the divorce of experience from risk, can be lethal; for them, it was life-giving. 'It's enlightening, to watch them play Second Life, to see them broaden their minds, and their creativity, and realise there's more to these people than their disability,' Kathleen Flaherty told me. 'I've just seen their personalities come alive. Not just when they're using the computer. The game has become a part of their being.'

Ever since January 2005, when June-Marie introduced them to her virtual hobby, Wilde had found a way to leave their bodies behind, to inhabit a single, capable self, and to transcend all the difficulties that have always hedged their real-world possibilities. Through their virtual self, they could achieve not just the normal life we take for granted, but something even more fantastical: a life where anything is possible. The nine souls of Wilde shared responsibility for planning different parts of the island. Scott and Mary oversaw the landscaping. Danny, who had always wanted to make money, took care of their virtual finances. Johanna and Micah handled island humour. 'In the real world, kids see them in the street and cry,' June-Marie said. 'They know shame their whole lives. But not in Second Life. Second Life makes them almost free.'

In our new virtual worlds, we are free from gravity and friction. Up can become down, and a personality disorder can become a distinct advantage. The members of Wilde had lived their life hungry for contact, unable to reject anyone. As June-Marie explained it, the group had a lifetime of enthusiasm and energy. Now they had been released into Second Life, they were bursting with things to share.

Over the next few days I got to know June-Marie, and I witnessed first-hand her constant and fierce support of Wilde. I watched her touch, encourage and cajole each member of the group towards a feeling of self-esteem. When – as often seemed to happen at Evergreen – there were raised voices or some kind of trouble or confusion, Nichole would hunch and mutter, 'I'm bad luck.'

'No, you're good luck,' June-Marie flashed back every time. ('If I say it enough, it'll stick,' June-Marie told me later. 'One day she'll repeat that instead.')

Over the hour or so each day they were allowed to inhabit Second Life, I watched June-Marie's relentless enthusiasm sweep Wilde along through the daily chores of maintaining and updating a virtual island. At home each evening, June-Marie spent hours making tweaks or larger changes to the island, on Wilde's daytime instructions. (Charlene's pride and joy, which she kept upstairs in her pink and purple house on the north side of their island, next to a cabinet and a canopy bed, was her 20-strong virtual doll collection. The day I arrived, June-Marie had been up at 4 a.m., working on a new doll.) June-Marie's job title was 'Senior Case Manager and Human Rights Officer', but she called herself their 'mascot'. It was a self-deprecation that both belied and drew attention to her own importance. Without her, their virtual life would be impossible.

And, through June-Marie, I began to get to know Wilde. I saw their innocence, when June-Marie asked me to cover my notebook – a *New Yorker* cartoon depicting a partially nude mosaic – and I also saw their burning drive to be understood. Wilde seemed to me guileless, forceful and direct. Their inner life had been held in so long, it seemed, they had no time to play games or withhold. Their every effort was focussed on expressing as fully as they could.

For all the members of Wilde, communication was a struggle. Micah could talk, Scott and John could manage little more than different groans for 'yes', 'no', and 'don't know'. In front of Scott's wheelchair was a picture-board, with a hundred or so tiny images: a glass, a telephone, a McDonald's logo. With a gesture, he could suggest a road trip, ask for a book, or ask June-Marie to call his mother. By the time of my visit, though, Scott's board was more of a security blanket than a communication tool. His cerebral palsy had progressed, and he couldn't stretch beyond the third row; his reach now ended somewhere around McDonald's. Danny's cerebral palsy was so bad, he hardly talked at all. 'A stranger in the street wouldn't understand what any of them are saying,' June-Marie said. 'Most of them are entirely mentally able – but people don't realise.' When June-Marie first met them, she explained, she was surprised beyond her expectations at how much they felt they weren't listened to, how much they felt they weren't part of something. Their passion to give out, to share, to spread their message, still overwhelmed her.

With June-Marie's help, I talked with a few in more depth. First, I spent some time with John S. After some practice, and with June-Marie's translation, I learned John's three main responses: 'Yes' – a wider sound; 'No' – a lower sound; and 'I don't know' – a longer, changing note. (Only when I began to talk with Scott directly did I realise how expert June-Marie was at drawing them out. Most of her questions were answered with a yes, so I had begun to suspect the group was simply agreeable; when my turn came to ask questions, though, many were answered with a firm no.) I asked John what most excited him about Second Life. Was it: Exploring? Discovering? Building? Talking? What excited him most, he finally agreed, was the ability to move around. Everyone near him stressed this with loud voices and wildly waving heads and arms.

Over the course of an hour, John communicated the following: 'Second Life is my favourite activity. I want more people to learn about Second Life. I had no idea how important Second Life would become to me. I'd like to access Second Life at home, and spend more time in-world. I am happiest when playing as a group. I feel like a pioneer. I like the way we look online. No, I don't want a green Mohican in real life. Playing Second Life together has brought the whole group closer. I don't feel more confident or more expressive in the real world now, only more confident and expressive online. My mother and father don't understand Second Life. I'd like my mother and father to understand more.' (This last brought a big shout from John, the most enthusiastic 'yes' I'd heard all day.)

As June-Marie drove me back to the transit station, she explained how frustrated she was that Wilde couldn't spend more time online. She herself, I knew, already spent most of her free-time making Wilde's virtual wishes come true. She explained how she hoped to change her job description so she could spend more time in-world with Wilde. 'It's hard,' she said, 'but all these other things take rank.' I commented on the militaristic term. 'Well, my father was in the military.' I asked if he still was. 'No. He's dead,' she told me. 'He worked in many other countries. Before he died he said he could no longer remember how many he'd lived in. Just before he died, I asked him what he had learned from it all. He said: Everybody dreams. Everybody fears. Everybody loves. Everybody hurts. It's true, too. They do,' June-Marie said.

4

LESTER PROTOTYPE
The beginning of virtual worlds

Virtual worlds, in the sense of computer generated places we can inhabit instead of our own, have been with us for nearly a third of a century. In the spring of 1979, on Essex University's DEC 10 mainframe – an early computer with 128K of storage space, which came in four refrigerator-size boxes – a young student named Roy Trubshaw constructed a text-based world that people could share: the first Multi-User Dungeon, or MUD. My own introduction to the ways computers could create a world was through single-player versions of these MUDs. In 1980, when my father worked at a technology mall in San Jose, I would visit him at weekends, spin on a swivel chair, and type 'Go East', 'Hit Dwarf', and laugh as I read about the dwarf knocking me dead in turn. I learned to type that way: rattling out basic instructions to my new virtual self. (For years, I could type the word 'examine' faster than any other word.) Back then, there was an experimental packet-switching system linking Essex University to ArpaNet, the US Department of Defense network that later became the model for the Internet. People who logged on were given a description of their starting place; our first ever view into virtual worlds: 'You are stood on a narrow road between The

Land and whence you came. To the north and south are the small foothills of a pair of majestic mountains, with a large wall running round. To the west the road continues, where in the distance you can see a thatched cottage opposite an ancient cemetery. The way out is to the east, where a shroud of mist covers the secret pass by which you entered The Land. It is raining.'

Despite the world's limitations, MUD was compulsive. Within a year, people were logging on from half way around the world. It was our first shared virtual space: even if they'd never met in the flesh, in this new text-only place, up to 36 players at once could meet, talk and fight. They could even alter the structure of the world by altering room descriptions and adding objects, described in text, that other people could use and alter in turn. (Their modifications soon filled up the DEC 10's 50K of useable memory; the assembly code had to be completely rewritten.)

Over the next few years, a few people made some profit – a developer called Alan Klietz wrote a game called Milieu, using a computer language called Multi-Pascal on a CDC Cyber main-frame, an early super-computer. Klietz sold Milieu as franchises for a few hundred dollars – but none of those pioneers had anything like the success of the multi-million-dollar financial success of later virtual worlds.

Richard Bartle, who took over MUD development from Roy Trubshaw at Essex in 1980, has fond memories of those early, text-only virtual worlds. Decades later, in an industry dominated by graphical worlds, Bartle argued the text-only form could handle concepts – like multiple perspectives, or more abstract narrative experiences – that graphical games struggled with. 'In a textual world, I can stand in my own mouth, seeing my surroundings get light and dark as I open and close it,' Bartle wrote. 'I can be part of a painting I am carrying under my arm. I can have internal organs. I can photograph an opinion. I can un-erupt a volcano, store the world in a box, hold a soul in the palm of my hand, dance with the colour cyan. Do that in your 3D world.

'I prefer text: the pictures are better,' he wrote.

Parallel to the emergence of text-based multiplayer games, though, was another kind of virtual community: Bulletin Boards (BBSs). BBSs were modems people could dial up to, connect with, and exchange software and messages with other members of the community. They were like virtual youth clubs or hangouts; early, localised versions of the Internet, except that often only one person at a time could be connected. (Recently, some of these original servers were discovered: text-world ghost towns, uninhabited for 20 years.)

These BBSs, early frontier outposts of our virtual worlds, were John Lester's first experience of a community outside the physical.

John Lester was a hacker kid, who had grown into a hacker man. He lived in Cambridge, across the river from Boston, and the day after I left Wilde, I met with him at his hacker den, near Harvard Square. He was 35 with a clean-shaven head. The room was like a stage-set from *The Matrix*: a jumble of wires, hacked computers, black-light rave props. We climbed through a trapdoor and he showed me his basement server room, a spider-web of cables and makeshift racks packed with grey boxes and blinking lights, sprinkled with fans to keep the servers cool. We sat upstairs and sipped coffee, as he explained how his interest in virtual communities, which began as a child, led him to buy Wilde an island.

In 1979, aged 12, he told me, John bought his first computer – an Atari 800. In 1981, aged 14, he discovered the online BBS communities. He hung his home phone on the cradle of his 300-baud modem (6,000 times slower than his current Internet connection), and dialled the numbers of local bulletin boards. 'I realised, wow! On these bulletin boards you would talk to people, you could communicate with people all around the world,' he told me, 'and it was like you were in the same room.' One bulletin board led him to another, and another. He began to log on to these early virtual communities all around the world. It got him into trouble with his dad. 'Once you start getting into this virtual, cyberspace environment, it's very post-geographic,' Lester told me. 'You get into a sense of, "Oh, I'll just call this number." And you don't think where it is. You just want to get there. It's just a number, and you go there, and you're there instantly. So the first month I had discovered all these bulletin boards, we got a phone bill. I remember my father saying, "We have to talk, John. You're on the computer all the time; I guess you've been using your modem."' The bill was $400.

Lester begged his father not to take away his computer. Rather than stop using the modem – it wasn't an option – he worked out how to dial up local computers to re-route his international calls for free. 'And that's when I discovered the whole sort of shadow world of people online. I discovered this whole underground of people who had exactly the same problem as I did. People who wanted to connect with other people on all these long-distance bulletin boards, but didn't want to pay. Not criminals, but people who were interested in trying to communicate more with people.'

Through the BBS underground, Lester learned ways to make long-distance calls for free. 'The simplest ways were special codes that would allow you to bypass the local telephone company's billing, and actually have it billed to some other company. There were other tricks: you could call the local computer at a university, because their security was always really crappy. That computer would have a modem connected to it, and you would use that modem to then call long-distance. So next time the phone bill came there were like no long-distance calls on the bill.' Lester persuaded his father he was making only local calls, and his time in these early virtual communities continued. 'We had one phone line, and I was busy on it every night.'

He played some bulletin board games, including 'Trade Wars', but these were turn-based; you had to log off before someone else could log on and play their turn. They were competitive, too, which didn't fit with Lester's excitement about the cooperative possibilities of these early virtual worlds. 'I was never into fighting,' Lester told me. 'I was always very much interested in people working together towards a common goal.' Then, in 1983, a friend who was a freshman in Dartmouth, Massachusetts, where Lester grew up, showed him a 'dumb terminal' – a basic computer hooked up to the college mainframe computer – and he had his first experience of Richard Bartle's MUD. 'And that totally blew me away, because you were communicating with people, but then you were also part of a game, and you were working towards a common goal.'

Then, around 1987, Lester took a break from computers. At the University of Fribourg, Switzerland, he studied religion, then evolutionary biology. It wasn't until 1991, when he found himself working at Massachusetts General Hospital, that he bought himself a computer again. 'I started calling bulletin boards again. I re-plugged in to the computer underground scene. People said, Count Zero! Where have you been!' (Many of Lester's real-world friends still call him Zero, after Count Zero, his bulletin board 'handle'.) It was as if he'd never left. For a while, he and a friend ran their own virtual community bulletin board. They set up the Boston branch of 2600 magazine, a hacker monthly. Lester still remembers their first meeting – the first time he encountered his virtual friends in the flesh. They spread the word about a meeting in Harvard Square: 'I remember I wrote 2600 on a piece of paper, and I folded it and put it on the table.' And people arrived. 'It was really intense for me. I mean I remember thinking, "Wow, this is the person behind the text on the screen."'

All this while, Lester worked as a technician in the neurological department of the Massachusetts General Hospital. Then, in 1991, his chief of department, Anne Young, asked him to find creative uses of computer technology to support medical practice. He looked online, to see what seemed to be needed. 'What I found, primarily, were the patients and care-givers trying to find each other.' He decided to found an online community to support people with neurological conditions and their carers. He named it BrainTalk, after the cult NPR radio show 'Car Talk'. In 2004, Lester – by then a research assistant at Harvard Medical School – moved BrainTalk, now one of the largest neurological websites, with over 200,000 members, away from Massachusetts General. By the time we met, BrainTalk was a non-profit organisation, funded by donations and Google ads, run by Lester in his spare time.

John Lester stood and pulled down a projector screen which filled one wall, and showed me the BrainTalk website, a message board crowded with discussions on conditions ranging from ADHD to vascular malformations. 'What excited me about BrainTalk was the intense sense of community. Every group is different. Some are about handling disabilities in real life. Some are about starting the staircase of getting back to where you were. We're trying to empower people, raise awareness, and let them know they're not alone. I'm not an encyclopaedia. I'm a hotel manager,' Lester told me.

That year, EverQuest launched. EverQuest was one of the first virtual worlds to offer a first-person perspective, and at the time it was by far the largest. 'Norrath' – as Steve Clover, co-creator and lead programmer, christened the EQ continent – now stood at millions of square feet of virtual real estate; at one point, EverQuest would have a per-capita GNP greater than that of China. At the start of development, though, the project team had no idea their creation was to become such a phenomenon.

Clover and his co-designer, Brad McQuaid, had been working as database programmers, developing a single-player RPG together in their spare time. The few offers they had fell through, so they posted the demo on the Internet. John Smedley, who co-founded Verant, the company which first developed EverQuest, saw the demo, and offered them a job. 'As much as we loved database programming,' Clover told me, when we spoke in 2004, 'we jumped at the chance.'

As Bill Trost, senior game designer, remembered, the team's saving grace was that they had no idea what they were letting themselves in for. 'When I joined the project, EQ was just an idea,' he told me. 'They wanted to create a graphical MUD, and had some idea about how it would look, but not many specifics. We had lofty goals but we were lucky: we were too young and too new to realise how difficult it would be.'

Steve Clover created the original map of Norrath, inventing the city names – including the branded capital, Qeynos (SonyEQ spelt backwards) – and, with McQuaid, wrote the main design document. They sketched three continents, accessible by boat, where players could fight, loot, barter and even learn a trade. 'No one had ever made zones of that scale in a 3D game before,' Scott McDaniel, EQ's art director, said. 'We didn't know what the impact of open geometry or 10,000 polygons would be. The programming and art teams got together, and through sheer trial and error we banged out a system that was robust enough to take dozens of players in a zone, but still allowed the freedom to create very different landscapes.'

The geography near the team's offices in San Diego (Clover told me he could 'go surfing and skiing in the same day without driving too far') offered inspiration for Norrath's varied terrain. And the eventual population explosion that made the EverQuest phenomenon unique was mirrored in the way the staff ballooned within their small office. 'Early on,' McDaniel remembered, 'there were maybe 14 people attached to the project. All seven of the artists shared one cube . . . It was a bonding experience.'

McDaniel told me Norrath, EverQuest's landmass, was 'Leviathan'. 'We shipped with 78 zones. Half of those were outdoors and averaged 3,000 by 3,000 feet across. After that came the Kunark expansion, which had zones that averaged 8,000 by 8,000 feet.' When we spoke, five years and hundreds of millions of dollars worth of revenue later, a team of 43 developers, supported by over 100 customer service staff, continued to expand their virtual world – which had more than doubled in size. At peak times, the EQ servers exceeded 1 gigabyte per second of bandwidth – a DVD worth of data every five seconds. 'You're in our world now,' was the game's strap line, and they meant it. 'None of our games is about playing for an hour and being done,' McDaniel said. When I spoke with the EverQuest team, there were over 430,000 residents, who averaged more than 20 hours per week as their EverQuest self.

At that same time as EverQuest was preparing to launch, John Lester had begun to explore the possibility of more visual communities for BrainTalk. He had spent time in EverQuest and another dungeons-and-dragons-themed virtual world, Ultima Online, but he felt they were limited: more like a 3D story than an entire world. Then, in a meeting on virtual worlds at MIT, he met Mitch Kapor, who had founded the software giant Lotus. Mitch told him about a new project he had invested in: Second Life. 'It's the beginning of the metaverse,' Mitch told Lester.

Lester – whose Second Life avatar, I later discovered, was as lively and as bald as his real-world self – was irrepressibly excited by the possibilities of this uniquely flexible virtual world. It was important to Lester that his communities have the possibility to remain private, but as soon as that facility was added to Second Life – through the ability to buy a private virtual island, in which you could choose who you allowed to visit – he picked up the phone. 'As soon as the private islands were set up, I called Linden Lab, and I said, this is great. I want to get a virtual island. They asked, What do you want to do with it? and I said, Hmmm, I'll get back to you.' Lester thought carefully about who in BrainTalk might benefit most from Second Life. 'I was thinking very pragmatically. Who would be the best group of people? Who would be unafraid of something new technically – maybe even fascinated by it?' He struck on BrainTalk's Asperger's group. People with Asperger's typically have detailed, often technical fixations, but in the ambiguous complexities of interpersonal relationships they can feel utterly adrift. ('In social situations, they're like fish out of water,' Lester told me. 'They have to learn social skills like we learn to play the piano.')

'One of the effects of Asperger's syndrome is, sufferers are really interested in how things work. They like to take apart clocks and put them back together again. In extreme cases, it becomes a very repetitive, obsessive behaviour, but in a milder form it's like an extreme geek syndrome. On BrainTalk, the Asperger's group were technically the most advanced in terms of their computer sophistication. Plus, the major problem they're dealing with is the problems of socialisation, of finding difficulty in social interaction. In Second Life, you can build an arena, or a garden, or a terrace on a roof, and you can explore how people sit around, how they congregate, how they physically arrange themselves as a group, how they look at each other, how they can change their appearance to reflect the different ways they feel, how they can communicate in so many different ways beyond speaking. It just fit.'

In July 2004, using money from BrainTalk, Lester bought a 16-acre virtual island (at the going rate of $1,000 in real-world currency, although he did qualify for the Linden's educational discount of 25% on the $200 monthly land fees). He called it 'Brigadoon', after the enchanted village in the 1954 film of that name. Lester decided to trial the new virtual world for people with In January 2005, Lester advertised the island on a section of BrainTalk reserved for those who live with Asperger's. Of those who responded, around 10% – 12 people – seemed suitably technically competent to handle Second Life. Participants were encouraged to build homes on the island; John Lester settled there too, in a custom-built Addam's Family themed home. Their island became a practice space, a place they could visit and rehearse their real-world social interactions. In Second Life, the physical cues were present, but more basic – the typing in mid-air, the exaggerated laughter, a hanging head to indicate the user was away. (Lester mentioned the now-ubiquitous email 'smiley face' as an expression of the need to add emotional context to words, which Second Life expressed more richly.) The experiment was a success; the group loved Second Life.

'There's a story about an autistic woman who couldn't tell how close to approach people when she wanted to speak with them,' Lester said. 'She just didn't have that sense. She would either run up too close, or stand too far away, and it freaked people out. What she discovered was that the automatic doors in her local supermarket opened at just the right distance, the same distance people felt comfortable with. So she practised. She went down to her supermarket every morning, and walked up to the doors over and over until she had the sense of how far she should stand when she said hello. It confused the supermarket people, to say the least – in fact, I think they called the police – but for the woman, the practice worked; she slowly learned how far to approach someone before saying "hi". For the people in Brigadoon, Second Life is like that. It's a place where they can practise themselves.'

(For a moment, I thought about my own time in virtual worlds. At times I too had felt awkward, eager to avoid misunderstanding. I wondered if virtual worlds, with their reduced range of expression, made us all feel a little autistic.)

Virtual worlds aren't just a window into another world; they become an instinctive extension of the self. Lester used the analogy of how people identify with their cars. 'Just as you would say, "I drove to his house", or, "he nearly hit me", instead of "I drove in my car to his house", or, "he drove his car and he nearly hit the car I was driving". In virtual worlds, like in your car, you are not looking at the avatar: you *become* your avatar.'

In September 2006, researcher Dmitri Williams at the University of Illinois at Urbana-Champaign, conducted a study that showed even basic human body language transferred into Second Life. Male virtual selves, he found, stood further apart than female virtual selves, and when virtual selves stood too close, they were more likely to avert their gazes. 'When people talk about what they do in Second Life,' Lester said, 'they talk about "I am walking over the bridge. . ." It's the same for people with Asperger's, and it means their practice inside Second Life has real meaning in the outside world.'

Brigadoon was a success. Then, John heard about Wilde and he decided to offer them an island too.

That evening, John Lester took me for ribs at Redbones Restaurant in Boston's Davis Square. 'This place has the best ribs in Boston,' Lester told me, and everyone seemed to know: the restaurant was full. As we queued, John told me about his new favourite property: a volcano. He'd been flying over Second Life, just gazing at the strange forms that littered the landscape, when he spotted a mountain. He flew down to what turned out to be an immense volcano, over four virtual acres, crowned with a pool of virtual lava. He swooped for a closer look, and there, sitting cross-legged in the pool of lava, was the volcano's owner. The owner couldn't afford the land fees, he explained, but he also couldn't bear to sell the property, and see the volcano – unique inside Second Life – divided into parcels, like a manor house converted into flats. Lester decided he had to have the volcano. He convinced the man to sell it, insisting he would never parcel or re-sell the land. 'So, now I own a volcano,' Lester said. 'Just for the hell of it. Sometimes I fly down and sit in the lava myself. Just because I can.'

The group behind us in the queue edged away.

5

LINDEN LAB
Dreamers of the dream

Virtual worlds, I had discovered, cast a powerful enchantment, and many residents were deeply attached to their virtual selves. Eventually, in my journeys into virtual worlds, I was going to step on some virtual toes. The only surprise was how quickly they took offence.

In LAX, as I waited to board the flight to San Francisco to visit Linden Lab, my cellphone rang. It was Catherine Smith, Linden Lab's Senior Marketing Manager. 'Something weird has happened,' she said. 'We read your column.'

Two months before, in a column for a UK magazine, *Edge*, I had written about my meeting with a Second Life resident named Torley Torgeson, in the period before I met with June-Marie and Wilde. Torley Torgeson had an online love affair with another Second Life resident, Jade Lily. (They were both playing as women; later, they both discovered in real life they were men.) Torley and I had met, but not officially, and not much was said. I had phoned Catherine Smith to talk about Torley. 'He's a nut,' she told me. 'We love him. But he's a nut.' I wrote about this conversation, and about Torley. Due to a

70

mix-up, though, a piece on a Linden Lab website written by Wagner James Au – aka 'Hamlet Linden' – wasn't credited as the source for some of the quotes. Torley, one of Second Life's most vociferous residents, felt I had quoted his words out of context. Linden Lab leapt to Torley's defence. In one deft move I'd stirred the wrath of the gods, the press, and the people.

Linden Lab was a small start-up company, named after the address of its first offices, 333 Linden Street. Philip Rosedale, the CEO, had begun the business with his own capital, along with investors and entrepreneurs who had made fortunes from tech companies like Lotus, Xerox, eBay and Yahoo. When I visited, there were 30 or so employees, and 25,000 residents. Most people in the real world had never heard of Second Life. But to Linden Lab employees, Second Life was everything. That's the thing, I discovered, about an artificial world: from the outside, you can't easily see it at all. From the inside, it feels like the whole universe. Linden Lab were unhappy about my infraction.

What made Second Life different to most virtual worlds was that Linden Lab sculpted only the landscape. Apart from some core elements (like Orientation Island), everything was made by the residents. For Linden Lab, this was a coup. It avoided the immense effort and huge start-up cost required to build the contents of the world; they just laid out the territory, and let the world's residents fill it.

This ability to create and to shape objects at will was the notion that first captivated Rosedale. He'd always loved to build things, but, even as a child, he'd been frustrated by the limitations of the real world. In fourth grade, Philip built his first computer from a kit. In eighth grade, he bought a retractable garage door motor, climbed into his attic, and sawed a hole in the ceiling so that when he pushed a button his bedroom door would slid upwards, Star Trek style, into the attic. It wasn't easy, though, to shape the world according to his dreams. 'I would imagine some neat thing and then I go to try and build it in the real world and it was rather difficult,' he told me. 'You run into problems like abrasion and friction and the fact that you can't just cut things. So as a little kid who didn't have a lot of money and had a lot of imagination, I always thought, "God, I can't make anything." I was very good with my hands, with wood-working and metal-working and so forth, but there's only so far you can go without like big shop equipment, so I was just always wanting to make stuff.' That year, frustrated by his growing ambitions, he began to yearn for 'magical machine', a super-technical tool-belt that would let him build whatever he wanted, without worrying about all the real-world practical limitations that stood between him and his imagination.

By June 1999 – after putting himself through college with his own software company – Philip decided what he wanted wasn't the ability to change the real world, but to conquer it and replace it with something better: a virtual world, with no barrier between thought and action. He left his position as chief technology officer of RealNetworks, which had bought out his video streaming software and developed it into RealVideo. He joined forces with an old colleague, and formed Linden Lab. Their vision was a renovation of Philip's childhood dream: a world where people could build whatever they liked, and become whoever they wanted.

Right from the beginning of online worlds, the players were quicker than the developers to recognise the possibilities in their new virtual lives. The designers of EverQuest were stunned when they discovered players were getting married online. In The Sims Online, you can combine objects, but not create new ones. The residents worked hard to overcome this limitation: in one case, a group of Sims residents decided they wanted a piano, so they built one out of a desk and chairs, with cigars for piano keys. Linden Lab decided to harness that creative force, and allow its users to build literally anything they liked. Compared to the amusement-park atmosphere of other games, where missions and goals are laid out like set rides – the same experience for everyone – this world would be more like a public park, with a minimum of rules. Linden Lab would create the physics, design the interface, and invent the basic rules covering ownership. With luck, a whole virtual society would emerge. Linden Lab christened its world 'Second Life', after what they saw as its unique benefit. 'We agonized over the name,' Philip told me. 'We got into this classic marketing thing, where you talk about features and benefits. So the feature is distributed computing environment in which you can build anything, but the benefit is a Second Life.'

I met Philip at Linden Lab's real-world office: a grey stone-walled, high-ceilinged, loft-style building, with 30 or so desks grouped together in clover-like fours, with huge, high-spec PCs on each desk. On the wall were pin-ups that looked like holiday destinations – a Japanese temple, a tropical island – but were, of course, pictures of places in Second Life. The atmosphere was part cutting-edge start-up tech company, and part hardcore gaming cafe. (To our right, one employee was busy blow-drying his painted fantasy figurines.)

Philip Linden, Philip Rosedale's Second Life self, looked much like his real-world body – cropped blond hair, wide blue eyes. Philip had a wide mouth, and light brown hair in a short fringe, and when he grew excited, his eyes widened. When he talked about Second Life, he grew excited a lot.

We sat at his desk, and Philip logged into Second Life. His other self, Philip Linden, appeared on-screen – co-incidentally, in the very same place as Wilde had been, at the same virtual church. He hadn't been online for a few days, he explained. His last visit to Second Life had been for the wedding of two long-time Second Life 'residents', Mash Mandala and Baccara Rhodes – the same bride Wilde had danced with down the virtual aisle. (The wedding was so well attended, Philip explained, that the server nearly crashed; to reduce the number of objects the server had to handle, the bride asked everyone to remove their hair.) Philip's avatar was still hovering beside the virtual chapel, dressed to the virtual nines: a tux and white bow tie, red virtual rose pinned to his virtual breast.

We talked about his clothes. He'd bought them himself, from a virtual mall in Second Life. Fashion, he said, was a great example of how Second Life residents created their world. In the two years since Second Life appeared online, the available outfits had developed from basic patterns to entire ranges of sophisticated fashions, some the work of successful real-world designers. Much of the in-world Second Life content that is for sale is also advertised outside the world, on websites like SLBoutique.com, where you can use your real-world credit card, or in some cases even your cellphone, to buy virtual haute couture, delivered directly to your virtual self, online (with, of course, no shipping charges). Philip showed me a few garments – skirts, garters, ball-gowns – and pointed out the complex folds and textures: realistic-looking effects generated with coding tricks that had surprised even Linden Lab employees. Residents can also shop inside Second Life itself; they can take a virtual stroll through one of the many virtual malls, hand over their virtual cash, and receive outfits from automated machines that let you try before you buy. It's not just clothes; you can buy vehicles – a virtual Ferrari will set you back 800 Linden Dollars, or about $2.40. They can buy accessories (a virtual Blueberry Apple iBook goes for 200 Lindens), and, of course, there's the largest market: property. (A prefabricated virtual beach house goes for 1,800 Linden Dollars, about $6, but that's before you've bought the land to put it on.)

Philip showed me maps of the Second Life landmass as it grew: from the virtual equivalent of around 140 acres, when the first virtual resident touched virtual soil in March 2002, to around 11,200 acres when I visited, in early 2004. Demand for virtual land was so high, Philip said, they were adding 160 acres a week.

And all this was exactly what they'd hoped for. They would never have had the resources to create such a complex world themselves, but because of the free-form nature of Second Life, they didn't have to. Buildings, vehicles, clothing, even custom-made gestures – a dance, a wave, a different kind of laugh – all designed by residents, are at the centre of most Second Life activity and trade.

As an example, Philip gave me a tour of third-party websites, run by Second Life residents, which sold virtual clothes for your virtual self. At these sites, with names like 2ndlook, and SL Boutique, you could input your credit card details and purchase a pair of socks (10p), a ball-gown (20p), or a furry bear-suit (£1). (I asked if Second Life experienced fashion trends. Philip didn't have the figures, but from what I had already seen in virtual worlds, hemlines went up, and they stayed up. In Second Life, where perfect body shapes were the norm, people had it, and they flaunted it.) He took me through a gallery of images of community-made dresses; they looked as varied and as fashionable as those from the pages of Vogue. Philip explained how fast they had seen fashions evolve in Second Life, in a kind of arms race between designers for innovations that would attract virtual business. Early clothes were just 3D shapes. Soon, though, designers learned to add images of real cloth to the dresses. At the time of my visit, the latest fashion was for hand-sculpted dresses, with carefully modelled creases and folds. The open attitude to currency exchange had created a whole virtual economy. Residents worked – as designers, event managers, pet-manufacturers, hug-makers, even virtual strippers – to earn

Linden Dollars. 'The market is getting very competitive,' Philip told me. 'There's money to be made.' At the time of my visit, 20 or so Second Life residents sold enough virtual clothes, property and animations to exchange their virtual profit for US dollars, and live off the result.

'All this really incredible stuff is coming from the community,' Philip said. 'I think that one of the surprises with Second Life is the degree to which people do tend to want to rebuild the world that they know. So people's first purpose is to make an avatar that looks like them, and their second one is to have a Ferrari, or a house on a cliff, overlooking the ocean, built with wood, and with high ceilings. People first rebuild the world that they know, and only then do they defy it or experiment with it.' Philip took travel as an example. In Second Life, you can walk, or fly, but you can also buy vehicles to travel faster and in style. 'So people start with the Ferrari, and then after that they think, Well, where could I go from this? How about a floating car?' Only later do they realise they can grow wings. (Philip told me how, when they first opened their world to residents, they began with 20 people in 140 virtual acres; each one immediately built a virtual house, even though there was not yet any virtual rain.)

'We're trying to create an environment where any kind of stuff can happen. It's their world,' Philip told me. He turned to his screen and showed me his new favourite web pages: online photo albums that captured Second Life residents' favourite virtual moments. Someone called Kit Calliope rode a giant green dragon; there was an arty shot of a flock of flying metal bubbles; someone else was dressed up as a cartoon squirrel (the poster of the picture asked: 'Is this the cutest squirrel in the world?'). Philip likened Second Life to Burning Man, the festival in Black Rock, Nevada. Once a year, for eight days, around 40,000 visitors build a fantasy town on the dry plain of an ancient lake-bed, to create a place where almost anything goes. Inside his virtual world, Philip Rosedale hoped for the same freedom of expression, the same freedom from day-to-day concerns.

Inside Second Life, above Philip, a beautiful woman with fairy wings looked down and waved. Philip grew animated. In the new digital frontier, he told me, people were *nice*. 'I'm actually pretty introverted. I was a really nerdy kid and definitely not gregarious,' he told me. To illustrate the friendliness inside virtual worlds, Philip imagined a situation where, in a strange place, he saw a beautiful woman. 'In real life if I came out of the subway in Paris or New York or London, if I saw some beautiful woman just standing across the way from the exit, I wouldn't just go walk over to her. I wouldn't chat her up, no way, that would be very hard for me,' Philip said. 'Yet in Second Life, you do that almost instantly.'

'I don't know if the general public understands the funda-mental love Linden Lab has for the community,' Philip said. 'When residents see a Linden, they think: "They have god powers. They could delete me." But it's not like that.' He laughed. 'Well, we *can* delete them – but we don't. We are more like custo-dians. We make sure the trees grow, the land remains, the ocean flows. We're not so much gods – we're groundskeepers.'

To Philip, the world of Second Life was a triumph of self over other, an opportunity to improve on the real. 'Second Life is the statistical average of all our dreams,' he told me. 'We get to rewrite the most basic rules again, from the perspective of the human mind.' Philip, the child with the *Star Trek* doors, frus-trated by the limitations of his tools, had grown into a man enraptured by his own vision of a perfect world where every-thing was possible. 'We get to write the most basic rules anew, from the perspective of the human mind,' he said. 'Second Life is a world which is perhaps in many ways identical to the world

we live in, but, in a number of significant ways, better. Second
Life can make us communicate. It can make us better.'

Philip had a world to run, so he passed me on to Linden Lab's
Chief Technology Officer, Cory Ondrejka. Cory showed me a
series of aerial maps of Second Life, as their universe grew – a
chart of the virtual explosion, a mushroom of creative energy in
a non-material plane. In Second Life, as in the real world, you
can only see so far – but, being gods, the Lindens could change
that, and they did. They showed me pictures of the virtual world
as it would look if you could see forever: a seemingly limitless
jumble of construction that looked as messy and as captivating
as any real-world city. (Philip told me the ratio of residents to
virtual land meant their world was 'already as dense as Tokyo'.)
All the while, though, I was acutely aware of tension in the air.
Second Life was a small world, with just 25,000 residents
(although 2,000 new residents joined each week, and they added
10 new servers each week to cope with the load.) Linden Lab's
employees were clearly protective over my trespass with Torley.
A bigger company wouldn't have cared – press coverage is press
coverage – but Linden Lab seemed more vulnerable and more
idealistic than most games companies. I faced a kind of immune-
system response: was I friend? Or foe? Then, I remembered a
remark Philip had made earlier that cast the whole experience
in a different light.
  We had talking about how easy it is in Second Life to broadcast your intended self, through virtual clothes, virtual property, virtual gestures and virtual body shape. 'It's a trap,' Philip
had said. I asked him to explain. 'I mean that, in Second Life,
your ability to project an identity is so high, that it's a trap. A
good one, but a trap. I think people come to virtual worlds
sometimes because they think they can be more anonymous,
and hide behind a pretended identity with greater skill than in

the real world. But Second Life is going to pull out of you a little more than you wanted to say. You go into it thinking you're in control. I think what happens is, you realise, you're not in control.'

I was at Linden Lab to observe, to see how people built a world. I'd approached the topic of virtual worlds as a detached observer, but Philip's remark made me see there was also something here for me. What he'd described was exactly what had happened with Torley. I'd thought I was in control, but the virtual world showed me otherwise. These people weren't pixels on a computer screen. They were outside my control, and they were real.

Philip told me that, at Linden Lab, they had worked hard for a practical solution to an old philosophical problem: what is real? 'The thing we concluded,' he said, 'is that something is real only if you can change it. If there's a pixel on the screen in front of you in Second Life, and you can't alter it, then why would we put it there? It just fades into some . . . neutral grey ether. There are more subtle answers, too. Is something real if you can't own it?'

Building a virtual world is a practical endeavour, and for that you need practical definitions. Things are real if you can change them, or you can own them. Both of these, I saw, applied to objects – but, in offending Torley, I'd discovered a new definition of what was real, one that also applied to people. Real things could be hurt, too.

As the day went on, the immune-system response to my arrival softened into a kind of wary half-trust. The ice slowly melted, but I still sensed some resentment. Robin Harper, Linden Lab's VP of Community Development and Support, talked me through how she helped to encourage Second Life communities. She related the story of a group of students, studying a class inside

Second Life, who posted conversations, including names, alongside some derogatory comments about Second Life residents, on a public webpage. The residents were hurt and angry, and the students were asked to come into Second Life and apologise in (virtual) person. 'It was a very uncomfortable situation for a lot of people. They learned the hard way,' she said, with a pointed look at me.

After I left Linden Lab offices, I slunk around the corner and nursed a coffee. I felt very uncomfortable. I had made a mistake with my article, and, although their response had been extreme, I felt culpable. A writer gets their education in public. I knew my journey into virtual worlds would become a journey into our own world. I knew, like any medium, they would change how we saw ourselves. What hadn't yet sunk in was how the world would change us; how a journey into virtual worlds also becomes a journey into the self. It wasn't just those with autism, or those with cerebral palsy, who were changed by their time in virtual worlds. I learned something else too – something a close reading of Nietzsche should already have taught me: when you gaze into the virtual world, the virtual world gazes also into you.

6

LOGAN'S WALK
Absent friends

While I was in LA, June-Marie emailed to tell me Wilde was about to receive their first visit from a Second Life friend, known online as Kage Seraph – who, a month before, had taken Wilde for their first plane ride. I'd met Kage before: on one of my meetings with Wilde and Lilone online, he'd turned up for a virtual snowball fight, among the scripted fish in the shallows of Wilde's virtual tropical sea. When I met him online, Kage Seraph was short and wizened, with a long nose and pointy gnome-ears, and a bulky tool belt. After Wilde had logged off, I asked him about the belt; he said he wore it because he liked to build. 'Mostly historical weapons and armour, and giant robots,' he said. Before my eyes, Kage the gnome turned into a winged robot. Kage was Wilde's best friend, June-Marie had told me; I wanted to be there when they met in real life.

I was looking forward to seeing Wilde again. But this arrival was no easier than the last. After a day on tenterhooks at Linden Lab and a sleepless midnight flight, I was exhausted. My flight landed in Boston at 6 a.m. The airport pavements were still slick with melting snow. I flagged a taxi and slung my bag into the boot. Slumped in the back seat, I gave the address of the

Evergreen Center. The driver told me it was a long way; it would cost over a hundred bucks. I knew it couldn't be that far. Bleary-eyed from lack of sleep, I told him something was wrong, and asked him to stop. I leaped out, grabbed my cell-phone to call Evergreen, and watched the cab drive away. Only after a few seconds did I remember my bag was in the boot.

There was no sign of the taxi. I ran back to the rank, where the controller told me there was no way to track down a cab without the license plate. He asked what it looked like. 'Yellow,' I said. He brayed with laughter. He gave me a list of the five main taxi firms, and told me to call each in turn. I walked back to the terminal door and dialled the first number. My phone beeped, then the battery went dead. I slid down the wall onto a pile of snow and held my head in my hands.

I bought a new telephone charger, and I called every taxi company in Boston. Although they all told me I would never see my bag again, I left my name and number with each. On the last call, the dispatcher sounded just as hopeless, until I mentioned my name. 'Did you grow up in a cult?' she asked, suddenly excited. 'I'm reading your book! I love it! Hey, guys!' she shouted out into the office. 'That book I was telling you about! I got the author on the phone! He's lost his bag!' (Did she think I'd find it again? 'Not a chance!')

To replace my belongings I needed a police report, so I trekked through the slush past three terminals to the airport police. Then, clothes-less and cold, exhausted and feeling like a failure, I gave up. I chose ease instead of struggle. I walked a mile to the airport hotel and got a room. With my nine new disabled friends waiting eagerly for my second visit, I stripped off my wet clothes, show-ered, and got into bed.

I wanted things to be easy. I wanted to evade my struggle. I too was labouring under a delusion, the dominant enchantment of my time. I was on the run from my own body, eager to flee

82

the absences of the past and the sorrows of now. 'You can hold yourself back from the sufferings of the world,' Kafka wrote in his *Blue Octavo Notebooks*. 'This is something you are free to do, and in accordance with your nature. But perhaps precisely this holding back is the only suffering you might be able to avoid.'

I switched on the porn channel, bought some non-existent company, and I held back my suffering for as long as I could.

The next morning, on the hotel's wireless network, I discovered I'd had the wrong address for Evergreen. I'd copied out the administration office address, 50 miles away. That morning, armed with the correct address, I set off in another a taxi.

The previous evening, when I awoke from my slumber, I'd called June-Marie to apologise for my no-show. When I arrived in the Evergreen activity room, June-Marie grabbed my arm and looked me up and down. 'We wanted to check. We thought you might have lost a limb.' Around her, Wilde erupted in delighted laughter.

June-Marie left to collect Kage – real name Logan Park – from reception. She returned with a young man in his mid-twenties, with a straight blond fringe and serious eyes. Micah – still wearing his gold plate necklace, but now with a blue tracksuit and white trainers done up with Velcro – strolled up and held his hand for a hi-five. 'Hey, Logan, what's up, my man?' he said.

To meet Wilde, Logan had driven four and a half hours from Vermont. When we'd last met in Second Life, I'd assumed from his gnome appearance he was an older man (there were few ugly people in Second Life, and I'd assumed it took an older perspective to choose to be odd-looking) but it turned out Logan was a college student. For years, Logan had helped out on Saturday mornings at a local centre for the disabled. Then he read about Wilde online. 'I first read of Wilde on the Second Life forums, on a thread that was discussing how Second Life can mean a lot to folks who struggle otherwise in real life,' Logan told me. 'So I poked around what was then a small kiosk of their poetry and pictures, and got in contact with them as a natural extension of that.'

After he met Wilde, Logan began to hang out with them in Second Life. The previous Christmas, after Wilde had mentioned they had trouble seeing their other self through the small window of Evergreen's only monitor, he'd sent them a gift: a huge computer screen.

Logan had spent the previous five months in real-world solitude, walking the Appalachian Trail, and he told me his return to civilisation had left him with sensory overload. He was ready to take humanity only in small bites, and, he told me, Second Life was helping him ease back in.

Once Logan had said hello, we made our way into the computer room. It was the first time Wilde's best friend had seen their projector set up. 'Wow, that's good. This is so cool, you guys,' he said.

With June-Marie at the helm, and the whole group shouting their desires, Wilde began to navigate Second Life. There'd been a few changes to their virtual self. The previous weekend had been St Patrick's day; the group had dyed Wilde's virtual hair green, and they'd all voted to keep it that way.

'What shall we do today, guys? Shall we hang out with someone?' June-Marie said. The group agreed. She pulled up a list of their Second Life friends. One, Ace Cassidy (in the real world, Rob, June-Marie's live-in boyfriend) was online. 'Shall we say hi to Rob?' June-Marie asked. 'Or do you guys want to go exploring?' Mary said something that sounded like Hi Rob. 'Alright,' June-Marie said. 'Your wish is my command. Shall we ask him for a teleport?' (In virtual worlds, if you want to see someone, you can instantly appear by their side.)

The screen blinked. Wilde stood in a Wild West poker saloon. Above their head swung a saloon-bar chandelier. Nearby were two long poker tables, complete with cards and stacks of chips. Along the wall was a row of gunslinger and Mae West lookalike cartoons. Like most virtual worlds, Second Life was regularly updated, adding new possibilities for your virtual self. The last Second Life update added the ability to play your own music on your virtual property. Honky-tonk piano tinkled out across Ace's saloon. In the distance, the virtual sun was setting over someone else's Egyptian-themed virtual property; an anomalous row of pyramids towered against the orange sky.

'Real quick,' June-Marie typed, and read aloud for Wilde, 'the room needs to know, is this PG safe?' (The Evergreen staff had to abide by conduct rules, which more or less parallel those of a PG movie.) Ace's reply appeared as text on the screen. 'It's mature, ma'am, but I think there's nothing around here that would be offensive,' June-Marie read aloud. Ace's fingers wriggled as the text appeared. 'Welcome to Pocket Bullet,' Ace typed. 'Under construction, as usual.'

Ace Cassidy's fingers wriggled again. A stream of colour stretched out, and, on the saloon floor, a cake appeared. 'Look, there's the cake he's trying to script for John's party,' June-Marie said. 'Remember I told you there were penguins on it?' The group was planning a surprise party, inside Second Life, for John Lester. Lester liked penguins, so the group voted to send a virtual invitation, which included a virtual costume. When the guest of honour clicked on a secret pile of snowballs, he would be teleported up to his party in the sky; there, they planned, he would be surprised by a group of his closest online friends, all dressed as Emperor penguins.)

A staff member appeared in the computer-room doorway. There was a real birthday party next door, and she'd brought cake. The group asked her to save their slices. For now, the virtual cake had their attention.

Ace Cassidy's fingers wriggled again. 'Want to see the wheelchair I'm designing?' June-Marie read from the screen. 'Let me explain about your idea,' she typed to Ace, then turned to face the group. 'He wants to know if you guys are interested in doing wheelchair demolition races,' she said. 'Where you drive your wheelchairs into each other and crash.' The group wailed and groaned in enthusiasm. (In Second Life, Wilde's wheelchairs were a choice the group could enjoy.) John S. moaned in a different tone – he was objecting – and June-Marie put a hand on his arm. 'Alright. John, I'm with you, OK? The day they do the demolition derby, we can be away.'

A passing staff member overheard. She shot June-Marie an accusing glance. 'Oh, he means this kind,' June-Marie said. She pointed at the screen.

'Oh, I thought you meant . . .'

'No. Never! No. You'd have to shoot me first!' June Marie laughed.

On the screen, Ace Cassidy moved his arms in a semaphore of gestures. He had created another new feature in the virtual world. In a beam of coloured light, a fully formed wheelchair appeared. Apart from John, the group cheered.

'OK, so what he's showing you is a wheelchair, but it's under construction,' June-Marie said. 'He's just playing with it to make sure he can make it do what he wants it to do. Then we can make it look pretty. So what do you want to say? Do you want to say something about it? He's gonna be looking for feedback here.'

Scott threw his mouth open and laughed, a gurgle that came from deep in his throat. Mary smiled and writhed her arms. June-Marie typed, and read her words aloud. 'Scott's laughing, Mary likes it, anybody else like it? Micah?'

'Motorcycle ride,' Micah said.

'OK, Micah, maybe we can go for a motorcycle ride with him tomorrow. If he's available. Do you guys like the idea of a wheel-chair bumper-car area?' Mary nodded a yes. 'The room seems to like it,' June-Marie types. 'But we're a little tired. We'll need to discuss it more.'

Ace Cassidy's hands were ghost-typing again. June-Marie read his words aloud. 'You folks can sell wheelchairs on the island so people can have wheelchair races.'

Mary cheered.

For some of the group, Second Life had offered their first chance to make real money. The money Wilde planned to make from selling virtual wheelchairs wouldn't just be virtual; if they chose, they'd be able to turn it into a real-world profit. A growing selec-tion of items on their island were for sale – 200 Linden Dollars (about 80 cents) bought you a virtual drum, which beat out a rhythm and animated your avatar wildly. Along with some in-world donations from their friends, the group exchanged some of their Linden Dollar profits and acquired a new computer and a projector, to facilitate both their virtual and their real-world lives. The new equipment helped them see their Second Life more clearly, but just as importantly, others at Evergreen could use the equipment too, for other activities. ('The projector was just like Christmas to us,' Kathleen told me.) Through Second Life, Wilde had given something back to the people who had cared for them for so long.

Once again, Wilde felt mischievous. Mary said she'd like to dance. June-Marie took a straw poll: the group agreed. June-Marie picked an animation, and Wilde leaped onto the virtual poker table and shimmied on the felt. Ace laughed, the same familiar exaggerated motion. 'You're supposed to do that after you win big money, not before!' he typed, holding his belly and doubling over. The room cracked up in laughter. Ace copied

Wilde's dancing animation, and the two wriggled and jived across the floor.

As he danced, Ace's fingers tapped away. 'I don't think I've ever danced with a green-haired man carrying a baby on his back before,' he wrote.

Then it was time to break for lunch. The group shouted their goodbyes. 'Charlene says thank you. Dan says thank you. Scott says thank you,' June-Marie typed. 'The pleasure was all mine,' Ace Cassidy replied. On the way to McDonald's, June-Marie talked to me about Wilde's plans for the future. 'Even the fact that they have plans is something amazing, and all down to Second Life,' she told me. 'When I met them, they were afraid to think about next week. Now, we're working with residents in all kinds of ways. They want to spread the word. Not just to people with cerebral palsy, either. Even the deaf are freed up by Second Life, because everything is related in text. It makes no difference how well they hear or how clear they sound. For the more severely disabled, the liberation is greater. But for everyone, it levels the playing field. I want people to hear about Wilde and think, "What if I got a computer? What would I be able to do?"'

Wilde hoped to reverse the pattern of care which has dominated their life by hosting their own virtual events, taking care of others this time. On their blog, John S. had written his own dreams for sharing their discovery with the world.

'I dream we are on the brink of a new time for people with extreme physical challenges,' John wrote. 'I see the vast online world as part of the answer. Virtual communities like Second Life [are] filling in the gaps that the physical world leaves gaping. For me, and I can only speak for myself, it has been the most transforming thing to happen to me in all my adult life.'

*   *   *

My time at Evergreen was coming to an end. At the reception, Logan said his goodbyes and left; he'd be coming back the next day. When we arrived back in the playroom, I asked if any of the group wanted to speak with me privately.

Mary nodded to June-Marie. Until now, Mary had been reluctant to speak. She tended to put the others first. (The previous April Fool's Day, June-Marie had told me, a friend at Evergreen had tricked Mary into believing she'd won the lottery. She tried to run the same trick on Danny, but she had barely finished before she blurted out: 'No sir! I can't lie to you!') In my group discussions with Wilde, Mary had always waited till last. Only when Scott raised his hand, and asked Mary to talk for him – 'Scott is Mary's most favourite,' June-Marie whispered to me under her breath – had Mary spoken up. Mary had not originally been part of Wilde. When June-Marie had arrived at Evergreen, Mary had spent her time alone. She didn't trust any of the carers enough to join a group. For June-Marie's whole first summer, when most of the Evergreen activities took place outside, Mary sat under a tree, and she kept a close eye on June-Marie. That winter, she watched from a corner of the playroom. The next summer, whenever June-Marie looked over, Mary looked back from under the tree: for two years, she kept up her distant vigil. Finally, one afternoon, Mary wheeled up to June-Marie and asked if she could join in. 'Do you remember, on your first visit, when we first went to the computer room, Mary asked me if she could come too?' June-Marie asked me. 'She asks that every time, for every activity. She has done for years.'

Mary had waited her turn, and now she wanted to have her say. The group filed out. ('Can I spend the night in the building?' Micah asked. 'I don't know,' June-Marie replied with a smile. 'There might be rats and bats in here.') June-Marie motioned for Charlene to stay behind – 'Charlene, I'm going to borrow your ears,' she said.

For the first 10 minutes, Mary stuck to a familiar line of conversation, and June-Marie had no trouble interpreting. Mary began by describing her life. She owned her own apartment, June-Marie explained. She liked computers – on a scale of one to 10, computers were a 10. She didn't have one at home, but she'd like to if she could: she'd spend three hours a day online. She moaned, a long sound of distress. 'I wish I could stand up,' June-Marie interpreted.

Mary talked on. She'd been married and divorced. She had personal care assistants (Cynthia was her favourite) who came to care for her basic needs a few times a day. She'd had no contact with her family for decades. 'Not all family relationships are helpful,' Mary said.

Then Mary indicated she had something else to say. This wasn't part of her usual conversation. June-Marie leaned in close to listen.

'You . . . Would . . . Like . . . To. Say. If everybody. Listens. To the disabled. It could change the world. Is that right?' Mary nodded. 'You,' said June-Marie. 'Think. Your. What?'

'Feelings,' Charlene said. Mary nodded.

'Feelings,' June-Marie said. 'Thank you Charlene. Are. Real.' Mary choked, coughed, and nodded.

'You,' translated June-Marie. 'Feel. People. Don't take you . . . seriously. You. Don't know. What. To do. To change things.'

'Do you think Second Life will help in that way?' I asked.

Mary writhed her legs and arms, nodded, and groaned. 'Yes,' June-Marie said. 'You. Love to play. Second Life. You. Feel. You. Have. The right. To be who you are.'

Mary coughed again.

'That's all,' June-Marie said. Mary started to cry. 'It's OK,' June-Marie said. 'You can cry.'

Mary cried herself out, and we sat in silence. Then Kathleen, the centre coordinator, stuck her head in the doorway: it was

2:30, and the van had arrived to take Mary home. As I followed Mary out the room, she groaned something to me over her shoulder. Without thinking, I replied, 'It was good to meet you too.'

'Did you hear that?' June-Marie said. 'He understood you.'

Mary nodded. She reached up and she pushed her fingers into mine.

On my final night in Boston, I took John Lester and June-Marie out to dinner. As we waited for our food, we talked about the decisions people make when they sculpt their virtual selves. John Lester, I knew, had modelled his virtual self identically on his real body. I asked June-Marie why she hadn't made her avatar like herself. Too late, I realised what I'd implied. 'You mean, why did I make myself hot?' There was an awkward pause. 'Well, I meant, hotter . . .' I said. They laughed.

I mentioned the difficult time I'd had with Linden Lab. John Lester insisted they meant well. 'They'll come around. It'll blow over. I've told them: you're a friend.' Again, his language – us, them, friend, foe; the clear line between those who shared the dream and those who did not – reminded me of my childhood.

Then, John announced he had some news. When we last met, Lester had told me he was in talks with Linden Lab to work with them in some capacity. In between my first and second visits, after an eight-hour interview in their San Francisco offices with eight of the top Linden Lab people – what Lester called 'the gauntlet' – John had been hired by Linden Lab. He was now their Community Manager. 'I am now Pathfinder Linden,' he announced. He reached under his sweatshirt and pulled out a medallion: a pewter hand with a black leather strap. It was the Second Life logo: an eye inside a curlicued hand. Every new employee was given one, he said. 'The eye observes the world, the hand shapes it,' a card which accompanied the locket explained. 'For this reason, many cultures embrace the eye-in-hand as a symbol of creation that springs from knowledge – as do we. Take it as your invitation to help create a Second Life that inspires ever more wonder, ever more imagination.'

'The pendant flashes when I say something against the Linden Lab party line,' John Lester joked.

We ate – when the bill came, John Lester joked about how virtual lobster was so much cheaper – and, at Harvard Square station, we waved goodbye. On the train, I couldn't help but still feel troubled about Linden Lab's reaction. On my visit, Philip Rosedale's messianic zeal – which informed the whole Linden Lab endeavour – had become apparent. 'We're not building a game, we're building a new world,' Philip told me. 'We can't understand why there aren't a million people in Second Life.' The zeal reminded me of my mother and her friends, who, in their mission to spread the word about the perfect new world they were building, sometimes ran roughshod over other people's feelings. Hidden behind Linden Lab's seeming liberal attitude, it seemed, there was an unacknowledged morality. They were, as Freud wrote about us all, 'far more moral than they thought, and far more immoral than they could imagine.'

There was some tension, I knew, between the Second Life community and their gods, the Lindens. Their power over the universe, and their tendency to make choices according to their own morality and agenda about what was 'fair' to their residents, had already led one resentful customer to christen the company 'KremLinden Lab'. And I wasn't the only one to receive Catherine Smith's wrath. In December 2005, CBC Radio reporter Lindsay Michael put out a request on the Second Life community website Dragon's Cove Herald, for Second Life residents in the Toronto area. One resident, known as Plastic Duck, announced on another website – Something Awful – his intention to 'expose just how filthy [Second Life] is these days'. Plastic Duck wrote to Lindsay Michael, but so did Catherine Smith. 'I noticed your call for interviews in the Second Life Herald and wanted to speak with you directly about Plastic Duck,' she wrote. 'You may or may not know that Plastic Duck has been banned from Second Life for griefing and generally anti-social behaviour . . . you probably won't get a very balanced interview from him. And he is certainly not representative of our community.' Linden Lab later amended their 'Research Ethics in Second Life' policy to instruct any reporters who wanted to interview Second Life residents to contact the Linden Lab marketing department first. I began to sense there was something else about the makers of virtual worlds, an insular protectiveness that would deserve investigation. If the makers of virtual worlds were gods, then their worlds would be made in their own image, and that image would also cast a shadow.

Once more, their underground morality reminded me of the idealised communes of my childhood. I'd felt the sharp end of Bhagwan's disciples' mania for positivity: they'd labelled me 'negative', the only sannyasin sin. Bhagwan's communes were intended as places of 'Life, Love and Laughter'. Virtual worlds, too, inspired a similar, almost religious, devotion.

The parallels were uncanny. My mother and her friends, for the most part, declared their devotion to their guru, Bhagwan, in a letter. In return, Bhagwan wrote back: 'Dear Beloved . . .' and, in his reply, gave them each a new name. And here, again, in this new, idealised corner of the universe, the virtual self of each Second Life employee was given a new surname. My mother and her friends wore a locket, with a picture of their guru; Linden employees, on becoming a Linden, were given a Second Life logo to wear around their neck.

*　　*　　*

Still, I couldn't help but think their reaction had rattled me out of proportion to the events. I was tired, and I'd lost a bag, and I'd offended people, and I felt out of my depth – all manageable problems, but together it all somehow felt much worse. My regret was like a constant cold burn, like walking through a cold fire that burned and froze and stripped everything away. Perhaps I was feeling a small echo of Wilde's own struggle, the loss and hardship that had stripped all luxury from their lives. My own difficulties were simply the troubles of modern life: disappointments, mistakes, thwarted hope. These were the everyday struggles people migrate into virtual worlds to avoid. And for members of Wilde, these struggles were magnified a thousand-fold. Wilde's struggle seemed to embody a hidden conflict in the life of the world: the darker side of the capitalist dream of ease. Despite what we are sold, we are vulnerable. Weakness and frailty were inevitable – important, even. Wilde lead a life full of jeopardy and loss, like the rest of us, only more so. My own instinct was to retreat into comfort, but Wilde could not retreat. Their frailty was a gift to us, and Second Life was where they gave it. 'i'm trapped i'm trapped but so are you,' Mary wrote on the group's weblog:

> tho perhaps you see it not
> your trapped inside frailities too
> your worries make you rot
>
> take my hand oh feeble friend
> for i am feeble too
> together we can make the world
> better for me, better for you

At Government Center station, I changed to the *Blue Line* northbound. On the platform, a balding rocker in a green corduroy jacket set down a portable amp and plugged in an electric guitar. The empty station echoed to the mournful chords of Pink Floyd's 'Wish You Were Here'.

There was one more airport train, scheduled for 12.49 a.m. I saw the train's terminus, listed on the departure board, and I laughed. I closed my jacket against the cold, and waited for the last train to Wonderland.

7

HACKING MATTER
Changing the world for fun and profit

After my visit to Wilde, I didn't return to Second Life for six months. I had begun my journey in a small virtual world, and found not just ease: instead, I'd discovered a new mix of trouble and consolation. Once again, though, the real world intervened with its own plans. On my return, all the loss and struggle of the journey – the plane flights, the insurance claims, the lost bags and cellphone, the 4 a.m. starts and the rainy waits for cabs – only added to my struggle with the daily tasks of real life. The world and its responsibilities reared up and threatened to swallow me again. In the burglary before I left, my laptop had been stolen. Disheartened, I began the slow process of reconstructing my notes from scratch. The relationship I had been in for five years broke up, and I began to search for a new home. The £1,000 I had spent on a PC, my gateway to virtual worlds, left a deeper hole in my overdraft. I took up smoking, another kind of narcotic to stave off my disappointment. I was partying too much, on money I didn't have. Once more, I was struggling to face up to the challenge of my mistakes and my history.

Virtual worlds had at first seemed an attainable, inhabitable ease: a smaller, safer world, where I might find some solution to the almost intolerable pressure of the real. But even there, I'd found strife. I was having trouble even spending enough time in the worlds themselves. Who had the time to lead two lives? I barely had time to live one.

To tell the truth, I was also ashamed. I'd offended the real people behind the virtual selves, and felt their real wrath. I hid from Second Life, in the same way I'd hidden from Wilde in my hotel room. It struck me, too, that this was always the way I'd responded to strife. As a child, faced with the antagonism of a commune that didn't understand my resistance, I'd armed myself with a science fiction novel and a Marmite sandwich, and taken refuge behind a commune sofa. I was already, unconsciously, taking up the same relationship with the virtual community as I had as a child, with the intense and idealistic community that had defined me. I was hiding like I used to hide: a witness, reluctant to participate. When faced with trouble, I retreated. I would discover something about myself, it seemed, on this journey too.

To add to my troubles, I discovered the cellphone I rented at JFK on my first visit to Wilde, which I thought had been lost, had in fact been stolen. In the 12 hours before my call to report the loss, the thief had made over calls to Africa. The cellphone company, Rentacell, billed my credit card over £2,000, and my bank refused to reimburse me.

The theft put me in mind of the now colossal economies of virtual worlds. Of the estimated yearly $400 million in virtual trade, I thought, there must be rich pickings for scammers and thieves. I wanted to move on from the virtual shallows of Second Life, a relatively small world, to spend more time in larger virtual universes. I logged onto EverQuest II – population, 300,000 – and I took on the role of virtual gumshoe. I put my foot in virtual doors, and asked awkward questions about virtual crime. That was how I met Noah Burn.

*   *   *

Noah, a pony-tailed 24-year-old aspiring writer from Myrtle Beach, South Carolina, had discovered a way to alter the very fabric of the virtual universe itself. In his real life, Burn worked as a showroom salesman, selling what he called 'upscale designer furniture'. 'It was well paying,' he told me, 'but not as well paying as EverQuest.' For Noah, who journeyed to the murkier side of virtual trading, virtual furniture became more lucrative than real furniture could ever be. Noah, previously a resident of EverQuest, was new to EverQuest II. Excited by the possibilities of the new skills, Noah set up an account, but he quickly grew bored of making virtual things. ('I was promised that trade skills would be more fun in this game than the last,' he said, referring to changes in the rules that supposedly made in-world construction more fun. 'I tried them; they weren't. It was a no-talent, button-mashing marathon.') For a while, Noah set up a basic virtual gambling den – what he called 'a ghetto casino' – where people would pay him and, using a random number generator inside EverQuest II, double their money if they scored more than 65. 'The odds were horrible, but they kept coming,' Noah told me. 'It was like Vegas, really – except, no free drinks, and the people weren't social.' Bored of dealing with money-grubbing strangers, Noah decided to move into a variation of a business he already knew. He set up a virtual furniture store. Noah's character, a gnome called Methical, found places in little-known areas (what he called 'the dark side of the game') to buy desirable virtual furniture – an oil painting, an ornate chair, a wine rack – for 50 pieces of virtual silver. He turned his apartment into a virtual showroom, and sold his furniture to residents with less virtual nous, for twice the price.

One afternoon, he bought a rare 'Gnomish Thinking Chair' to sell on at a slim profit. He opened his inventory – which appeared as a window on his screen – clicked 'Sell' to put the item up for sale, then closed the sale window to better see his virtual showroom. Normally, when Noah put an item up for sale, it disappeared from his possession until it was sold, at which point the object reappeared in the possession of the buyer. Unusually, this time Noah found he could return the chair to his showroom, even though it was for sale. He thought nothing of it, until later in the day when he got a message from another EverQuest II resident called JimBob. 'This chair isn't as cool as I thought it was.'

'What chair?' Noah – Methical – messaged back.

'The "Gnomish Thinking Chair",' JimBob replied. Methical looked over: the same chair was still on his showroom floor. In his real-world room, Noah started laughing. 'It was the kind of laugh you have when you're a kid and you just hit a house with an egg,' he told me. Noah contacted his 'guild', a group of friendly players. 'I think I just duped something,' he said. Noah had discovered a bug in the game's code, which meant he could copy any virtual item whenever he liked. He could buy one expensive item, copy it, and sell it to as many buyers as he could find.

Finding a way to duplicate virtual items was the equivalent of a virtual printing press for dollar bills, Noah realised. If he played his cards right, he could find himself sitting on a very real gold mine. He called on a friend, Liz, from Beaverton, Oregon, also an EverQuest II resident, and the pair set out to build a career as virtual forgers. They copied a few items to confirm the Gnomish chair wasn't a fluke. Then they set up a production line.

To maximise their profit, the pair focused on the most expensive items, beginning with candelabras. (After all, Noah knew the virtual furniture market inside out.) Noah offered 10 candelabras for sale, placed them in his showroom, then Liz bought them; they had 20 candelabras. Then they had 40 candelabras. Finally, they owned more candelabras than they could store in Noah's virtual apartment. They sold them on to other residents for two gold pieces each. After a day of trading, they had sold a hundred candelabras, which netted them two platinum pieces of virtual money. This was at a time when virtual item trading sites sold platinum, one piece at a time, for £150. The next night they copied furniture, Noah said, 'until our eyes bled.' Bored of candelabras, they switched to high-end paintings, which went for five gold pieces (about £10) each.

In virtual terms, the two were rich. The pair worried that the authorities – Sony Online Entertainment, who run EverQuest II – might notice their forgery and confiscate the profits. To launder their virtual money, they bought virtual mansion houses, the best spells, the most expensive in-game horses they could find. 'Hell, I even bought stuff and then just destroyed it. I had a crazy idea that the more I spread the money around, the less chance I would get banned. It started to feel like *Goodfellas*,' Noah recalled. 'You know, that scene where they rob the airport, then all the mafia members are told to lay low and not spend any money. Then one guy shows up with a fur coat and a Cadillac.'

Each morning they prepared to discover they had been caught red-handed, and each morning they found they could continue their forgery. The excitement kept them in EverQuest II for up to 20 hours straight. 'I can't even describe the almost magical feeling – of just being some mad scientist while everyone just walks past you on the server, not knowing what you're up to.' Noah found the single most lucrative item: a rare virtual pet dog, called a Halasian Mauler. They forged those. They bought more copies of EverQuest II, running multiple copies at the same time, all the better to forge their dogs. They were making two platinum pieces – worth £300 – every few hours. On six of EverQuest II's 23 servers, their level five characters – in the EverQuest II level hierarchy, which continues up to level 50, these were the virtual equivalent of pre-schoolers – were the richest in the game. They had so much money that they considered just copying items for fun: setting up a houseful of expensive baby dragons and just giving them away. 'We actually had about 20 or 30 baby dragons duped before we decided that this plan made no sense,' Noah said. 'And, well, money is cool. I like money.'

Then, the pair took the step that would make them a real-world fortune. They began to sell the proceeds of their virtual counterfeiting for real dollars. They hit the auction sites, selling at 50% of the market rate just to shift more platinum. Noah knew he was doing something questionable, and every day he expected Sony to fix the bug that allowed them to copy items. Weeks later they were still selling They spoke on the phone to negotiate with virtual currency brokers – sometimes taking 10 calls an hour. Worried about real-world consequences, they confessed to many of the third-party virtual currency brokers where they were getting their platinum; none cared. 'They said things like "We can't know that",' Noah said. 'And then they would follow it up with "Keep cranking out the money".' (No wonder. 'Judging by the buy and resell prices on some of the companies, I probably made them close to $300,000,' Noah told me.)

Noah and his co-conspirator sold so much virtual currency, they floored the market. Platinum prices dropped 60 per cent. They too were scammed: six times they sold virtual cash to buyers who refused to pay; they lost a total of around £2,500. But they kept on selling. So much money began to accumulate in their real bank accounts that Noah consulted a lawyer and an accountant to make sure they weren't risking prosecution. Both professionals just threw up their hands. 'Needless to say, neither of them had any idea what we were talking about,' Noah told me.

Ultimately, the dogs were their undoing. Anyone who strolled into Noah's virtual showroom – and there was no way to lock the door – might see 24 of the most expensive dogs in the game lined up ready to sell. When discovered in this way, Noah made excuses ('I'm quitting EQ2. I figured this would be a fun way to blow my money'), but not everyone was convinced. On EverQuest II websites, players began to post complaints about the sudden deflation. Then one morning, three weeks after Noah had copied his first Gnomish chair, he logged on to find a message from Sony: 'Merchants will no longer have any interest in purchasing your pets.'

It was a change aimed squarely at the pair's dog-forging operation. They knew the game was up. They decided to dump their virtual booty, selling their dogs, horses and mansions at a quarter of the usual price. To cover their tracks, they destroyed whatever they couldn't sell. Nonetheless, the next day, some – but not all – of their accounts were banned. Sony emailed Noah. 'Greetings. I regret to inform you that your account has been banned for duping items in order to generate large amounts of coin. Your account will be closed from this point forward.'

Publicly, Sony announced they had tracked the duped money and made it disappear from the world, but they never made any further contact with Noah or Liz. Other residents whom Sony believed had ties to the duplicated money – to determine who had received what, they sifted through their logs of all activity in their virtual world – also had their accounts banned. The company introduced a number of new economy reporting tools to avoid a repeat of the incident. But there was no way for Sony to recall the real-world money Noah and Liz had made. (When we spoke, Noah told me he still had nine virtual selves in EverQuest II – and some of them still possessed a share of their forged virtual booty.)

The problem of rectifying virtual deflation is not trivial. Sony decided to remove as much of the forged platinum as they could find; other virtual world makers chose different solutions. In 1997, a player in Ultima Online, a fantasy virtual world, discovered a gold-copying bug like Noah Burn's. The economy collapsed, and residents found their once-valuable virtual objects were worth almost nothing. After they had fixed the bug, the Ultima Online team faced the challenge of how to remove the currency from the game. They decided to release a new item, a red hair dye, which altered the appearance of residents in a unique way. Because the dye was rare, everybody wanted it; prices rose. Slowly, the duplicated money leaked back out of the hands of residents and into the hands of automated shopkeepers. The economy stabilised.

I asked Noah how much money the pair had made. Initially, he was reluctant to reveal the total. 'It's allowed me to go to both Hawaii and Paris, as well as pay off student loans. Just know, it's more than some people make in a year. Hell, maybe three years.' Later, he told me the pair made almost $100,000.

I asked Noah what he had learned from his days as a virtual forger. He related it to a scene from *The Matrix*, in which a character inside a virtual world bends a virtual spoon with the power of their mind. 'There is no fucking spoon,' Noah said.

Others have found similar loopholes in other virtual worlds. One group of World of Warcraft residents discovered another method: they handed a friend a large amount of gold, but didn't click 'Trade' to complete the transaction. Then they left that area of the virtual world, returned, and both residents would have the gold; they'd doubled their money. The bug was fixed within days, but in the meantime they, too, made a profit. In another case, EverQuest II residents discovered another loophole and made so much virtual cash, they caused a 20 per cent deflation in the virtual economy; the amount of money inside the virtual world increased by a fifth in just 24 hours. To stop the virtual market crash, Sony temporarily closed the entire virtual world.

With now over a million virtual residents inside EverQuest II, tracking every potentially fraudulent virtual transaction is unrealistic. In June 2005, Sony opened the Sony Station Exchange, where players could trade certain items between one another, without prejudice. In a statement explaining their decision, John Smedley, one of the original EverQuest designers, told his residents: 'Dealing with fraudulent transactions of one type or another takes up roughly 40% of our customer service people's time.' When word of his story got out, Noah told me, he received death threats, from people whose virtual items lost real-world value in the massive deflation the pair had provoked. He accepted those as an inevitable consequence of his life outside the virtual law. 'It is like the Wild West right now . . . and we're kind of like these outlaws,' he told me. 'I feel like Billy the Kid.'

In Noah's case, it seemed as if he had made something from nothing. It wasn't immediately obvious that the real world profit he made was at the expense of others who owned virtual items, which went down in value after he flooded the market. But in some cases of virtual profit, I discovered, the victims were clear.

Another 24-year-old, Thomas Czerniawski, worked for his father's dental technology company, Exceltec Dental Laboratory, on the outskirts of Toronto, Canada, crafting crowns. In his other life Tom's virtual alter ego, Istvaan Shogaatsu – who, along with 100,000 others, inhabited a space piracy universe called Eve Online – knew about the technology of a different kind of pain. Shogaatsu, who described himself as 'a cut-throat without morals or mercy,' had long enjoyed causing havoc in virtual worlds. In his last virtual residence, a relatively small online space-combat universe called 'Darkspace', he claimed he had been single-handedly responsible for obliterating a quarter of the universe's players (he'd killed over 4,000). When we met, Thomas was Istvaan, the CEO of Guiding Hand, a mercenary corporation of 10 Eve Online players that made their virtual living destroying other players' characters for profit.

In May 2005, Istvaan was contacted with an anonymous offer of 1 billion ISK (around £350 worth of Eve currency) for a 'Pearl Harbor' style attack – a massive, surprise assault causing irreparable damage – on another player's corporation, Ubiqua Seraph. The client, who wished to remain anonymous, had been scammed by Ubiqua Seraph, and wanted virtual revenge. For the attack, Istvaan chose Arenis Xemdal, Guiding Hand's 'Valentine Operative' – so named because of his charm, which enabled him to work his way into enemy corporations. Xemdal spent four months wooing the Ubiqua CEO, Mirial. They drew charts of Ubiqua Seraph's corporate structure, and found gaps where she was likely to be hiring. She hired Xemdal. To make him look good, Istvaan staged a number of artificially crippled raids, in which his Guiding Hand battleships underplayed their hand, and Xemdal saved Mirial. Guiding Hand operatives fed their Valentine Operative secret information on competing corporations, which Xemdal fed to Mirial in turn; Mirial profited from the information, and her trust in Xemdal rose. Meanwhile, the Guiding Hand plotted their attack. 'We mapped the locations of their most bountifully stocked asset hangars,' Istvaan told me. 'We took down the locations of their privately owned stations . . . and we waited.'

Four months later, Mirial appointed Arenis Xemdal as her lieutenant. She gave him access to the corporation's resources, and gave him the access codes to Ubiqua's warehouses: the key to her virtual safe.

When Guiding Hand received a message from Arenis with the attack signal – 'Nicole' – they made their move. A Guiding

Hand battleship appeared near Mirial's position. The Guiding Hand had a reputation for fierce piracy; the appearance of the battleship, far more powerful than her own ship, warned Mirial something was up. She fled for a nearby space station, but before she could reach safety, Arenis Xemdal turned his 'Navy Apocalypse' battle cruiser's pulse lasers and combat drones on her. 'She was killed by her lieutenant, who she trusted – dare say, even liked,' Czerniawski told me. Across the galaxy, timed with the attack, Guiding Hand operatives looted six separate Ubiqua Seraph warehouses, stealing virtual minerals, cash, and all the Ubiqua Seraph corporation's valuable battleship blueprints. In a last-ditch attempt to save her virtual self, Mirial jettisoned an escape capsule, but she was quickly killed. Her frozen corpse was scooped on board by Istvaan himself. It was all over in 15 minutes. Istvaan delivered Mirial's corpse to the client, but kept the stolen property as spoils of war. ('He still has it,' Istvaan told me. 'He treasures it.')

What made this different from just any space-fight inside a computer game was that, now virtual currencies have a real value, their haul was more than just pixels on a screen. The cash and merchandise stolen by Guiding Hand amounted to 30 billion ISK – about £10,000. They decided not to sell, though; instead they invested the cash in rare Eve Online ships, which have since increased in value. 'Overall, we've done very well with the money, multiplying it many times over,' Istvaan said.

Thomas invited me on a tour of the crime scene. I logged into Eve Online, so he could show me where it all took place. I launched my new ship, and Istvaan guided me to his own location in space – luckily a sparsely populated sector of the universe, where his virtual enemies were unlikely to pass by and attack while he was switching ships. He showed me the ships he had bought and stolen: a Raven class battleship, Navy Issue, with a regenerating shield and seven cruise missiles, each capable of taking out any enemy battleship. (The battleship was worth 3 billion ISK, Istvaan told me – about £1,000). He showed me another ship, which seemed 10 times the size of the first. 'This is an Apocalypse Imperial Issue. Only two exist in the entire game, and we [Guiding Hand] control both.'

I flew my tiny trading ship in close to the war-scarred metal of Istvaan's prize ship; I felt like a fly on the hide of an elephant. 'No more of these ships will ever be released, making them next to priceless.' Istvaan said. Guiding Hand paid 9 billion ISK (about £3,000) for each. 'They've since appreciated in value to about 25 billion a piece.' That meant Guiding Hand could sell those two ships, together, for around £14,000.

The Eve developers, CCP games, based in Reykjavik, Iceland, looked fondly on Istvaan's operation – not least because, as the story spread through the Internet, Eve Online gained thousands of new subscribers. But many players were outraged. After the heist, back in the real world Thomas Czerniawski received nine email and telephone death threats. To Mirial and others connected with the Ubiqua Corporation, the loss felt very real.

Istvaan's attack shone a bright light on the wild-frontier-style ethics of the virtual world. It had taken Mirial over a year to build up her virtual empire, but she had no recourse: the virtual items she lost had no legal value. Games developers need it to remain that way, otherwise every bug or server closure could be followed by a class action suit by players for compensation. The games would become true economies; every player would have to fill in a tax return. The games developers, CCP, decided the scam was in the spirit of the game – after all, it was a space piracy universe. ('We would like to remind the players of Eve

Online that game masters are unable to assist players who have been involved in any sort of scam,' they announced. 'We have taken measures to prevent scamming by making it easier for corporations to see exactly who has access to the shipyards and equipment pools, but it is up to the officers of the corporation themselves to ensure that they fully trust the individuals they recruit.'

In spite of this, Czerniawski told me he and his Guiding Hand co-conspirators were concerned they might be accused of breaking a real-world law, such as wire-fraud, so they were careful to keep all contact within the game. Others, though, haven't been so careful.

In October 2005, another player, known as 'Nightfreeze', pulled off a more complicated confidence trick. 'This is a story of deception, intrigue, and double-crosses,' Nightfreeze wrote, in his own account of the scam. 'It is a story of liars, bandits, and greed. This is the story of my life in Eve Online.' Eve Online was Nightfreeze's life. He spent more time navigating the Eve universe than navigating his campus hallways. Bored and restless, he and his best friend Trazir decided to form a partnership. Another trader, HardHead, lent them 3 million. They bought a colossal ship, poured their cash into computers, and within three hours had doubled their money. They were in business. Their only obstacles were pirates. Every trade run, privateers homed in on their lumbering ship and demanded payment. When they refused, the pirates lasered their ship to ashes. With hardly any firepower, all they could do was run – so they learned to run in style a with expensive engines, micro-warp drives (MWDs), which could rocket their ship to safety. The pirates ate exhaust fumes. Within two weeks, Nightfreeze was worth close to 85 million ISK. Then the universe changed the rules. One morning, two months into his lucrative new career, Nightfreeze baited the pirates as usual, waited until they closed in, then activated his drives. Which didn't work. The enraged pirates destroyed his ship – 35 million-worth of hardware and 40 million in cargo. In revenge for his insults, they shot up his escape pod, too. The pirates, unhappy with the MWDs, had complained to the gods – the developers – and the gods had listened. Suddenly, the drives barely worked. But nobody had told Nightfreeze. His fledgling career – and two months of his life – was in ashes. He was about to log off permanently in disgust, but then had a better idea. The rules didn't care for him; why should he care for the rules? He made a call to his friend, who agreed. They would perpetrate the biggest scam the universe had ever seen. To establish their con, they paid 20 new players 10,000 credits each to join their 'corporation', named ZZZBest (after an infamously fraudulent carpet cleaning firm). In-world, on notice boards and in instant messages to all their trading partners, the pair announced their mission: to acquire the blueprints for an Apocalypse battleship, the most powerful in the game. These cost 1.2 billion; by combining their purchase power, they claimed, they would offer the same blueprint to each investor for just 100 million. Slowly, their offer began to attract potential partners. They populated bulletin boards with fake investors, and arranged a fake chat-room 'investor confer-ence'. One investor – the largest – insisted on speaking with Nightfreeze in person. Nightfreeze gave the number of his local library payphone, and sprinted to catch the call. The investor said yes. By 9 a.m. the next morning, Nightfreeze's account held 480 million credits (worth nearly $3,000). He transferred the money to a dummy character. Then, with one click of his mouse, he deleted his account. After gloating in reply to a few instant-message death threats, he cancelled his IM accounts too. It was the perfect crime – the criminal no longer existed. But what now? His half of the money belonged to a new character without pilot skills; he had hundreds of millions, but nothing to buy. He toyed with a few passing ships, and was instantly killed. Somehow, it barely seemed worth it. Nightfreeze hailed a passing player, Frosttt, in a beginner ship, asking: 'What would you say if I were to offer you 300 million?' 'I'd say pretty cool,' said Frosttt. Nightfreeze wired all his credits over and logged off. He never logged in again.

After it became clear there would be no payback for Nightfreeze, the Eve Online bulletin boards erupted in fury. That's how virtual worlds affect us: once the borders with the real world are threatened, we feel threatened too. Only one level-headed commentator, on the message boards of the website Something Awful, pointed out the double standards: 'You can be a pirate in this game, but you can't be a white-collar criminal?'

Virtual worlds, with their heady combination of experience without attendant risk, were starting to get real. Greed, corruption and human weakness threatened to turn paradise into a lawless frontier world. Czerniawksi, though, had a moral stance too. Although his virtual property would fetch $34,000 on the open market, he refused to sell, or move into other virtual worlds where his actions could be more profitable. For those who profited from virtual worlds like Second Life, he had only scorn. 'If I want to make money, I'll buy my stock broker a bottle of good cognac and watch the magic,' he said. 'Not try to peddle real estate and virtual pornography to some dancing cretin in a CGI raccoon suit.'

In the real world it was autumn, and everybody was anxious. The Geneva Conventions, a protection against the return of our savage history, had been replaced by a new global doctrine of pre-emptive war. In my home town, London, tube trains and busses exploded. The actions of my government – involving us in a war the majority of the population did not want – hung like a pall over everyone I knew. On my part, I longed for time away from these anxieties. I wanted more time in my virtual shoes. As I walked the grey streets of London, I daydreamed about Second Life. I longed for escape. I wanted to rise up above the grey roofs and bare winter trees, to free myself from gravity and from sorrow, to push up off the ground and fly.

As people hunkered down in the cloud of new global anxieties, virtual worlds seemed far away from the chaos: a safer place than the real world. Through the electronic looking glass, there was no pollution, no global warming, and – as I believed then – no terrorism. I heard rumours, though, that more clearcut virtual crime had found its way into Second Life. Some Second Life residents (including that world's richest, Anshe Chung, who reportedly made upwards of $200,000 a year from virtual land sales inside Second Life) had complained of underhand attempts to force land sales at deflated prices. In one case, Anshe claimed, a group known as the W-Hats had intimidated potential buyers, erected unpleasant or intimidating billboards – anti-Anshe posters, and tasteless and angry images which included real-world photos of a naked man with children's toys over his groin – on small, cheap parcels of adjacent land, and built towering structures which slowed her own land to a crawl, all in an attempt to obtain her virtual land at below market rates. (Another resident, Bakuzelas, who approached Anshe to buy the land on behalf of the W-Hats, claimed they had offered a fair market rate.) Others, too, complained groups like the W-Hats had used similar tactics with them. The CEO of a corporation inside Second Life claimed the W-Hats had built towers so high he couldn't even enter his own land. There was more at stake, too. Like the real universe, virtual worlds were expanding. When I'd first entered Second Life, the land covered 120 virtual acres, with 25,000 residents; in the six months since, this virtual world had inflated to over 300 acres, and nearly 100,000 residents. More people meant more profit: in May 2005 alone, Second Life residents traded $1.47 million-worth of virtual property. Now a seedier side of the virtual world had moved in for a cut.

'These are basically blackmail and mafia methods,' Anshe said, of the intimidation.

Also, I wanted to do more than hear about virtual crime. I wanted to take part. After his raid on Ubiqua Seraph, Istvaan stole another battleship, worth 3 billion ISK (£1,000) but since then – despite his claim to have secret operatives planted inside every major Eve Online corporation – Thomas Czerniawksi had hung up his virtual space-pirate hook. His virtual self had taken a back seat to his real life. Elsewhere Noah, the forging gnome, still hoped for another opportunity to bend the rules of virtual worlds and make a killing, but as yet he'd found nothing – instead, he told me, he was considering a 'how-to' book, to help people discover similar exploits and make money themselves.

A different, more organised kind of crime was emerging in virtual worlds. Not long before, one resident of There, a web-based virtual world with 400,000 members, put up a 'For Sale' sign in front of a virtual home he didn't own. Many new players didn't know how the property system worked; he sold the house many times over, and pocketed the virtual cash. Now, I discovered, the same kind of fraud had taken root in Second Life. 'Do I need to get in this game and bust some heads together?' wrote one J.C. Soprano, in the comments section of an interview with Anshe about her harassment, on the Second Life newsletter site 'Dragon's Cove Herald'. Soprano included a link to his website, the Sims Mafia, where he advertised his services. For the right virtual price, they would assault another Second Life resident. (Because physical violence in virtual worlds is mostly harmless, in practice the assault included a barrage of instant messages, harassing them with scripted objects, and bad ratings which can affect everything from a character's virtual reputation to their virtual credit.) They would blackmail, bribe, or collect debts from your virtual enemies.

It was time to return to Second Life, to talk with the Sims Mafia. Embarrassed by my previous difficulties, I considered creating a new virtual self, with a different computer and someone else's credit card. Linden Lab would never know. (When I'd visited their offices, Robin Harper had hinted they had ways to track the real people who inhabited their virtual residents. They were secretive about how they did this, but they seemed confident they could; a mixture of IP addresses, unique to most Internet connections, plus the credit cards, and financial transactions between in-world residents, would make most identities clear.) Like the Asperger's sufferers on Brigadoon, I thought, perhaps I could practise virtual worlds until I got it right. But also, it seemed that accountability and reputation were intrinsic to these worlds. Plus, I didn't have another credit card. Errol Mysterio would live on.

When I logged in again, I reappeared on Wilde's island. Things had changed. They'd built a platform over the sea, to house a shiny blue virtual Spitfire. Across the bay I could see they had neighbours: two new islands, one tinier and deserted, the other mountainous. There were wood huts, palm trees, a blue avant-garde bubble-domed apartment. Everything was covered in drifts of virtual snow. It was nearly Christmas. To my left, a choir of snowmen, hymn books open in their mittened hands, were frozen in mid-carol. I walked the island looking for Wilde, but they weren't logged on. I hadn't wanted to make a splash, to upset people in virtual worlds. But here I was, and I couldn't help it. Even my avatar left crisp footprints on the fresh virtual snow.

8

VIRTUAL MAFIA
My life as a foot soldier

When I met J.C. Soprano, the virtual mafia don, he tried to hustle me too.

In the real world, Soprano was Jeremy Chase, a 28-year-old customer service manager and IT specialist at a Sacramento, California, financial company, with hair spiked down across his forehead, a thin-line goatee and tattoos on each arm. Chase began his life of virtual crime in 2001, in the virtual world called The Sims Online. 'Behind every fortune, there is a crime,' reads a traditional Sicilian saying. The saying implies a basic balance in the universe – a great wealth, which upsets the balance, must take a great act of violence to accrue. The phrase, which Mario Puzo used as a preface to his novel *The Godfather,* was originally coined as an argument *for* the mafia: a warning against the ruling principalities in feudal Italy. Under the restrictive and capricious martial law of ruling powers, which changed with the seasons, Italians grew to distrust those who ruled over them. When disagreements or vendettas arose, rather than turn to the latest despot who wouldn't understand their plight, the Italian people chose to mete out their own rough kind of justice. Out of this tradition arose the twentieth-century mafia (the Cosa

Nostra – 'this thing of ours'). What the mafia taught the world was that sometimes, when the powers that be don't have your best interests at heart, strength and security have to be forged by the people.

Chase believed this was true for virtual worlds too. Even the basic in-game laws, known as the 'Terms of Service' – which generally included basic rules such as don't swear at other characters, and don't cheat them out of virtual currency – relied on players to lodge complaints, and seemed to Chase poorly policed.

This absence of virtual law enforcement led Chase, a long-time mafia movie fan, to set up his own alternative: The Sims Mafia. He named his virtual self J.C. Soprano – J.C. from his initials, and Soprano from the HBO crime family series. Players could hire Chase and his virtual employees to protect their virtual interests. The Sims Mafia used its virtual muscle to perform all the services you might expect from a bona fide crime family. The Sims Online, though, was never a runaway success. In 2004, Chase's mafia family upped sticks. In the same way Vito Corleone shifted his crime family from New York to Las Vegas in *The Godfather*, Chase decided to move the operation to another virtual world. He tried Star Wars Galaxies, but that world disappointed. ('The most you could do was kill someone,' he told me. 'There was no way to gamble or extort like we had in The Sims Online.')

Chase sold his J.C. Soprano Sims Online self on eBay, and moved to Second Life. When Chase joined Second Life, the surname 'Soprano' wasn't available, but 'Wallace' was; he named his Second Life self Marsellus Wallace, after another kind of fictional gangster, from the movie *Pulp Fiction*.

In Second Life, for the right amount of virtual currency, Chase's family offered all the services they used to offer in the Sims Online. There, they used to hire virtual escorts, but Chase – who once ran a porn site in his spare time – closed down the prostitution rackets because there was too great a risk of underage players hiring virtual hookers. In Second Life, however, where all the other residents are over 18, hiring a virtual escort is as easy, and about as expensive, as buying a virtual pair of shoes.

'Essentially, I look at myself, in a way, as like Gotti,' Chase told a Second Life website, the 'Second Life Herald'. 'He fought the law, like I do with Electronic Arts and other groups. And he was very respected . . . he gave to the community. Sure, he was violent and ruthless. I am not saying these guys are saints. But they do some good in the community. That's all. With the bad, there is always some good.'

Inside Second Life, I ran a search for Marsellus Wallace. 'This is who I am and what I do,' his profile read. 'My basic philosophy is don't start none, won't be none. Show some respect! Even if you don't like someone, they should never know it. Get them when they least expect it. I'm the face of online Mafias and the real-life press calls me the Boss of Bosses. Deal with it.'

I contacted him via Second Life instant message, and, after a long, suspicious exchange, I finally managed to meet Marsellus. He received me in his virtual marble-floored mansion. His broad frame, in a virtual tailored suit, was sprawled on a virtual leather sofa. (His mafia family had already built up a reputation in Second Life; an interior designer, eager to curry favour, furnished his mansion for free.) 'Currently, I have myself, the consigliere, the underboss, three Capos and several soldiers who work under the capos,' Marsellus told me. 'In total, with the foot soldiers, about 15 people.'

Marsellus explained how he makes his virtual profit. He offered no-questions loans, at 25 per cent vig. For a price, he offered mediation (a 'sit-down') to settle a virtual beef. For 'a very high price', he said, you could hire him to do what he called a 'Moe Green': a virtual hit, which removed a virtual character from

116

the game completely. I asked how they did that: 'You'll see,' he told me. As well as the paid services, which accounted for about 35 per cent of his revenue, Marsellus also ran sports spread-betting, and back-door card craps games in virtual VIP casinos, with the virtual equivalent of about $4 as minimum bet. 'We are working on a new gambling operation that's not up yet. We hope that to be our cash cow. I have a game here no one else has. I also am doing a website hosting and design business soon that accepts cash and Lindens: 2L Hosting. That's my legit side. My not so legit side consists of various scams – mainly real estate extortion (very small money in this though), protection, bribes (I can't go into details on this one but I have many, many connections with top players). We dabbled in prostitution here for a bit, but I prefer to stay out of the sex stuff. Too much competition anyway.' Virtual war occasionally broke out with the other online mafia crime families, Chase explained, until both sides incurred enough losses that they were forced to sit down and make the peace. Sometimes, to build their rep, wannabe Mafioso took shots at Chase. (He invited me to search for 'Marsellus' in the directory of Second Life residents. Other players with a vendetta had created alternate selves with first names like 'MarsellusWallaceThe', and last names like 'Prat'.)

Marsellus told me about his latest virtual strong-arm move. An associate called Drax Lemiuex, who owned a Second Life establishment called the Red Dragon casino, had asked Marsellus to go into business. Marsellus operated a profitable virtual dice game, and Drax wanted to share his expertise. Drax paid Marsellus 5,000 Linden Dollars (about £20), and agreed to pay another 19,500 (£75) when the dice games were making a profit. The two grew close; Drax even acted as groomsman for Marsellus's virtual wedding.

Marsellus's Second Life bride, Mackenzie Draper, was Chase's real-world girlfriend, who he'd introduced to Second Life.

Mackenzie, a pretty redhead, worked inside Second Life as a virtual photographer. As Marsellus and I talked, she strolled over to say 'hi'. Marsellus had mentioned she didn't like his being 'in the life'; I asked Mackenzie how she felt, being married to the mob. 'Well, he's right, I don't approve,' she said. 'But that's his thing.'

'She's my voice of reason,' Marsellus said.

After the wedding, Marsellus and Drax planned to split the casino dice-game's virtual profits. According to Drax, though, the casino began to make a loss. Drax refused to pay the second payment of 19,500 Linden Dollars. Marsellus sneaked in and installed himself as a dealer; his table made money. A vendetta was in the offing. Even though Drax had been a groomsman at his virtual wedding, Marsellus couldn't let the disrespect stand.

(At this point, as Marsellus was talking, another player contacted him to ask if he would 'rub out' a high-profile Second Life resident. I mentioned to Marsellus I'd like to follow him on the hit. 'I'm not going to take the job,' he said. 'See, this particular person if what happened, happened, would become a martyr. I do not like this person either, so I don't want that to happen. Anyway, back to the casino.')

Drax's casino was famous in Second Life for the unique facade: a huge sculpted red dragon, with the casino door in place of the mouth. After a 'heated discussion', in which Drax refused to pay up, Marsellus chose his revenge. He persuaded Drax he needed to move the dice games around to make them more profitable. Drax made Marsellus an 'officer' of his group, which automatically gave him the ability to alter his virtual property. Marsellus gave Drax one more chance to follow through with their deal. Drax passed, and Marsellus went into action. He deleted a partition wall, just to let Drax know what was coming. Drax panicked, and fumbled with his windows to try to change the casino, piece-by-piece, so Marsellus couldn't delete it.

Marsellus sent him a message to keep him busy typing, then, while Drax was writing his reply, Marsellus did the virtual equivalent of torch the place. With two mouse clicks, he deleted the Casino's huge red dragon facade.

In the real world, time is money; in the virtual world, money is time. Drax had lost the months it took him to construct the casino and its reputation, but he had no recourse for its loss: his virtual den of iniquity had no real-world legal value. Still, when I met Marsellus, the two had put the beef aside. They were in talks to go back into business. 'We have rules to live by very similar to real mafia,' Marsellus told me. 'Our goal is to make money. All that other crap just gets in the way of business.'

In the real world, Chase's mafia activities would be against the law, but through the electronic looking glass, the rules of conduct are less clear. Chase seemed to make little attempt to hide his virtual crime family. In Second Life, every character's name and group is displayed for all to see. Chase's second self walked around with a sign above his head: 'Marsellus Wallace. Sim Mafia Boss.' Chase was known to Linden Lab – he applied, ironically, for a Second Life community liaison job – and had become a minor celebrity within some virtual circles. 'EA Games and me didn't get along,' he told me. 'Second Life seems to embrace it.' His only worry, he explained, was that through some confusion between the real world and the virtual world, he would get himself into real trouble.

Privately, Chase admitted to me he was worried about the possible real-world consequences of his virtual crimes. 'The money in this game is worth real money,' he explained. '[Linden Lab] say so. In Sims Online, EA said it was not legally protected. However, in Second Life I am worried that somehow my gaming could result in legal action. Even if I keep it in game.'

Chase planned to consult a lawyer, he told me, 'just to cover my ass. Because a game is not worth jail time.' He even called up Linden Lab to speak with their legal specialist, who advised him caution.

Despite his anxieties, Chase modelled his virtual mafia carefully on the real thing. A week after we met, he emailed me. 'If you can make it, we will be swearing in a new member tonight.' The ceremony was to take place at 7 p.m. his time – 3 a.m. London time. I hurried home from a night out to witness a virtual mafia member being made.

As soon as I logged on, Marsellus emailed me. The rules of the ceremony were his greeting. '1-Inductees may not talk until prompted to do so or the ceremony is over. 2-Only members of management and those getting made may attend the ceremony. (Making an exception for you.) 3-No one repeats what is said or done during the ceremony. (Once again, you're the exception.) 4-All in attendance of a ceremony must dress in a nice suit.' (I hoped my white tux waiter suit would suffice.)

'5-No pictures may be taken except by pre-authorised existing members. 6-No guns are allowed to be displayed unless security requires it.'

When I arrived to the site of the ceremony – a concrete basement – Marsellus introduced me to his underboss, Tony Caligari. Tony had been in online mafias, he told me, including under Marsellus, for three years. All of a sudden the subject of the ceremony, Shadow Tokhes, appeared beside us. Forgetting my commitment to remain quiet, I asked what he'd done to 'make his bones'. 'He will be our consigliere,' Marsellus said. 'He whacked the last one. Which is how he earned his stripes to get in.'

The hit had gone down in classic mafia style. 'I called the guy over to our casino and said that the family needed some money,' Marsellus said. 'I took all his money with the promise of it being returned, and he sent me a screenshot to show he had nothing.' (I thought for a moment about my own virtual money, still in Marsellus's pocket.) 'Then I walked him outside where Shadow was waiting – under the dock.' (Of course under the dock.)

'I took out my gun and shot him.' Shadow told me. 'After, I told him what the boss said, which was, "Next time you keep an oath, make sure you fulfil it."'

(It all sounded authentic enough. The only distraction for me was the former consigliere's name: Gandalf.)

Before Shadow could be made, there was a little stage-craft. In Second Life, objects need to be prompted into action. Marsellus had prepared a ceremony, but it needed a push to get going. 'Shadow, see that circle by your feet? Choose the ceremony option.' Shadow shuffled into place.

'All right, you all know why we're here,' Marsellus continued. 'So if you got any doubts or reservations, now is the time to say so. No one will think any less of you. Because once you enter this family, there's no getting out. This family comes before everything else . . .

'Everything. Before your wife and your children and your mother and your father. It's a thing of honour. And, God forbid, if you get sick, suspended, or something happens and you can't earn, we'll take care of you. That's part of it.'

'If you got a problem, you just gotta let somebody know,' Tony, the underboss, chimed in. 'This man right here.' He pointed to Marsellus. 'He's like your father. It doesn't matter if it's with somebody here or on the outside. You bring it to him, he'll solve it.'

'You stay within the family,' Marsellus said.

Shadow raised his hand, and in it appeared a playing card.

'That is St Patrick, our family saint,' Marsellus said. 'He is the Saint of Sacramento, where I am from, and New York, where the heart of the mafia lies . . .

'Ignite,' Marsellus said, for the card's benefit. The card burst into flames.

'Those flames represent the flames of hell. Now, as that card burns, so may your soul burn if you betray your friends in the family . . .

'Now, repeat after me. May I burn in hell.'

'May I burn in hell,' Shadow said.

'If I betray my family,' Marsellus intoned.

'If I betray my family,' Shadow echoed.

'Congratulations, you may step off the ceremony stand as a Made Man,' Marsellus said.

'Thank you,' Shadow said.

'Welcome to the family,' Tony said.

'Now no one can touch you,' Marsellus continued. 'But that don't mean go around starting nuttin', either. Don't start none, won't be none. This is still a business. Now, Tony has some things he wants to cover real quick.'

'You're a made guy now,' Tony said. 'It's your turn to make some real money, and I get to relax a little. Your only problem in life now is you give me 25 points of your take every settle-up day. Other than that, you got no problem. My only problem in life? I gotta kick my points to that man over there. And onward goes this thing of ours.'

Slowly, Marsellus drew me into his mafia world. Even in the supermarket, he found a way to reach me. The morning after the ceremony, Marsellus sent me a message inside Second Life, which was forwarded to my email account, which was forwarded to my telephone. I received it in the frozen foods aisle. 'Ahh the life,' Marsellus wrote.

Over these weeks, my virtual life had already begun to blur into my real life. I had met Istvaan, the Eve universe's most feared warlord, who showed me his prize battleship's laser cannons; I had met Noah, the virtual world's richest gnome; and I had met the virtual Godfather, sprawled in virtual luxury. My diary was full of appointments with people called 'Eight Bar Masher Algernon Spackler' and 'Biscuit Carrol'. I felt the kind of dizzy head induced by too much travel, only this time it wasn't a whirlwind of airports, it was a whirlwind of worlds. Which universe was I in? One evening, I had to meet Marsellus, but I also had to cook dinner; my girlfriend sat at my laptop and pretended to be me. I'd told her he was part of an online mafia; while I fried the fish she tapped at the keys nervously, imagining a different kind of fish nailed to our door.

Over time, Marsellus began to make me nervous, too. He scolded me for missed appointments, although he skipped his fair share too – a boss's perogative. 'Just as in real life, intimidation is our biggest weapon,' he'd told me – and I suspected he was trying the weapon on me. He had told how, at his virtual wedding, a Second Life resident had disrespected some guests. As Marsellus, he strolled over to the resident's property and claimed the resident owed him money. The resident didn't owe him anything, and said as much, but after a few visits from mafia footsoldiers, their virtual guns drawn, he paid. Now, Chase began to try some of the same tactics on me. When I asked him again to let me work for him, he asked what was in it for him – 'writers must get Bank!' he said. Later, after a documentary team borrowed my virtual self for a TV short, the director mailed me an update. 'Marsellus came and had a few words,' he said. 'We told him we weren't you and we were making a film with you in it – and he started asking for money!'

There were surreal moments, too. I asked permission to take virtual photos of Marsellus and his mafia. They agreed, and gathered in a basement, dressed in dark suits (bought from 'a friend of ours', at a Second Life store called 'Made Men') and posed – with bling, with and without guns – for the virtual camera. I took up various positions around them, framed them on my screen, and saved image files of my virtual view to my laptop. It was awkward and disorganised, like a real-world photo-shoot. I found myself saying things like: 'Candy, can you move in a bit?' and 'Getting some great shots here. Marsellus, keep looking at me please.'

I began a campaign to persuade Marsellus to hire me. I wanted in on a virtual mafia job, to see what was involved, and what effect Marsellus could actually have on his virtual enemies. He dodged the issue, asked for money, and accused me of being too 'flaky' – because of Internet problems, I'd missed two appointments – for 'the life'.

Then, just when I thought I was out, they pulled me back in. Marsellus contacted me. He had overcome his objections, and decided to let me to do a job. We met in his new virtual home, a palatial development that had yet to be furnished. It turned out Marsellus had a network of characters designed to give the impression of an entire mafia family. He logged on as another of his virtual selves, Raymond Polonsky – who, in his black suit and jewellery, looked more than a little like Marsellus. Raymond was Chase's 'legit' character, he explained, a lawyer 'with a few mafia ties'. (In Second Life, you can click on a character for more information. I clicked on Raymond. 'I am your virtual legal representation,' his description read. 'IM [instant message] me if you need contracts written up and notarised, or if you need representation in-game for a crime you did not commit!')

'So, you want in and want to do some things,' Polonsky told me. 'First . . . you got any questions? Now is the time to ask them, because once I agree to this, if I don't like you, you will be part of the house foundation in-game.' I nodded. 'Let's step inside,' Polonsky said. 'Less ears there.'

I followed him in. There was another concrete floor. 'OK first a couple of ground rules. Common sense shit, but necessary.

'First off, watch what you say in-game. Never refer to avatar names, initials, description, things like that. If you have to, name a name, but once you say it, don't say it again. Refer to them as the guy the girl or whatever.'

'I'll keep my mouth shut,' I said.

'Although it cannot be proven, I believe the Double L Mafia has the ability to monitor conversations, and does.'

When I visited Linden Lab (the target of Chase's oblique reference), Philip Rosedale had explained that it was possible to record everything that happened in a virtual world. Technically, as the entire world was computer-modelled, they could record every single movement, gesture, and interaction that took place. (In that virtual world, it would be easy to find out whether, if a tree which fell when no one was around, any noise was made.) In practice, though, Philip told me the amount of data storage required to record everything was far beyond their capability. What they did record, though, were a set of 'logs', which included a record of every word, and every transaction.

I knew they could read the logs if there was any dispute, and I imagined it would be easy to monitor troublesome characters – or writers – should they become concerned their community was threatened. The UK, where I logged on from, has the highest public CCTV coverage in the world. In January 2004, there were over 4,285,000 CCTV cameras in the UK – about one for every four households – and the Metropolitan Police had ordered a trial of head-mounted digital video cameras. The average Londoner – me included – was caught on camera 300 times a day. Still, in virtual worlds the world's makers could theoretically record everything, all the time, forever. The heightened potential for surveillance in virtual worlds made me nervous. It felt strange to exist within a world where someone could watch everything you did.

Raymond Polonsky led me down to the basement. 'Another thing. You are going to do some odds and ends shit at first,' he said. 'Just for a week or two. We've gotta get you used to the slang, introduce you to a few people. After that things will pick up, I'll get you running a crew, or part of a crew, depending on what we determine your specialty is.'

I had to be willing to do anything, Raymond said, even if it jeopardised my virtual self. 'The Double L Mafia may try to eliminate you, in other words.' We agreed I would remain incognito. To the rest of the virtual mafia, I would be just another foot soldier.

Then it was time to talk cash. 'How much money do you have?' Raymond asked. When I'd originally logged on to Second Life, Linden Lab gave me a small weekly stipend. I'd bought some of my own currency, and over the year I'd hardly spent any, so virtual cash had accumulated in my account. I had 61,590 Linden Dollars – worth, at IGE.com, about £90.

'Give it to me,' Polonsky said. I thought for a moment, then, because I hadn't earned the money, and I wanted Chase to trust me, I handed him the cash.

'OK thanks for your money. Have a nice day!' Polonsky said. Then he laughed. 'Just kidding. A little mafia humour.'

As it turned out, though, he did keep most of the money. He explained how, just as in the real mafia, new members paid for the privilege. 'Normally, if no one is vouching for you, we require you buy your way in. That is 25,000 Lindens alone. Normally most guys make it back over a period of time. A decent earner can pull in 5,000 to 10,000 Lindens a week. Now, before you decide, there are some perks you need to be aware of.'

He gestured to my clothes. I still wore my white waiter's tuxedo.

First – 'no offence' – I had to get a new suit. 'I will contact a tailor. Basically you go pick out some suits and I'll get you a discount. We get a lot of discounts.' He told me to get some jewellery too, although not too flashy. 'Please don't gangsta your-self out.'

I told him I planned to set up an office in Second Life. 'Go to Home Depoz,' he told me, referring to a virtual superstore furniture chain. 'Make a shopping list. Anything and everything you need. Give it to me, I'll make it happen. No cost.'

'So. You getting nervous you ain't got the money back yet?' Polonsky said. I nodded, and he paid me back the difference. I was in. I would have to pay the vig, 2,500 Linden Dollars (about £4.00) a week, come virtual rain or virtual shine. I asked what kind of work he had in mind. 'Police department for wiseguys, all we are,' he said. 'Most bosses come to us to handle disputes.' His upcoming jobs included a little corporate espionage. 'For example, this one guy who runs a very popular business. In fact, he was recently in *Business Week*. He turned to us to spy on a rival business, see if they were competition. Paid 30,000 Linden Dollars – that's for a few days of work.' First, though, he had a bigger job in mind. 'I already have your first real mafia job lined up. A warning message to someone.' He didn't want to say too much, in case Linden Lab was listening. He told me he would describe the job now, then name names at another time. It was like having a conversation with a real mafia member, taking routine precautions against phone taps. 'The guy's name is Tommy Fitzsimmons. Just remember that.'

The coming weekend was his girlfriend's birthday, and Chase was heading out to Vegas. In true mafia style, he would co-ordinate the job while he was out of town. He gave me some homework, too. As well as order a new suit and get some gold, Chase told me to watch *Goodfellas*, *Godfather* I and II, and '*Donnie Brasco* for sure. It teaches the structure and rules.'

'Just remember one thing, Errol,' he said, as we parted. 'Don't fuck me over.'

With that he disappeared. I stood in his concrete basement, feeling more than a little paranoid. I wondered if I could trust Polonsky. Was he trying to set me up, get me banned from Second Life? Did he really charge that much to new mafia members? I hadn't earned most of the money I'd given to Polonsky – it had come free into my account from Linden Lab – but it still felt like a real loss. Was he double-crossing me? Still, these anxieties of trust seemed suitable for a new mafia member.

Afterwards, I couldn't sleep. What would my other virtual friends think of this? Who was the person, the target of the job? In real life, were they vulnerable? Would I cause real pain? It was OK, right, because this was all a game? I logged back on and looked up some information on Tommy Fitzsimmons. A Google search brought a couple of results: an advert for a poker game (with 20/10 blinds, run at the 'Eiffel Tower casino' by Tommy, and someone called Salvatore Muromachi); the next result was an ad for the grand opening of the Il Calabrese Casino ('Free prizes and other fun!'). Tommy's Second Life profile included information on his company, Platini & Co. 'Want to create your dream company, but don't know how to get started? Our crack team of businessmen will meet your needs no matter what you need done, be it a casino, club or something else.' That 'something else' sounded ominous. His profile had links to more people with intimidating names: Tommaso Ludovico, Carlo Platini. What was I stepping into?

It crossed my mind, even, that Chase himself might be Tommy Fitzsimmons. A few months before, a friend, Matt D'arcy, had logged on to Second Life. I took him to a strip bar, and a stranger asked him to join his club; my friend agreed, and the name of his new group was attached his virtual name, which followed above his head at all times: 'Jimmy DeFarge, Hardcore Lover'. Within minutes, he was approached by another resident, a complete stranger. 'You can't fool me!' the resident said.

My friend looked at me. 'What?!?'

'I know who you are,' the resident said. He had mistaken Matt for another resident, who he believed was trying to sneak back into the group. 'You're banned!' Jimmy DeFarge was a Hardcore Lover no more.

I'd had my own share of this confusion, too, after the TV company borrowed my virtual self for its documentary. I logged back on to find myself, as if after a virtual binge-drinking blackout, in an Ikea-style furniture store, wearing unfamiliar clothes, with no memory of how I got there.

A few weeks after my laptop was stolen, I suddenly realised that were the burglar to start up Second Life, my automatically saved password would allow them to walk in my virtual shoes. Unnerved by the possibility, I changed my password. In the virtual world, there's no easy way to tell if someone is who you thought they were. (When I called Linden Lab to confirm my password change, to verify my identity, they asked me which magazines I wrote for. The information they had on file for me was out of date, but it showed the importance they placed on verifying the real people behind their virtual selves.)

The next morning, my worries were gone. After all, Chase wasn't in the real mafia – 'I love Mafia movies and books and it's a culture that fascinates me,' Marsellus had told me, that first night in his mafia mansion. 'It's something I will never get to be as I am not Italian.' The morning after our meeting, an email arrived from Chase with more details of the job. It was a big one, a 'Moe Green': a hit.

'Errol: Good afternoon. You already have the target name. Hopefully you have not forgotten it. From this point on, refer to the target as, 'young buck'. This avatar is going to be hopefully whacked by yourself. We use the term whack to define getting an avatar removed from the game. It is something we rarely do as it is hard to pull off most of the time, and we believe it is an extreme measure. No hacking is involved, just using the games Community Standards and Terms of Service in our favour.' It turned out that the virtual equivalent of a mafia hit was to get a resident removed permanently from the game. It made sense. My job was to somehow talk 'young buck' into breaking the rules of the game, or admitting something which showed he shouldn't be inside Second Life. He could then be reported, and banned from re-entering Second Life.

Marsellus had some leads as to how the job could be done. 'At some point an informant came to me and advised me that this young buck was just that . . . young. He was only 14 or 15 and should not be playing on the main grid, which is for adults only.' Marsellus explained: I was to persuade Tommy Fitzsimmons to admit he was underage. Then, armed with a copy of the conversation, I was to report this infraction to Linden Lab. 'You are going to use his age against him and file an abuse report once he confesses this to you. I'll setup a meeting between you two. You will have to use your own finesse at that point to get him to confess.'

The email also contained some background information on the target. 'The young buck was at one point a friend of the organisation. He came to us one day and asked permission to use our name as a reference for a deal he was doing. In exchange for this he would pay us part of what he earns. He wouldn't give us many details. We have mutual friends and have known each other for a while so it was reluctantly agreed he could use us as a reference and we got our Lindens. That is how all this started.

'It turns out his version of using us as a reference was using our name as a weapon. Basically, trying to intimidate avatars by saying he knows us. That is something we do not condone. He was warned nicely and told not to do it again. He then mistakenly sent me a screenshot of him talking to another mafioso trying to stir shit up. This screenshot almost caused our organisation to go to the mattresses with this other organisation. Someone was talking out of school and it was the young buck.'

As always, Marsellus gave me ominous warnings. 'DO NOT CONTACT anyone in the organisation about the completion of the job until 24 hours after it has been completed. We believe in warnings, in working things out diplomatically. We use these types of retributions as a last resort. If you mess this up, it will probably be the last time you participate in this type of job.' He signed the email 'Marsellus Wallace, Boss, The Sim Mafia'. Since our last chat, though, Chase's real-world anxieties had moved him into action. He'd added a new signature to the bottom of his email: 'DISCLAIMER: This email is only part of a game and does not represent any real-life illegal activity even if it seems so. It is for a game called Second Life and we role-play mafioso. Please do not interpret otherwise.'

Chase was out of town for the weekend, but he promised to arrange a sit-down with the target soon. I had some time to think about the ethics – even the legality – of the job. If the target really was 14, that seemed to make him vulnerable. Also, was this typical of Marsellus's mafia life? The virtual mafia don liked to brag ('I am now pretty much the second most famous gamer in the world, next to Fatal1ty,' he wrote me in an email – whoever 'Fatal1ty' was) – but when it came down to it, his first mission was for me to rat out a 14-year old loud-mouth. Marsellus had turned out to be a rather theatrical mafioso.

Still, he'd already made a $100 out of me. Maybe he knew what he was doing, and maybe there was more to this job than met the eye. I decided to take the job – but I wouldn't see it through. I wouldn't report the target to Linden Lab. Instead, I would play the target against Marsellus, who seemed a much more robust target. I had done my homework, and watched *Godfather I* and *II*. I'd learned that it's good to have a war every now and then. It clears the air, gets rid of bad blood. I would see if I could start a mafia war. I would go to the virtual mattresses myself.

In the meantime, though, more serious crime had come to virtual worlds. Until now, I'd begun to believe the ideal of virtual worlds as an escape from the more serious anxieties of our own world. Even the virtual mafia, it seemed, caused no real harm. But something had changed. There was more news on criminal behaviour inside Second Life. This time, though, the offence was being taken more seriously. There had been a series of attacks from inside Second Life, apparently designed to damage the infrastructure of the world itself. Terrorism had come to Second Life, and, it seemed, Marsellus hadn't been entirely paranoid in his worries about real-world law enforcement. This time, Linden Lab called in the real-world FBI.

9

CYBER TERRORISTS
Attacking thought

When I visited Linden Lab, Philip Rosedale had told me he couldn't help but admire the ingenuity of people who cause trouble – known as 'griefers' – in his virtual world. 'Everyone at Linden Lab is in awe of the residents. When a 'griefer' with many alternate characters causes trouble, we try to control him. Our overarching priority is to support the culture of our community – still, at the same time, we also think, 'Isn't it amazing? What this dude did?' But, since my visit, their stance had hardened.

In early December, 2005, at a virtual Christmas celebration inside Second Life, Philip Linden made an announcement. They had tried banning a few culprits – rumoured to be members of the W-Hats – but the attacks continued. Each time their servers were shut down it cost them money, and they regarded this as a real crime. Dressed in a virtual Santa's hat, Philip Linden announced their harder line: 'This seems about a good a time as any to tell you that I am turning over names to the FBI.' The night before Christmas Eve, Linden Lab made an official announcement: 'In the last month there have been several attacks in which users of Second Life have intentionally released objects or taken actions intended to disrupt activity in the Second Life grid. These attacks result in substantial real-world economic harm, and Linden Lab intends to protect its interests using all legal means.'

Part of Second Life's flexibility as a virtual world stems from residents' freedom to create. When someone designs an object in Second Life, they can choose how it appears, but they can also sculpt what it does. Any object can be 'scripted' to interact with itself and other objects and people. The W-Hats had discovered how to create something simple but devastatingly effective: a kind of virtual bomb. They'd built an object – which looked like an orb, with a picture of a character from the popular computer game Half Life on it – which was scripted, when triggered, to copy itself. Then, each copy would make a copy. Soon the world filled with copies; then, the world overflowed. The Second Life servers crashed, and every resident was ejected.

Anyone who possessed one of these objects could crash the world at any time. Linden Lab developed a virtual firebreak, an impassable virtual barrier that contained outbreaks to certain areas of the map. But the attacks were repeated. Some days, over the last few months of 2005, it was hard to log into Second Life at all. The group had refined their scripts into a device shaped like a block of C-4. Like a real terrorist attack, when the virtual bomb went off, the world went dark.

Between October and December 2005, a group of Second Life residents – who cannot be named for legal reasons – persisted in these 'global attacks'. In Linden Lab's eyes this was a step too far. The attacks cost money and time. For a real-world crime to have occurred, the relevant UK law (the Misuse of Computers Act) requires actions which cause damage to data to be 'unauthorised'. Whether actions permitted by the Linden scripting language, on a server to which access is allowed, are 'unauthorised' is arguable, and at the time of writing has yet to be tested in the UK courts. US law is clearer: US Code Title 18, Section 1030, drafted to outlaw Denial of Service attacks, where web servers are taken out by a barrage of requests for information, says, in effect, that if you knowingly transmit information to a computer involved in interstate communication, and cause at least $5,000 of damage, you will be liable for a crime that may be punished by a fine, or imprisonment of up to 10 years, or both.

'These attacks affect the ability of our servers to provide a service for which people are paying us money,' Linden Lab's legal counsel, Ginsu Yoon, told me. Yoon was eager to play down the virtual nature of the crimes, and focus instead on the real-world effects. 'I don't think of these denial of service attacks as taking place *within* the virtual world. These attacks affect the ability of our servers, which are physical and located in the real world, from providing a service for which people are paying us money. It doesn't really matter to me what the attack looks like in the virtual world. What matters is that the effect denies access to our service.' Yoon told me Linden Lab had warned the perpetrators prior to calling in the Feds (although he stressed they were under no obligation to do so. 'If a burglar breaks into your house, do you warn them that you will be calling the police?').

In Linden Lab's eyes, at least, planting a virtual bomb was a real crime.

In the real world, terrorism attacks thought as well as property; in virtual worlds, the same appeared to be true. Instinctively, Linden Lab's step seemed to me an overreaction. The zeal I'd felt first hand on my visit to their offices was now being turned on a few trouble-making residents. On the other hand, I could see the events from Linden Lab's point of view: they'd tried to stop the attacks, and warned those involved, who really were threatening the stability of their world.

One group kept being mentioned in connection with the attacks: the W-Hats – the same group accused by the world's richest resident Anshe Chung of attempting to intimidate her to force her to sell virtual land. In a world where the politeness and positivity sometimes grew cloying, the W-Hats were determinedly perverse. I'd read about their exploits: they'd built a communist-red van, with hammer and sickle, and the slogan, W-Hats: Cyber Terrorists since 2004. They had littered some areas of virtual land with swastikas and giant virtual penises. They had built a scale model of the 9/11 attacks, complete with flames and crashing planes. I visited their website, full of pictures of Second Life avatars, including Transformer robots with penises, called 'Optimus Dong'.

The W-Hats, and a splinter group called Voted 5, were closely linked to the scripting attacks. Publicly, the W-Hats insisted their scripted objects were only ever intended to annoy other residents, not to crash Linden Lab's servers. In September 2006, Linden Lab announced they had banned 60 accounts associated with Voted 5. Since then, the W-Hats had adopted a new, less confrontational tactic – more Dada than Weathermen – which I had witnessed first-hand: they followed people around, and mocked them with virtual hand-puppets.

Plastic Duck, a former member of W-Hats – and one-time target of Catherine Smith's wrath – seemed central to the story. Catherine Smith, in her concerned email to CBC reporter Lindsay Michael about W-Hat member Plastic Duck, had listed his infractions as follows:

– Stolen scripts and republished them on the web
– Hired residents to negative rate other residents

– Dropped the infamous Goatse image all over Second Life

– Harassed the furry community

– Sexually harassed female residents

– Spammed others with penis images

– Was part of the group that recreated a flaming World Trade Center in Second Life with a smashed plane and falling bodies.

The W-Hat HQ was inside Second Life; I went to take a look. They lived in an area of Second Life called Satyr, which seemed to fit their priapic ethos. When I visited, there was a giant statue of what looked like a hatless Hamburglar, with a penis attached. There were fan-club areas for classic computer games. There was a terminal for W-Hat applicants: 'Welcome New Goons!'. In the sky, written in giant, flamingo-pink letters, was the word: 'FAGS!'. Inside their warehouse-style HQ was an auditorium, two rows of chairs and a giant bone throne. ('Like being inside the mind of a crazy person,' another W-Hat tourist, here to check out the view, told me.) In one, oddly psychedelic corner of their workshop, everything I said fell out of my mouth to roll around on the floor.

I waited around their property. A few tourists, who had heard about the W-Hats by reputation, dropped by to take a look, then moved on. Finally, a W-Hat member arrived: it turned out to be Masakazu Kojima, a short woman, dressed up like a Japanese 'otaku' anime cartoon fan, with a pink off-the-shoulder top, jeans with heart and star prints, pink pig-tails and a bright yellow 'Hello Kitty' style cat-themed cap. Kojima, it turned out, was co-founder of the W-Hats. She wanted to make clear she hadn't encouraged the global attacks, or any of the other troublesome behaviour perpetrated by her members. 'W-Hat is the non-griefing 'SA Goon' group in Second Life,' she said – referring to Something Awful ('The Internet Makes You Stupid'), a mischievous prank-based Internet forum. 'Although I always want to put 'non-griefing' in quotes. It's more of a goal than a reality.'

Kojima admitted that some W-Hat members had been behind some of the recent attacks, but she insisted they were no longer members. She told me the latest trend among her trouble-making members was to find shared objects, which could be altered by anyone in the right group, and set them to copy themselves and destroy the world: that way, it was harder to track down the culprit.

I asked if Plastic Duck was behind some of the recent attacks. 'He would probably deny it,' Kojima told me, 'but yeah. He can put you in touch with the other grid crashers too. Most of them hate me, quite a lot, for kicking them out of W-Hat.

'Crashing the grid is not quite in line with our ideas,' she told me.

Kojima gave me instructions on how to find Plastic Duck. 'Just keep in mind that he likes to mess with people,' Kojima said.

Kojima gave me details of an obscure chat channel, dedicated to reconstructing the Second Life client outside the reach of Linden Lab's control – so users could alter it – where Plastic Duck lingered under the name of 'GeneR'. It was my best shot at getting a straight answer, she told me; in more public areas, she said, 'he's more likely to just mess with you.' I lurked in the chat channel for two days before Plastic Duck replied, although once we had exchanged emails, I found him very willing to talk, and the facts chimed with his CBC radio interview.

Plastic Duck turned out to be Patrick Sapinski, a 19-year-old high school student from Ajax, Ontario. Patrick first logged on to Second Life in January 2005. 'When I was 17, I was constantly ill and basically spent all day either in bed or in Second Life. I avoided school and constantly caught shit from my parents for "skipping", as they called it. I'll admit that a lot of the time I wasn't sick enough that I couldn't go to school, but I preferred staying at home and logging into Second Life.' Exhausted by the symptoms of a disease that had yet to be diagnosed, Patrick saw an interview with Philip Rosedale on the niche cable gaming channel TechTV. Then, Second Life became a topic of conversation on one of his favourite websites, Something Awful. Patrick had enjoyed playing with level designers for small online games, but he was frustrated by the weeks it took to release a design, spread the word online, and get people's comments on his designs. He saw the more flexible Second Life as a place to build and try things out straight away.

It took doctors a year to figure out Patrick's illness. 'It turned out to be Crohn's disease,' he told me. 'At that point it had gotten so bad that I pretty much didn't have a life outside of my room. Crohn's disease is an immune disorder where your immune system attacks your bowels. The pains are often compared to those of birthing pains, but constant throughout the day. It was pretty bad, but looking back, I wouldn't have changed a thing.'

After a long post on Something Awful about Second Life, the 'goons', as the website's regulars called themselves, created virtual selves, and they began to enact the jokes they'd talked about online for so long.

'One of the first organised projects was when we took a Something Awful real-life idea called a "fauxtest" into Second Life,' Patrick told me. 'A fauxtest is basically a fake protest. Some goons organise these in real life and for example, on a rainy day make signs to protest the rain, silly stuff like that.' As an early virtual prank, Patrick's friends organised a 'fauxtest' in Second Life, where they dressed in black mime outfits and made blank signs, then stood around in the welcome area doing absolutely nothing.

Not everyone enjoyed it. 'This absolutely enraged the Second

Life community,' Patrick told me. 'It was never done before and wasn't normal, people didn't like the change. Since its inception, Second Life has mostly consisted of people who generally treat it much like real life. They build homes, buy clothes, and hang out with friends. They take things like virtual guns very seriously and don't take kindly to anything that wouldn't normally belong in real life.'

Second Life residents weren't afraid to report people who offended them. (Each month, about 6.5 per cent of logged-in residents filed one or more abuse report, Linden Lab had announced. By the end of 2006, Linden Lab was receiving close to 2,000 abuse reports a day.) Virtual residents who were bumped or jostled by the mock-protesting mimes reported them to Linden Lab. 'You can bet that every single one of them was reported repeatedly,' Patrick told me. Within weeks of joining, many W-Hats were banned from Second Life.

Those who survived, or came back under a different name, began to make new kinds of virtual mischief. 'We had fun,' Patrick said. 'A W-Hat member would randomly stumble upon a couple having virtual sex. They'd attach a chimney avatar and sit on the couple's house, then they'd mention the fact that they are doing this in the W-Hat group chat. Soon enough a goon would show up soliciting bible sales, or dressed as a fire hydrant. To us, it was silly fun; to others, it was horrible griefing.'

W-Hat members posted videos of these pranks to YouTube, under the title 'Second Life Safari'. Predictably, the victims were incensed.

Across virtual worlds, other residents were defining by trial and error this dividing line, between one person's fun and another's suffering. To retain the attention of their residents, virtual worlds like World of Warcraft hold regular events – fourth of

140

July fireworks, fancy-dress nights at Halloween. In these more themed worlds, events are mostly under the control of the companies who make the world, though players do make their own fun, sometimes at the expense of others. In February 2006, the real woman behind a popular World of Warcraft troll, Fayejin, died. On 4 March, her online friends decided to hold a virtual wake; they lined up by a snowy virtual lake, the Frostfire Hot Springs in Winterspring. 'Because she loved to fish in the game,' her virtual funeral announcement read. 'She liked the sound of the water, it was calming for her, and she loved snow.' Her virtual friends queued by the lake to pay their respects to the dead woman's virtual self, who was controlled by a real-world friend. As a mark of respect, they decided to attend without weapons. '$10 on somebody fucking with it,' World of Warcraft resident Stanos wrote, under the funeral announcement. He would have won the bet. An opposing band of players, ironically named 'Serenity Now', decided to take advantage of the vulnerable moment. They stampeded through a cavernous tunnel and attacked the ceremony, their weapons drawn, and killed everyone there. The first virtual resident to be killed was the dead woman's virtual self. Serenity Now posted a YouTube video of the attack as a 'recruitment video'.

By March 2005, when I travelled to Boston to meet Wilde in person, Patrick was forging a virtual reputation as Plastic Duck. Among his already mischievous W-Hat peers in the virtual world, he stood out. 'I participated in a large majority of these outings, which is likely why people even know of my existence. In early 2005, I was known to actively play Second Life at least 10 hours a day. I would show up as a lost robot, oompa loompa or some-thing equally silly. The name was also easy to remember. People didn't remember Operating Thetan, Louis Neutra, or Dave Eisenberg; half the time, when listing suspected griefers, people listed completely wrong last names, but they always got Plastic Duck right.'

His antics came to the attention of Linden Lab, and Plastic Duck began to accumulate the first of his eventual double-digit rap-sheet of suspensions. 'I recall that one of my first suspensions involved me following a woman around the welcome area who was trying to get away from my avatar (an oompa loompa from *Charlie and the Chocolate Factory*) because she claimed it was ugly,' Patrick said. He thought the Second Life community too sensitive about the W-Hat's playful attitude. 'It's hard for non Second Lifers to realise the severity of these "crimes". I can guarantee you that if I did the same thing in real life, I could likely get a laugh out of anyone who saw it. But in Second Life, people are living a very sheltered life. They can't stand the smallest change.'

Despite Patrick's insistence that the W-Hats were just out to have fun, their antics did stray into offensive, and later, damaging activities. W-Hat member Ol Fitzcarraldo liked to change his virtual shape into what he called his 'black' avatar: a racial stereotype, complete with watermelon slice, bucket of chicken and an afro. I asked Patrick about these. 'There are goons whose intent is to harass,' he told me. 'That's against the Second Life rules, and those goons get kicked out and come back on new accounts. Then there are those, which I guess I sort of fall into, that like to have fun, and sometimes get a kick making fun of some really weird people and communities out there. On my Plastic Duck account, I pushed the boundaries and rules, but I rarely if ever broke them. Almost all of my suspensions were for Disturbing the Peace – words most goons have seen many times. If you get reported enough in Second Life, no matter how innocent you are, you'll eventually get a suspension for Disturbing the Peace.'

I asked whether the W-Hats, with their provocative 'Cyber Terrorist' slogan, were out to destroy Second Life. 'Someone on the Second Life forums made a claim that W-Hat are cyber terrorists because of what we do,' Patrick told me. 'The group found this rather funny. The "W-Hat Cyber Terrorists since 2004" moniker is a complete parody. Not a single person in the group believes they are really cyber terrorists.'

Patrick then told me the W-Hat side of what he called 'the drama with Anshe Chung', on the Baku area of Second Life, where the W-Hats built their first HQ.

'When Baku was put online, I believe half the land was first land, which consists of small parcels made available to Second Life newbies,' Patrick said, referring to a common term for new residents. 'The other half was purchased by land baron Anshe Chung, who divided it up into small chunks to resell for profit. A number of goons bought up the first land parcels and joined them together to be used for the W-Hat land, and added to that were a few Anshe parcels we purchased.'

'Anyway, W-Hat as a group did what they did,' Patrick said. 'The land was very colourful, with random 'newbies' leaving all kinds of offensive crap around, swastikas, penises, bombs, etc.' ('It's a common joke that in Second Life, Star Wars fans build their first lightsaber; goons build their first penis,' Patrick had joked.) 'That'll lower the value of any land around it.

'I'd bet that more than a few new goons tried to extort Anshe, no doubt about that. But their perception of Second Life,' Patrick said, quoting the Linden Lab slogan, '"your world, your imagination", made this acceptable.'

I enjoyed the stories of some of the W-Hat pranks, but some – Ol Fitzcarraldo's 'black' avatar, the intentional grid attacks – seemed genuinely offensive. In the real world, terrorism attacks thought, and cyber terror too disrupts dialogue. Still, as a group, the 'terrorists' seemed to have a place in the virtual world. They were the anti-Lindens, the amoral shadow of the Linden's crusade for community and calm.

'A lot of people want to live perfect lives in Second Life, but I don't think those people could stand it if Linden Lab did somehow manage to rid the grid of any drama or griefing incidents. They may not like it, but in the end, it's a part of the world.'

At this point, Patrick had to take a break; it was time to travel to his clinic for an infliximab infusion, a treatment for his ongoing Crohn's disease. When he returned, our chat continued.

Over time, Patrick told me, their bans added momentum to the W-Hat's more disruptive side. 'Usually when a clean account got banned I'd be left with nothing, no land and none of the content I created,' Patrick said. 'This pissed me off, so in turn I would make throw-away accounts which I would just mess around on. Squat other peoples land, and build stuff that I didn't really care if I lost.'

I asked if this was when the attacks against the whole world began. 'I remember the first grid crash like it was yesterday,' Patrick told me. 'We were doing a top hat, monocle and suit theme at the time. It happened in October 2005. Ol Fitzcarraldo, a member of W-Hat and a W-Hat splinter group, was working on objects called 'griefspheres', which were balls that randomly flew around and tried to place themselves at the location of an avatar, in effect swarming and surrounding unsuspecting players.' The griefspheres, a metre across, were painted with a picture of an evil character from the video game Half Life 2, grinning manically. Another W-Hat brought up the idea of making them replicate. After some reluctance, Patrick told me, Ol Fitzcarraldo altered the griefspheres so they copied themselves. According to Patrick, Ol didn't want his new invention to spiral out of control. He built a self-destruct command, the letter 'd'. The first time he released the new, improved, griefspheres, they quickly filled the room. 'They were replicating pretty fast,' Patrick said, so Ol flew around shouting "d". After a few minutes, he got rid of all the griefspheres around the area. He thought he was safe.'

About 10 minutes later, another W-Hat sent a message: Hey Ol, What the fuck are these griefspheres? CLEAN THIS SHIT UP. Patrick checked the map; that particular W-Hat was on the opposite side of the world. 'That was when we realised the severity of what was going on.'

According to Patrick, the Second Life servers, interconnected on a grid, are surrounded by a buffer zone, the 'space server'. 'When something crosses into the space server,' Patrick said, 'it is deleted and sent back to your inventory. Now, all these self-replicating griefspheres overloaded and crashed the space server. Because of this, any object that left the grid would warp to the next closest server as it never made it to the space server. This caused just about every single server in Second Life to be packed full of griefspheres.' (Some reports put the total number of grief-spheres at 5.4 billion.)

'Within about half an hour, the space server had crashed, and so had about half of the other servers. So while others may believe it was a planned attack, the first griefsphere incident was definitely an accident, one that the creator attempted to clean up but had managed to get out of his control.'

'There have been many grid attacks since, maybe around five to eight that appeared well thought out and planned, and were often successful, and about 20 that appeared to be spur of the moment: "hey we made this big foetus object, let's make it attack people!" Or more, "let's see how 500 of these spinning around flying at people will look!"' (One of the 'Second Life Safari' showed this kind of grief: in a Second Life nightclub, a W-Hat filled the dance-floor with body-popping Gremlins.) 'I recall a few of the smaller random "attacks" were sometimes colour-changing cubes called "lolcubes" and a few times a brown foetus object was used called "chocolate foetus". I recall a specific chocolate foetus incident where one of the Live Help goons was pasting us chat logs from Live Help. One resident complained that he was being "hugged by big brown bears". A Linden employee told this resident to restart their computer as a means of fixing the problem. Most of us found this reply rather funny.'

Attacks actually shutting down the grid was rare, Patrick claimed. 'Only a few of them caused any actual crashes. I think out of all of the grid attacks that have occurred, a group of about five vengeful goons have been responsible, with maybe two to three grid outages that we weren't able to find a responsible party for.'

'I know most of the grid attackers pretty well,' Patrick told me. 'Most of them were former W-Hat members. W-Hat kicks people who attack the grid.'

In the end, bored by his regular bans, Patrick told me he decided to return to the straight and narrow. As his new character, Gene Replacement, he had even earned bounties – 10,000 Lindens, about $30 a time – from Linden Lab for reporting possible exploits: mistakes in the world that other residents might have used to cause trouble. 'On one occasion I had a chat with Philip Rosedale himself,' Patrick told me, 'where he personally thanked me for turning in a pretty big exploit, one that let you generate unlimited and untraceable amounts of Linden Dollar currency.'

After he told Linden Lab about the exploits, Patrick said, a Linden Lab manager even considered hiring him as a security consultant. 'I was put in contact with some management, and we discussed a possible consultation contract for about a month or so, to see how things go.' The idea didn't go down well with some other Linden staff. 'From what I gather, the other management just shot the idea down as soon as they found out who he was talking to,' Patrick said.

146

I asked about the email Catherine Smith had allegedly sent to CBC reporter Lindsay Michael, listing Plastic Duck's infractions. 'Some of them are partly true, overall everything is exaggerated,' Patrick said. 'For example, I might have sent the Goatse image [a notorious sexually explicit photo] to a few people, but they were friends within W-Hat, not all over Second Life. Anyone can be guilty of being in a group with another griefer in it. Most Second Life groups are public. It's sad that Catherine would stoop to that level, and stupid of her to actually think that such an email would change Lindsay's mind.' (In the end, Patrick was interviewed on CBC. He showed them a model he was working on, a virtual Mac-10 sub-machine gun. He read out his notice of termination email from Linden Lab. 'Apparently they seem to think when I make fun of someone I'm causing them intense mental anguish,' he said. 'I don't believe that. It's a video game.')

Despite his attempts to stay clean, Patrick's new virtual self, Gene Replacement, was dragged down by his friends. 'In the end, I was banned for associating with a grid crasher, including about 60 other people banned for the same reason. There were one, maybe two people involved in the grid attacks. In an effort to make it look like Linden Lab was working on the problem, they pinned the blame on a group of 60 goons and banned them all. Then they reclaimed our entire land, which they resold on the open market.'

When we spoke, Patrick still had a few Second Life accounts, which he and friends had created when they discovered a simple loophole in the registration system. (In 2005, Second Life accounts cost $9.95; banned W-Hats would just pay a friend to set up an account for them. Later, first accounts were free, but you needed to establish your identity with a credit card, PayPal, or cellphone authorisation. A Something Awful goon discovered you could just click on the form button twice to register an account without any authorisation. 'The Second Life client does use various unique parts of your computer to identify you,' Patrick told me, 'however those are easy to get around once you know what you're looking for.')

But it wasn't the same. All his friends had been banned. By the time we spoke, he spent less time in his virtual shoes. He wrote a website posting for his friends, called 'I miss Second Life'. 'I miss it all,' Patrick wrote. 'It was silly, it was pointless, we didn't really accomplish much, but we had fun.

'The furries, the goreans, the griefers, the sexual deviants, the builders, the scripters, the thinkers, you, my friends, your friends, everyone. I miss all of you.'

'I definitely made a connection with these people, and I still care for them very much,' Patrick told me. 'We've mostly lost contact, outside of a few who still idle in our Ventrilo server and one person who I often visit in real life. It's a shame that Linden Lab had to ruin that for us.'

'The whole thing was like being back on the gradeschool play-ground for me,' one of the banned Voted 5 members, 'fiddy' – one of Patrick's closest friends from Second Life – wrote on Patrick's website. 'Just being a total inner child and doing ridiculous silly things and having our own immature little wars and drama. It was also kinda like being at the kid's table at a big family Thanksgiving or something. A few yards away everyone is trying to be real mature and stuff, then you have a bunch of kids flinging food around and making fart jokes. It was the most fun and best laughs I've ever had on the Internet. I guess the big adults finally had enough though, and sent us all to our rooms.'

'I know the real people behind a lot of the anonymous accounts used for grid attacks,' Patrick told me. 'I would consider a lot of them friends. No one is really afraid of the FBI threats. We've had Lindens tell us anonymously that the FBI threats were fake.

There's really no reason to believe that the FBI is even remotely interested to hear LL's cries for help.'

Patrick saw the FBI announcement as 'a bad PR move'. 'I doubt there are more than a few people in SL crazy enough to want the FBI investigating grid crashes instead of real crimes relating to national security,' he said.

Earlier, Masakazu Kojima had backed up Patrick's comments. 'As far as calling in the Feds,' Kojima had told me, 'I can tell you for sure that the Big Bad Guys have yet to hear from anyone.'

Linden Lab had hoped a real-world prosecution would intimidate others tempted by similar trespasses against their universe. A Linden Lab contact told me the FBI had in fact visited Linden Lab three times. (The first two visits, the FBI apparently had trouble grasping whether a crime had taken place. The third time, after Linden Lab gave them a list of the credit cards involved, they returned to report the credit cards were stolen, and there was little more they could do.) Linden Lab had at least pushed its security to the point where it required breaking a real-world law – in this case, credit card theft – to persistently disrupt their universe. But the lack of real-world consequences for these disruptive activities made me wonder how the virtual community might handle these infractions themselves. Virtual worlds like Second Life were now full of crimes and misdemeanours. Linden Lab published a weekly 'police blotter' – lists of offences committed by residents. In the real world, many of these crimes would have led to a jail sentence; in the virtual world, where stakes were lower, they mostly led to warnings or a short-term suspension. In one day, 14 June 2006, two resident logged into other residents' accounts and stole their virtual cash; Linden suspended each for seven days. On 21 September 2006, one resident was warned for wearing a giant penis attachment in a PG area. Another was warned for harming a virtual pet; a third, suspended for seven days for wearing a KKK outfit, yelling Sieg Heil and waving a Confederate flag.

When I visited the Linden Lab San Francisco offices, I had broached this subject. 'We always thought that there would be a lot of disputes,' Robin Harper said. As part of her work as VP of Community Development at Linden Lab, Harper tried to encourage Second Life residents to get along. 'We believed that part of complexity was intrigue. Part of why we like the world is because it is complicated. The explicit feature set of Second Life is so open, there's always going to be people defining what making you miserable means in different ways. I think we expected to get asked to resolve disputes.' Linden Lab employees told me, though, with just 30 employees, they did not have the resources to handle every argument; they hoped the watchful eyes of the virtual community would begin to police themselves, 'to delegate that responsibly, wherever we can, to the people who live there,' Robin Harper had told me. With the aim of fostering community spirit, Philip Linden held a weekly 'town hall' event, in which he discussed Linden Lab plans, and threw open the floor to questions from concerned residents. But for some residents, who wanted freedom, but didn't want the attendant responsibility, Linden Lab wasn't doing enough. 'Some people are very unhappy that we haven't put a system of governance in place,' Harper said. 'And we keep saying governance will come when it's ready. There is one small community, called Neu Altenburg, that does have a system of self-governing. I'd say you will probably start to see more of these local jurisdictions in Second Life. A group of all the landowners in a large area, saying, Hey look, if you don't play by the rules, guess what, you'll never come to this place again, you'll be exiled from that part of the world. I can see that being a very powerful motive. If you go against that and lose you might have interests there, that would be very serious, that would be nearly the same as death.'

To build any society, you need a world-pillar, a foundation for the structure to come: a constitution; a senate; a guru. Linden Lab see its 'Terms of Service' and 'Community Standards', both of which new residents have to read and agree to, as equivalent to a basic constitution, designed to foster a co-operative culture based on mediation rather than arbitration. 'Basically we have three rules,' Harper said. 'One is the golden rule: do unto others. Then growing out of that is the second rule, which is that we support and promote tolerance and so we don't allow any hate speech. The last rule is that we don't allow you to reveal other people's real life information.' By March 2005, Robin Harper had told me they'd only ever had cause to ban 20 people – many for credit card fraud. But the idea of emergent arbitration seemed to excite them. 'In a decentralised way, local governance is all that makes sense. Sometimes that's a bit painful and chaotic but far more fundamentally right.'

'Where there's no law, there's no bread,' Benjamin Franklin wrote. The converse is also true: where there's bread, there's law; and where there's law, there's disagreement. Now that people made actual dough in virtual worlds, the ways in which those worlds were policed seemed increasingly important. Virtual residents knew, though, that real-world courts rarely offered recourse for virtual damages. Even in Korea, where the phenomenon of mass population of virtual worlds had reached its peak, real-world cases rarely extended beyond violence caused by games. There, the Seoul Police CyberTerror Unit, which polices real-world crimes related to online gaming, told me that virtual objects had no legal value. If you paid someone for a virtual sword and they didn't deliver, it was fraud – after all, you'd lost money. If you delivered a virtual sword and they didn't pay, well, that was just a disagreement inside a game.

So what options did virtual residents have when they felt they had been the victim of a virtual offence? How were the rules enforced among those who played? Virtual worlds liberate us from our bodies, but not from each other. In Second Life, to take two actual examples, a sniper who took pot-shots through a school window was a mild nuisance; someone who skinny-dipped in a PG area was far more frowned upon. The usual path of action for disagreement in virtual worlds was to plead with the game developers, usually via a 'Games Master' (the virtual equivalent of the local councillor), in the hope the gods – the world's makers – would intervene. (Often, they didn't. Spokesman Jeff Brown of Electronic Arts, developers of the virtual world The Sims Online, admitted that, in their world, the rules 'are enforced about as well as the rules are enforced on the Massachusetts Turnpike.') When I visited Linden Lab, Robin Harper cited some examples. A resident who threw a fire-bomb at a wedding, she said, might get a few points against their record, whereas someone writing a self-replicating, heavily scripted object which caused a whole section of Second Life to crash – a kind of terrorist attack against the infrastructure of the world – would be suspended. (Later, their stance against this kind of attack toughened considerably.) The community-focussed Linden Lab said it took the decision to ban someone seriously. Residents who committed more serious infractions would have their accounts put on hold, while a randomly selected jury of 12 residents reviewed the anonymous facts of the case; those convicted by their virtual peers would have their Second Life selves permanently banned. But what about more subtle forms of disagreement? What if your neighbour builds a huge tower block and puts your virtual garden in the shade? Who can you turn to?

'Do what thou wilt shall be the whole of the law,' Aleister Crowley wrote. In virtual worlds, to some extent, this was true. But our virtual worlds had begun to highlight the inherent contradiction in Crowley's famous exultation. What if people wilt make laws? In September 2005, two law school students, Judge Mason and Judge Churchill, took it upon themselves to solve this problem: they built a virtual courtroom, and opened the Second Life Superior Court. Residents could take their arguments, large or small, to the court. The judges would, with reference to the Linden Lab Community Standards, and their own knowledge of real-world law, resolve the disputes. The court followed basic legal procedure, including brief and counter-brief, and any decision by the court was intended to be final. (It was the formation of this court which led Marsellus Wallace to create Raymond Polonsky, his virtual legal counsel.)

Not all Second Life residents agreed the court was a good idea. 'What a mind-numbingly futile exercise,' resident Tony Walsh wrote on the 'Second Life Herald' website. 'So now we have yet another level of tedious bureaucracy to Second Life, one administered by self-appointed "officials" with no recognised real-world powers, let alone make-believe ones. I'm in contempt of this kangaroo court.' Others wondered whether the court would have teeth to back up its judgement, or even what would happen if a Linden employee was the target of a case. 'Perhaps even the Lindens themselves will take action to stop this,' wrote another resident, Dygash Talamasca.

In fact, Linden Lab did step in. Not to stop the court, but to request the pair change their court's name, so as not to confuse residents about the court's authority. The court was renamed 'The Metaverse Superior Court', but the lack of authority did cause problems, and the court never heard a case. Others were exploring possible solutions to the lack of virtual law. Second Life resident Zarf Vantongerloo realised most legal agreements are founded on signed documents. Using cryptographic keys and secure communication with a server outside of Second Life, Zarf designed a notary service, providing signed, un-tamperable documents, for virtual agreements and business deals.

The legal status of virtual trespass has yet to be established. At real-world conferences like State of Play: Law, Games and Virtual Worlds in 2005, real-world lawyers have begun to examine the new legal frontier. As yet, although virtual items have real value, those with virtual income do not pay real-world tax unless they convert their virtual earnings into real currency. Most virtual world developers try to stem this problem by banning the sale of virtual items through eBay: Sony Online Entertainment, which owns EverQuest and EverQuest II, insists all the content of its virtual worlds, including items and even the virtual selves, remain its property. All new residents must agree to the Terms and Conditions, which state as much. The Terms and Conditions of Ultima Online, another massive fantasy-themed virtual world, state: 'You acknowledge and agree that all characters created, and items acquired and developed as a result of game play are part of the Software and Service and are the sole property of EA.com.' Lawyers, though, are not convinced these disclaimers will hold forever. For legal and copyright purposes, European and American legal systems equate lines of computer code with narrative prose; this stance implies ownership remains with the companies that own the worlds, although once creative input takes place on behalf of the player, it isn't always clear who has made the content, and therefore who owns the virtual self. Virtual worlds have created a whole new nexus of legal debate; copyright laws, laws of identity and, in the case of well-known virtual selves, rights of publicity, are all arguably relevant, and each branch of the law reaches a different conclusion about who owns what in the virtual world.

Virtual worlds give us an opportunity to observe the development of society again, from basic tenets. ('In Second Life, we are free of everything but the need for community and novelty,' Philip Linden had told me.) In medieval times, banishment from your community was the worst possible punishment; it cut you off from your collective self, which held both your earthly and heavenly connections. It was a fate worse than death. Ever since, police, moral philosophers, and criminals themselves, have all wrestled with the thorny problem of what to do with those who break society's moral codes and repeatedly hurt others. In the real world, our attitudes to punishment evolved. When banishment stopped being a punishment worse than death, we switched to using death – now seen as the most extreme exclusion. Later, the British tried banishment en masse, sending convicts across the world to Australia. In the modern world, social conditions have changed; we're no longer tied into the body of our local community, so that to be removed from it is no longer to be cut from your heart. Now we exclude people 'humanely'; we hold people – in prisons, in detention centres, in borstals – inside the world, but outside society. Murderers get imprisoned or deported. Ghosts get sucked up by Bill Murray and kept inside a toaster. Whoever you are, society's greatest punishment is still to remove you from itself.

As a rule, though, in virtual worlds the medieval approach prevails: those who break the rules of the game are banned. (In December 2005, Blizzard banned 18,000 residents for trading virtual gold for real money.) For those who identify primarily in their virtual selves, nothing could be worse than a ban. To be cut off from Second Life or World of Warcraft is to be cut off from the heavens of their virtual lives, exiled into the purgatory of the real world.

Some virtual worlds, I discovered, were working to make the punishment fit the crime. The Egyptian-themed world 'A Tale in the Desert' has a player-run legal system, modelled on the ancient

155

Egyptian system, which allows residents to vote on the banning of another player. In other virtual worlds, the punishments played a dramatic role in the stories of the worlds themselves.

Cynewulf, a barbarian and resident of a new online game set in Roman Britain, AD180, called 'Roma Victor' – developed in the UK by virtual world company RedBedlam – is perhaps the only living American to survive crucifixion. In the real world, Cynewulf was a 27-year-old electrical engineer from Flint, Michigan; in the virtual world, he was a bloodthirsty barbarian. Throughout the summer of 2005, Cynewulf had raided the areas where new residents, and residents who had been killed, rejoined the virtual world. These defenceless young Romans, fresh to their virtual sandals, were easy prey, and other residents complained. Finally, the rulers of the virtual empire decided enough was enough. As punishment, the world's gods (RedBedlam) decided Cynewulf would spend seven days nailed to the cross.

Where we used to gather, outside the reach of commerce, was in the church. Religion has made an appearance in virtual worlds already. The Anglican Church has set up an 'i-church', with its own virtual pastor, to explore ways to worship online. At St Philip and St James' Church in Bath, the Reverend Alan Bain runs regular sermons streamed over the web. Meanwhile, the Meenakshi Temple in Madurai, in India, offers 'E-pujas', for people who can't make the real-world pilgrimage. One Second Life resident, OmegaX Zapata, conducted a Catholic Mass, dressed as a virtual priest, with his congregation of 10 or so reading along from a virtual book. Another retired Episcopalian built a church and handed out virtual T-shirts which read, 'Jesus had a Second Life, too'.

On their website, Christian organisation Ship of Fools has built a tiny virtual world, 'Church of Fools', which you can inhabit, as a Ned Flanders lookalike, a bearded, Gap-shirt-wearing teenager, a raver, or a smart black man in an Oswald Boateng suit. You can wander among the other virtual parishioners, virtual pews, and virtual pillars – hung with rebellious Christian modern art like Albert Herbert's Jesus Falls Under the Cross – that turn transparent so you can watch yourself pass. There is no virtual collection plate, but, for a while, visitors could contribute funds from their mobile phones. As your virtual, Cluedo-piece shaped self, you can attend a sermon, talk, whisper, kneel in prayer, extend a hand or raise both arms in rapture, all without leaving your living room. (One visitor arrived with her five-year-old son in her real-world lap. 'Who's on my team?' he asked. 'Which ones do I kill?') From May to August 2004, an average of 8,000 virtual people (the size of a cathedral congregation) visited each day. Even in the virtual church, though, trouble arrived. As Richard Chartres, the Anglican Bishop of London, addressed the virtual church's opening congregation, some of his virtual flock wandered around, pointed at him, and swore. People arrived with racist names, or tried to get close and personal with the female congregation. More than once, 'Satan' himself logged in and climbed the pulpit.

Apparently, even religious apparitions had come to virtual worlds. In August 2006, one Second Life resident, Kali Zeluco, claimed to have had a virtual vision. Kali had created a 'prim', a single block of Second Life virtual material (in this case, virtual wood). With no modification on her part, she claimed, on the wooden block appeared an image of the Virgin Mary. (She apparently considered donating the block to a local church, but instead decided to offer it for sale on a website called SLExchange, for 30,000 Linden Dollars – about $100. 'People will flock from sims around to see this "prim", to touch it, to be healed by it's holy aura,' she wrote in her sales pitch.)

*   *   *

'I was raised in a fairly religious upbringing, but I don't view this game or this method of punishment as an insult against Christians,' Cynewulf told me, of his virtual crucifixion. 'In fact, the era being represented is rife with possibilities for Christian gamers to role-play being among the early faithful who died for the faith. A Christian player could decide to be another Perpetua and face lions rather than renounce her faith, or another player could role-play an early church father and re-enact with other Christians the debates that formed the various sects of Christianity – this could actually be a great opportunity for religious players wanting to relive that rather momentous time in their history. My chosen preference, however, is just to step away from the modern world and pretend to be a Woden-worshipping Germanic warrior. It's just a game, after all.'

Cynewulf's punishment was untested, and there were a few glitches. The sinning barbarian should have been firmly nailed to the cross, unable to speak or move, but as a crowd watched the cross being pulled erect, Cynewulf raised an arm and waved.

Still, Cynewulf told me, being nailed to a virtual cross for a week wasn't fun. 'It was surprisingly agonising for just being a game,' Cynewulf told me. As the virtual crucifix was raised, a fellow barbarian ran from the crowd and attached the guards in a rage. Cynewulf watched helplessly as his compatriot was put to death. 'Being jeered at by the Romans while immobilised is not much fun. Particularly since they are all weaklings who deserve to die by my sword.'

When I visited Linden Lab, they had hinted at their hopes for new forms of punishment. ('It's a really interesting area,' Philip Rosedale had told me. 'I don't know yet, do you go to jail or do you go to virtual jail? I love that.') A year after my visit, they tested a new approach, designed to rehabilitate, rather than just punish, offenders. Also, their solution was designed to amuse.

Early in January 2006, Second Life resident Nimrod Yaffle broke the Second Life 'Terms of Service', by hacking into the Second Life code to steal items from a virtual store. Instead of a suspension, Yaffle was the first resident to be sent to 'The Cornfield'. Every time he logged into Second Life, where there once was a whole world, suddenly all he could see were endless rows of corn. (The scenery was inspired by a classic episode of the TV series *The Twilight Zone*, in which an omnipotent child rules a town in terror. Anyone who offends his infantile sense of right and wrong is banished to the 'cornfield', never to be seen again.) Yaffle walked the rows for what seemed like days, under a full moon that never seemed to wane. No one else came. He found a tractor, but the tractor was 'insanely slow'. He found a TV, but all it ever played was a 1940s cautionary film, about a troubled teenager trying to avoid a life of crime. Nimrod's crime wasn't too serious, and nor was his punishment. ('The cornfield is not used often,' Catherine Smith told *Discover Magazine*, 'and it is only for white collar crimes. It is supposed to be funny more than anything.') Nimrod knew he would be seen again. He was temporarily cut off from his heavenly connections, but he still had his earthly ones. (He posted pictures of the cornfield on Second Life bulletin boards.) Nimrod even tried, unsuccessfully, to create a scripted object that would crash the world – an echo of the crime that had him teleported into the cornfield in the first place. Nimrod was being asked to consider the effect of his actions, but mostly what he did was drive the tractor. Also, he kept half an eye out for the virtual Children of the Corn.

10

VIRTUAL RICHES
Where there's money, there's an addiction

My time in the lawless virtual underworld had made me conscious of my own security. When I'd met Wilde in person, I'd told them I planned to set up a virtual office. 'Make sure it's burglar-proof!' June-Marie had joked, and the group had laughed.

As it turned out, even in the virtual world, home security was a concern.

In the real world, my housing situation was turbulent. I had read stories of homeless people in New York City scraping up change to maintain their virtual mansion, but I no longer believed these tales. I was having enough trouble building my own virtual life, on the short security of six-month tenancy agreements. To build virtual stability, I had discovered, you needed real stability. You needed to have something before you could want to escape it. Over the last 10 years of living in London property prices – already among the world's most expensive – had tripled in value. The pressure on young people to rent or buy their own accommodation was phenomenal. In the city, the buildings I most coveted were large and full of light, but my own accommodation was now a string of rented and shared apartments. At the same time, I longed for a place in the country, away from every-thing and everyone. My daydreams were of penthouses with views of the city, or quiet places by the sea: homes above or outside the crowd.

I made a few small steps in these directions. On a trip to Brazil, a friend and I seriously considered putting down £10,000 for a plot of land overlooking the sea. A local hotel owner led us over the brow of a hill, still thick with near-jungle, and we paced out the plots (one to eight had been snapped up by French investors; nine, 10 and 11 were still available). We could build homes there, we thought – share an Internet connection, and live our real lives in a tropical paradise. I knew enough about paradises, though, to know things would be hard there too – plus, neither of us had £10,000. Closer to home, I considered moving to the British seaside. I visited a lighthouse keeper's cottage in Dungeness, a low-rent single-story building, with little insulation and no heating. The view from what would have been my office was a long, low, shingled beach, grey stones and sea and sky as far as you could see, broken only by the boxy silhou-ettes of Dungeness A & B, which together housed four working nuclear reactors. But London was three hours away, and here again there was no Internet connection; I would have had to end my virtual life and settle exclusively on the real. I wasn't ready to make the sacrifice.

The channels on my TV seemed packed with documentaries following people moving from place to place: to France, to Australia. Through so-called 'reality' game shows, we stranded our celebrities on sunny, deserted beaches, as stand-ins for our own desire to be elsewhere. Technology had made it easier to work away from others; it had never felt easier to relocate – and it had never been harder to choose our new location.

We hadn't just chosen to live in virtual worlds; we'd also been driven there, in the same way American colonists were driven to leave Europe. People were living alone because they chose to do so – for so long we had wanted to be free, and, we found, part of being free was being alone – but we also lived separately because our 'free market' system had pushed us apart. We had been divided by the forces that profit from our separation – the companies that made the washing machines, which profited when they sold more to people who lived alone; the car manufacturers like General Motors, which, in the 1930s and 40s, bought up electric streetcar systems across the US, and replaced them with buses – and then, in 1949, was convicted of using its subsidiary National City Lines bus company to buy up only General Motors vehicles, so people would use more G.M.-made combustion engines. The resulting separation from these kinds of pressures had helped drive people to leave their real cities to reside in cyberspace – the place William Gibson, who coined the term, called 'the city of lights'.

In the real world, we were surrounded by space, glass, dreams of light and freedom of motion – but our access to those valuable resources was restricted. We needed money and influence to reach those spaces. In our commercial culture, the big lie is that money and success bring happiness. Even the wealthy struggle; even the famous are unhappy. In virtual worlds, we can live out our material hopes much faster, experience an echo of the hollowness of mansions and Ferraris, without spending a lifetime to achieve them. Even those who had achieved material success in the real world suffered from the attendant separation: money created access to space, but eroded our access to each other. In our individualistic culture, success was measured by the amount of space we could place between ourselves and others. We wanted each other, and we didn't want each other. Virtual worlds were a kind of solution to that tension, between self and other; a way to be together when we felt so alone. In virtual worlds, we could come together, but also keep each other at a safe distance.

(These thoughts of the real-world economy that underpinned our virtual worlds made me wonder if our new frontier was in some sense a gated community of privilege: after all, I'd invested £1,000 for a PC that helped me spend time in virtual worlds; for real-world residents from poorer nations, that would be a significant barrier to virtual lives. But, in November 2006, the charity One Laptop Per Child announced its first 21,000 laptops – designed to cost just $100, and subsidised by bulk orders from the governments of Argentina, Brazil, Libya, Nigeria and Thailand – had rolled off a Shanghai production line. The laptop, designed to assist IT education for the world's poor, ran Doom, a classic 3D video game. It couldn't be long before virtual world technology would be able to transport the Third World too.)

When my mother and her friends decided to set up a commune, to build their own solution to the problem of how to live, their zeal for a better world drove them, after a long year of fund-raising, to buy Herringswell Manor, a mock-Tudor manor house in 14 acres of Suffolk countryside. They knocked down walls, and filled the space with each other. Coincidentally, the week I visited Dungeness looking for my own space, a Herringswell resident who knew about the commune sent me a brochure. In a 'sympathetic refurbishment', the manor, our old commune, had been converted into luxury apartments. Walls had been rebuilt, so the new residents could shore themselves up against each other. When my mother and her lover travelled to the Suffolk estate agent to sign for the commune property, they carried a cashier's cheque, the pooled money of hundreds of fellow devotees, for £250,000 – the entire purchase price. Then, that money bought a home for 400 adults and 30 children. Now, the cheapest one-bedroom apartment was being sold for exactly the same price.

In the society where I lived, status was indicated by the amount of space you were able to put between yourself and others. I wanted some of the space for myself, but space, above everything, was at a premium. Along with almost everyone I knew my own age, I was priced out of the market. Instead I would build a temporary solution to these problems of space and need. To find space, I would have to go online.

In my time as an adult, separation felt familiar. Through the last century, the century of the self, we found ourselves, but we lost each other; now, we need each other, but we are afraid to lose ourselves again. To keep people at a distance can now be a comfort. We keep our friends on the other end of an email, our families on the other end of a phone call. We keep them at a distance, both far away and close, where everyone can remain comfortable. For now, and for me – and, it seemed, for millions of others – virtual worlds were a perfect solution. They were a way to be together, but also to keep others at a safe distance. It was time to build a virtual home.

Getting a seaside home in a virtual world wasn't as easy as I'd imagined. For a start, there was so much choice. I logged on to Second Life. Each time a resident enters Second Life, while the world loads, a 'tip' message appears. This might be a reminder about a town meeting, or a reminder of a useful but little-known feature. This time, coincidentally, the log-in message was a warning about castles in the air. 'If you build a castle in the air, be sure to buy the land below it. If someone else buys the land, they can delete your castle.'

I considered a whole island, but, at $1,250, plus $175 a month – about the price of a car loan – they were beyond my budget. (Within a month, prices would rise to $1,675 per island; residents, of course, complained – suddenly every message board was full of people who had been 'about to buy an island'

– although the new prices were still a snap compared to the real world. That same day, I read Richard Branson had bought an entire island, shaped like Great Britain, in Dubai's as-yet-unfinished man-made Earth Archipelago – a different kind of virtual landscape, laid out as a faux earth atlas – for around £3.5 million.) I browsed through the in-world classified ads. One caught my eye: 'Private sims, tropical island views: $39.50 US a month.' But the price seemed high. I looked at a mountaintop retreat, above a private bay resort (17,600 Linden Dollars, plus $15 a week to Linden Lab). Some land that claimed to be a stone's throw from the ocean . . . well, in virtual worlds, apparently you could throw stones a lot further. Not all the ads were placed by Linden Lab. In fact, most were from other residents, private property speculators who had bought desirable land – a snowy cliff, a sandy beach – in order to re-sell at higher prices.

It was a business model, I knew, that extended across other virtual worlds. For example, in 2004, David Storey, a 22-year-old graduate who lived in Sydney, Australia, bought a virtual island in a game called Project Entropia, for £13,700 – not for fun, but for profit. Every month, for the next 12 months, he could sell five plots of land on his island, which he hoped might nett him as much as £40,000. There were people in Second Life, too, already making more than that. The classified ads for virtual land I had seen were full of ads from Anshe Chung, Inc. (When I later met Anshe, her current account balance – that day's virtual turnover – was 1.6 million Linden Dollars: about $5,500 real world. That would put her annual turnover at just over $2 million a year.)

In the end, I fell in love with a new development: a series of hillside plots, similar to the ones I'd looked at in Brazil, although the landscape was more autumnal. On each plot, the virtual developer had built cantilevered glass and concrete homes, once again clearly influenced by Frank Lloyd Wright's Fallingwater, each one with a sea view. I clicked on the 'For Sale' signs to learn more. A property here would cost me 14,000 Linden Dollars – about £20 – plus $15 per month. Even after Marsellus had cleaned me out, the price fit my budget. A passing resident swooped down out of the virtual sky to ask if I was interested. I nodded. He began to show me around the homes. It was like being taken round by a real-world estate agent. ('This one has a lovely terrace,' he told me.) It became clear, though, that he himself was another kind of profiteer. Spotting a smart investment, had bought half the properties from the developer, and was offering them for rent. But I wanted a home of my own. He told me numbers seven, eight, 10 and 12 were still available; I chose 10, a modest, split-level building with room for an office and a lounge upstairs.

I clicked 'buy', and paid 14,000 Linden Dollars to someone called Rocky Rutabaga. (His profile showed a buff man in jeans and nothing else. According to the accompanying text, he was a member of '3 Feet Under Scuba Divers', 'Busy Ben's Vehicle Lot', and the 'Bareback Woodsmen Gay Club'.)

I was now the owner of a new virtual home. I could ban people, charge people money to access my land, play loud music. But first, I needed some virtual furniture.

As it happens, that evening my girlfriend had persuaded me to go on a trip to the exhausting Swedish furniture superstore Ikea, to choose chairs for our real apartment. I cut a deal; I would go, if she would help me choose virtual furniture for my virtual office.

We went first to Home Depoz, the virtual superstore – 'Define Your Space!'. It was the place Marsellus had offered to wrangle free furniture from. These days, though, Marsellus seemed barely available – perhaps he was in the avatar protection programme

– but it seemed a good place to start. For 300 Linden Dollars – $1 – we picked out a pair of easy chairs, which you could customise with the click of a mouse. At another store, Belle Belle furniture – 'Everything you need to make your Second House beautiful' – a virtual resident was earning a tiny wage (150 Linden Dollars, about 50 cents, an hour) to stand on a ladder and go through the motions of dusting. The cleaning had no use (in virtual worlds we have conquered housework as well as taxes and death) but the motion gave the place some authenticity, and, to the virtual storeowner, the ambience was worth the money. In the end, we picked up a pair of Louis XV chairs, a daybed, a private-eye-style desk and chair, a laptop, and an ashtray with smoking cigarette, for effect.

In this world, land seemed more plentiful, and therefore relatively cheaper, than furnishings. My house and land had cost £20; all my furniture together cost almost a quarter of that.

Then, it was time to shop for real. The roads surrounding the west London Ikea are a masterpiece of hard work, slap in the centre of a vast industrial area: factories, businesses and warehouses, split by an almost impassable arterial road. From the car on the way, we saw the angular jumbles of industrial estates and business parks, great grey blocks, some with bright neon blue and red logos: it looked to me like Second Life, only uglier. This was the landscape of urban consumption after hours, empty of promise. In our virtual worlds, we had already replicated this landscape; perhaps soon, we would replace it. When we arrived, Ikea itself didn't seem too different from Home Depoz, except it took twice as long – and, in the real world, there was a lot more arguing about the route.

When we arrived back in our real home, we watched a BBC TV arts show, *Imagine*, about J. M. Barrie. Barrie's own life was full of loss. ('To be born is to be shipwrecked on an island,' he

167

once wrote. I thought of Wilde, who had been shipwrecked their whole lives, only to be washed up, whole again, on their virtual shore.) Barrie conceived of Neverland as his refuge, 'a place where people never die'; a place – along with the real-world children who inspired it – which became Barrie's hard-won consolation. Virtual worlds – our own never-lands, where people never die – seemed like much less effort to create and inhabit.

Later that night, after we unwrapped our new kitchen chairs, I set up my armchairs and TV in my new virtual apartment. It felt sparse, but adequate; just like it had done a few weeks before, when we'd set up the TV and sofa in our real-world living room. I turned on my new virtual TV, and watched 'StrangerHood', a piece of machinima – machine-made cinema – filmed with a virtual cast inside The Sims 2. In it, the characters wake up in their new virtual neighbourhood, with no memory of how they arrived. I watched and laughed; Errol laughed along with me. I was sitting in a virtual world, watching a virtual TV show made in another virtual world. Almost nothing here was real.

Now I could sit at my virtual desk, in front of my virtual laptop, and stare into space – just like I did at my real desk. Only, in the real world, my view was of our garden wall; in the virtual world, my view was an autumnal landscape, orange leaves, the sea, and a view of the rising full moon, blood-red against the night sky. (I looked more closely: faded discreetly into the moon was the Linden Lab logo.) I had bought a virtual cigarette, for show; I placed it in my virtual lips. Virtual cigarettes couldn't be addictive, but this one made me want a real cigarette. I put it out. The air was quiet. I turned the TV off. Around me, I could hear the virtual world: the faint wind, the flutter of a nearby flag, the first few spots of coming rain.

But I had forgotten Wilde's advice. My virtual home was not yet burglar-proof. Right then, behind me, my automatic door –

a logical descendant of the Star-Trek-style door Philip Rosedale built in his childhood bedroom – slid open, and a passer-by strolled in. My house had come without a manual, and it turned out I had forgotten to lock my virtual door.

From the beginning, Linden Lab decided to encourage ownership and trade of virtual items. Second Life was the first world to grant intellectual copyright to residents for the items they created in-world. (Early in 2005 one Second Life resident, Kermitt Quirk, sold the real-world rights to his popular in-world game, Tringo – a combination of Tetris and Bingo – to a cellular provider, for delivery on cellphones.) Linden Lab makes most of its money through taxes on virtual land. A newcomer who buys a half-acre plot of virtual land pays one Linden Dollar per square metre, plus a monthly land fee, depending on how much land they own, to Linden Lab. Just like in the real world, once property has been developed, it increases in value; whenever it's sold on, Linden Lab charges sales tax. The company also encourages trading in Linden Dollars, the Second Life currency. When I first visited, Second Life saw $250,000 worth of real-life currency conversion per month, and to protect its investment, Linden Lab has to monitor its virtual world for inflation. (When I spoke with Philip Rosedale, he told me Linden Lab was hoping to recruit its own 'Alan Greenspan', but until that happened, they planned to handle the economy in-house.)

So those who wanted to profit from the unprecedented mania for non-existent things (young, urban professionals, who would laugh at the suggestion of a job in a real-world shoe factory, would, it turned out, spend hours making a virtual boot) had to turn to third-party item brokers, and risk being banned for breaking the rules.

From the start, Linden Lab had taken a more risky, but potentially more rewarding stance: all the copyright in Second

Life virtual creations remained with the resident who created them. Encouraged by this vested interest, in the time since I'd visited Wilde, Second Life residents had driven a huge growth in their economy. In November 2006, virtual currency was changing hands inside Second Life to the equivalent of half a million US dollars a day. ('The US has had a GDP growth over the last century of like two per cent per year,' Philip Rosedale told me. 'Ours is more like two per cent per week.') I wondered exactly who was creating and trading this much imaginary property.

When we met, Philip had used the example of Second Life fashions to illustrate the entrepreneurial side of his virtual worlds (the top fashion designers earned in the region of $75,000 a year from their virtual creations). I knew that some residents made a living from organising events – there were even Second Life tour guides, who charged a real-world hourly wage – but the most obvious way to earn money in virtual worlds was by making virtual things.

I'd experimented with building myself. In Second Life, building objects is like sketching in three dimensions; with a few clicks you can create basic shapes, stretch, push and rotate them, join them together to make new shapes. To help people learn the process, Linden Lab provides a 'Sandbox', a vast empty area where you can build as much as you like, without paying land charges. Like a 3D Etch-a-Sketch, every night the Sandbox was wiped clean. When I visited to try my hand, the Sandbox was a vast, dusty plane, overgrown with a forest of oddball creations. Blue square whirlwinds, rideable yellow griffons, oblongs, two wooden cubes a quarter-mile square. A pink pig surrounded by a pink force field. A jumble of random vehicles piled together, like a child's Matchbox collection: a Ferrari, a Batmobile. A flying shark. Pegasus. A Chevy Malibu. A colossal blue marble bowl, like an Anish Kapoor installation, tilted toward the sun. Here and there, more professional builders were honing their skills, preparing developments for paying clients: in one corner of the Sandbox was a meticulous recreation of palatial Roman gardens, a high jet of water at the centre; the illusion was punctuated only by the three bright red motorcycles parked against the fountain.

Although the act of building is easier than in the real world, virtual worlds can't help with the inspiration. I found an empty spot, created a huge wooden triangle, and sat on the top.

Mankind has always used objects to explore and enact ourselves – to extend our abilities and to broadcast our self-image to others. Now, through our sponsored media, we were encouraged, for the benefit of others, to solve our dilemmas with concrete, marketable – hence profitable – objects and services. In virtual worlds, we can do this without actually investing our limited resources.

Building virtual objects was easy, but not *that* easy. I decided to go shopping.

All good reporters need a Dictaphone. I searched on a Second Life website, SLBoutique, 'Second Life's Premier Web Shopping Site'. (When I visited, the top-selling items included a cherry tree, a wrist computer, and a device to follow other people around and record their conversations.) Payment was a complicated procedure; to verify my Second Life identity, I had to sign up on the website, then visit a virtual terminal inside Second Life. After some confusion, I bought the Dictaphone for 250 Linden Dollars. As far as I could tell, the terms and conditions stated that anything I bought could disappear at any time, and no one would be liable. I wondered how far a real-world retail outlet would get with a disclaimer like that. I opened my inventory, selected the Dictaphone, and clicked 'wear'; what looked like a cardboard box appeared on my wrist, and did nothing.

Not all virtual purchases were so complex, or so unrewarding. Earlier, on my second ever visit to Second Life, shopping had been an easier experience. I had wandered the virtual malls. I bought a Panama hat, then a roll-up cigarette, which, when placed in my virtual mouth, looked like a cartoon joint. I tried to play automated poker, but the table told me it was broken. I had been warned by the tailor of the Panama hat that there were few places to buy clothes for men, but I wanted something writerly: a scarf and tweed coat – or maybe, for my mafia missions, some bling. Still, everywhere I looked, almost everything for sale was lingerie. There was even what claimed to be a cash machine, which seemed to work a little differently to the ones I knew from the real world. I put some money in. 'Thank you,' it said.

Eventually, I found a showroom, run by Thai Greenacre, that catered for the 'discerning gentleman'. For 20 Linden Dollars (prices were lower then) I bought a pair of 'Black Brushed Oxford Lace-ups'. In some cases, the virtual manufacturers had made no bones about the brands they were copying; for another 20 Linden Dollars, I bought a purple pair of Converse lace-up sneakers. In other cases, the designers copied brand names with the same oddly transparent attempt to avoid prosecution as the Devi-Krauss jeans you find at a Thai market-stall: in a virtual electronics showroom, I found a wall of 'Sono' TVs.

In Greenacre's store, I ran my virtual hands along the rails. Fifteen Linden Dollars got me two pairs of boxer shorts (I passed on the penguin and polar bears, and bought the tropic print). I skipped the thongs, the bowling shirts, and the pyjamas (I didn't even own a bed yet). I did decide to splash out on a smart suit; this was when I decided to spend 80 Linden Dollars on my white, cruise-ship steward tuxedo.

As I walked through the shop, everything seemed to slow down; the pressure of so many objects on the servers, perhaps, or the pressure of so much consumerism on Errol Mysterio.

Near the clothes shop was a sign: 'Monkey Mafia Gun Store'. I clicked, and found myself teleported to an iron fortress. I clicked on the portcullis, and a claw dropped a ball to open the cantilevered gate. As I entered the castle, I saw a record sleeve on the wall; I clicked it, and death metal – the kind of music I imagined trench-coated American kids cleaning guns to – filled the main hall. I browsed through the shelves: a paintball gun, a skateboard (at 100 Linden Dollars I couldn't resist, although when I put it on it just stuck to my feet, and wobbled a little as I walked around). One wall was covered in blades: 'A Sword'; 'A Big Sword'. Under the swords was a butterfly knife, just like those carried by the kids in the comprehensive up my road. At 100 Linden Dollars, the butterfly knife seemed expensive (as any local Hackney kid would tell you, in France the real thing costs £5). Deeper into the store, the weapons became more outlandish. An automatic turret, designed to shoot people who trespass on your land. A belt to make you fly faster. Landmines. In one corner was a 'nearly' free sales bin: handguns for a knock-down one Linden Dollar.

None of these weapons could hurt other residents, although in certain, 'damage-enabled' areas, you could mock-fight; those attacked might crumple to the floor, but they'd wake up immediately in a nearby safe place.

Upstairs – the music still playing, sounding now like the noise that came out of Sigourney Weaver's fridge in *Ghostbusters* – there were more weapons: a flamethrower, a sniper rifle, assault weapons, shotguns. A missile launcher. A remote-controlled 'Predator' armed drone. Who wants these kinds of things in their idea? I thought.

Years later, prices had risen considerably. After kitting out my virtual office, as an offering to tempt my (real-world) girlfriend to take another look into Second Life, I decided to buy her some virtual shoes. I searched on the Second Life classified ads, and teleported to a smart virtual store called Shiny Things, run by a resident called Fallingwater Cellardoor. There, a shiny green pair of sling-back heels cost me 300 Linden Dollars.

Second Life fashion wasn't just about residents making their own clothes. In January 2004, a British company called Rivers Run Red had brought the first real-world designer label into Second Life: Mrs Jones, who designed Kylie Minogue's dress in her video for the single 'Can't Get You Out of My Head', designed an exclusive virtual collection. Since then, virtual fashion had become big business. By July 2006, when American Apparel launched a virtual store inside Second Life, 40 per cent of items traded in Second Life were items of clothing. (The most popular items were shoes.) I wanted to talk to a virtual fashion designer, to see what kind of work – and profit – was involved.

Fallingwater Cellardoor – in real life, 42-year-old Alayne Wartell – first joined Second Life in October 2003. Her stall, Shiny Things, sold fashion, mainly for women – shoes, handbags, cocktail dresses – which she had designed inside Second Life. After I bought a pair of her heels, Alayne visited my virtual office. ('Ah, cool, you bought from Szabo,' Alayne – or rather Fallingwater – said, eying my virtual furniture with a professional eye. 'He's good, and he's a friend of mine.') By then – in October 2006 – Alayne made her real-world living solely from Fallingwater's Second Life store. She had been a computer programmer, but, although she had no background in fashion, or 3D design – just some web design experience – she began to feel her way, and she found she enjoyed designing clothes. 'I was programming for 20 years,' she said, 'and at times, because I got to do new things over the years, it was very fulfilling. But I was a bit burned out. This is fulfilling because I get to be creative in a different way from programming, and I love being my own boss, making my own decisions about what to do, not having set hours. And, honestly, the feedback I get from my customers – such nice things they say. It's an ego boost.'

At first, working sometimes days and sometimes nights, she made a hundred bucks or so a week. 'It took a year before I could say I was making a real income,' she said. 'I remember early on I was making about 5,000 Linden Dollars [then about $20] a day – calculating how much would constitute a living wage, and wondering how on earth I'd ever get there. I couldn't even imagine how I'd manage 10,000 Lindens a day.'

She didn't advertise, relying instead on word of mouth – and a few virtual fashion shows – and business grew. By the time Fallingwater and I met, in October 2006, her sales of non-existent clothes and accessories earned her an average of $1,000 a week.

In the real world, space for others to meet and fabricate objects costs; you need both money and the will to risk losing it. In virtual worlds, space – to reside in, to meet in, to work in – costs almost nothing. The material costs are literally zero. With no barrier to entry, any resident could set up a shop, and begin to sell the things they had made. For Alayne, the liberation from the restrictions of the physical meant she could turn a profit. 'I started my businesses here because I loved building and was good at it. I didn't need anything more than that. That's not possible in the real world.'

Fashion design is creative work, though, and sometimes she struggled for ideas. 'I run dry sometimes,' she told me. 'Nothing works, or I'm trying too hard, or something.'

When we met, she was working on a messenger bag. She'd finished the woman's version, and was customising it for men. That didn't take too long, she said, although she had spent up to five days crafting a single pair of virtual shoes. (Once the design is complete, she can sell as many as she wants; in Second Life, there are no production costs, apart from her labour as a designer.) I asked about her sales. 'It varies a lot; some things hit big, others don't,' she said. 'I just make what I like and see what happens.' I showed her the shoes I had bought my girl-friend. 'Ah, the lady slingbacks!' She said when she spotted them. 'Those are one of my proudest creations.' A product like the slingbacks might sell 150 pairs a month, she told me, at the Linden equivalent of $1 per pair – all through automated sales at her virtual store. (Although her accountant barely understands how she makes her money, nonetheless she pays her taxes.)

She gave me a freebie: a recent creation, a pair of brown leather shoes. They didn't quite fit, but, like a real pair of shoes, I couldn't change the size. 'If your feet are too big, you'll have to modify those,' she said. I laughed, and adjusted the size of my feet to fit the shoes.

To promote her virtual wares, Fallingwater had tried a few ads on 'SecondStyle', a Second Life fashion website, with little effect on sales. 'As Second Life grows, using that stuff as brand awareness becomes more important. I may actually hire a marketing consultant, someone I know here with that back-ground.'

By that point, in October 2006, a new class of virtual profes-sionals had emerged: the land baron.

I visited another virtual world, to speak with a virtual land developer. Project Entropia, later renamed the Entropia Universe, was a world somewhere between EverQuest and the more free-form worlds like Second Life. (In Project Entropia, you can buy EverQuest-like role-playing items such as 'Kobold Thigh-Guards', but you can also acquire buy-to-let property for a profit.) The Entropia universe was constructed specifically to tap into the global mania for virtual funds. With the 'Entropia Universe Cash Card', residents could even visit real-world cash machines in the US, or Post Office counters in the UK, and withdraw real-world currency, at a fixed exchange rate, directly from their virtual Entropia account. In October, 2006, over half a million people called Entropia Universe their virtual home, and in 2005 their in-world turnover – the amount of virtual currency that had traded hands between Entropia residents – was reportedly 1.6 billion Project Entropia dollars ($160 million in the real world). I spoke with David Storey, the 22-year-old Australian PhD student who, for 265,000 PEDs (about £13,700), had bought Treasure Island, 25 square kilometres of land, with three human settlements.

David Storey's virtual self, Zachurm 'Deathifier' Emegen, was a dapper, crisp-suited man in a button-down shirt and shades. As the owner, landlord, and host of Treasure Island, Storey offered spaceflights, and, in his island mansion and bar, regular Full Moon parties, with music and competitions.

Storey pegged out some areas of the island for virtual residents to hunt in, sold mining rights to other areas – part of his income comes from a four per cent tax on any hunting bounty or mining rights – and he developed the remnants into estates, including 'Lake View': 'perfectly suited for those looking for a nice home or place of business close to a teleporter'. Residents rented these areas to establish virtual shops, in the hope of turning a profit. Storey told me the island earned him around $100 a month. 'Right now the island is the only thing that really earns money,' Storey told me. He hadn't expected to earn so much, Storey told me, but he put the earning down to the work he'd put in to develop the island. When he bought it, he told me, Treasure Island was 'a few fairly standard creatures scattered amongst lots of trees and grass, and mineral resources that bordered on nonexistent.'

'Initially its income was to be through estate sales; however, over time, that's transitioned over to tax income from people hunting and mining on the island. This transition also brought with it extra costs as hunters want to hunt cool creatures, and finding the DNA materials to create said cool creatures is somewhat expensive (ranging from a few hundred to thousands of US dollars).' Since his success, others had offered unique properties for sale; when we spoke, an Entropia Universe space station was on sale for $100,000.

Second Life, I knew, had land barons too. When I met Philip Linden, he had shown me a list of the world's richest residents: at the top was 'Anshe Chung'. In the years since, I'd heard more about Anshe. Anshe Chung, real name Ailin Graef, was a 33-year-old Chinese woman living in Germany. Anshe began her Second Life in March 2004, after time as a powerful player in other virtual worlds, including Shadowbane, an apocalyptic fantasy-themed universe. Anshe didn't think Second Life would hold her attention for more than an hour, but she was intrigued by the possibility of residents owning copyright to their virtual creations. She stayed. At first, Anshe supported herself by teaching languages, both in the real and virtual world (she spoke German, English and Chinese). She supplemented the virtual side of her operations with another business: virtual escort work. Anshe's escort ad described herself as 'a material girl with a money fetish', and for 1,000 Linden Dollars (then about £2) an hour, she offered 'exotic massage'. Anshe also taught people, for a fee, how to have better online sex, and she sold virtual animations to accompany her lessons. In July 2004, Ailin's husband, Guntram Graef, joined Second Life, as Guni Greenstein; together, they began to buy and sell virtual land. 'Somehow I ended up sending money to my parents in China, coming from this,' Ailin later told me, in slightly awkward English. 'I also helped one boy in one poor country. Suddenly the SL economy become very real.' (Through a German charity, Anshe donated some of her virtual profits, translated into real

178

cash, to a Singapore boy, to support his family until they found work.) Anshe's business model was simple: she bought large plots of newly available land, separated the areas into lots, and sold or rented the property at a profit.

In November 2006, I joined a press tour of Anshe's latest virtual developments, built by her team of 25 employees in Wuhan, China, which included three ex-architects. We followed Anshe, a medium-height Chinese-looking virtual self, with straight black hair, a smart trouser-suit, and a dragon tattoo on her back. She strolled through a huge white latticework nightclub, elevated over a pastoral field, and a clean-cut mall, with water features and olde-worlde clock towers – like an American mall, only even cleaner. (There, the virtual press corps moved slowly, as if we were flying through treacle. I quite liked the effect, although Anshe said it was a technical problem. 'This sim need reboot badly,' she said.) Anshe said she was already working to provide virtual developments to real-world corporations. 'Last night we rented 12 sims to one major TV station for example,' she said. 'We also have several universities as clients and other companies, small and large. We also had RL billionaires as clients live in our lands. But they prefer stay anonymous.'

Next on the tour was her in-world HQ, still a building site: a sci-fi office tower block surrounded by domed gardens like the tropical houses at Kew. (Because the site was still under construction, I got pinned by the lift. 'All systems online,' a calm, robotic voice stated, over and over, although, as I struggled to escape the lift shaft, I felt less than calm.) The futuristic tower was designed to be Anshe's business HQ, for meetings and press conferences. In London, where property prices were among the most expensive in the world, I'd grown used to seeing tower blocks rise up over the space of six months; Anshe's headquarters would take just two weeks to complete.

In a desert development, a Second Life prostitute, Antje

Achterbahn (her job was clear: written above her head was her group name, 'Peaches Escort'), in a short plaid skirt, bright red heels and a silver necklace that said 'Slut', flew down, sucked a lollipop and listened in. Even the virtual 'ho' was business-minded. 'Really too bad I hooked in this late!' she said. (She told me she'd just been passing by, and she'd recognised Anshe Chung's name; she'd read about Anshe in *Business Week*.)

When I'd looked for my own land, I'd toured a few of Anshe's properties. She bought land in bulk – by November 2006, her territory, christened 'DreamLand', covered 36 square kilometres, about 10 per cent of the total land area of Second Life – and she re-let her property to residents for real-world dollars. Anshe's rates varied, depending on location and the kind of development she included in the price – but even her most expensive land was only 20 Linden Dollars (about four pence) per square metre. Her revenues were small-margin and high-volume. ('We move very, very huge volumes, so that is how relatively small margin help us grow fast,' Anshe later told me.) By June 2006, *Business Week* estimated her land holdings at £135,000; Anshe Chung Studios, her company, put the figure for 2006 close to $2.5 million. ('I'm like Wal-Mart,' Anshe told *Business Week*. 'The margins are small, but the volume isn't.' Rocky Rutabaga, the developer of my virtual office, called her 'Anshe Cha-Ching'.) In May 2006, Anshe made the cover of *Business Week*. 'Dreamland' had become a kind of democratic fiefdom, something akin to Robin Harper's vision of a self-policing community. In November 2006, after consultation with her residents (she polled each one using an in-world vote, she later told me), Anshe banned any organisation new to Second Life who claimed to be 'the first' – the first radio station, the first tabloid – at anything residents had already been doing for years.

*　　*　　*

Those, like Anshe Chung and David Storey, who made their living from the actions of their virtual selves, were in a relative minority. When I visited Linden Lab, Philip Rosedale told me 20 or so residents made their living from inside Second Life. At the time there were 25,000 residents, which meant less than 0.08 per cent of residents made their living that way then. By October 2006, Linden Lab estimated over 13,000 – 1.3 per cent – made a profit in their world.

In a consumer society, the American sociologist Ivan Illich observed, 'There are two kinds of slaves: the prisoners of addiction and the prisoners of envy.' Computer games, which offer a favourable ratio of reward to effort, have always presented the problem of the first; now, our virtual worlds offer us the chance to become enslaved by envy. Virtual worlds play to our longing to be accepted, to be a success, to overcome all obstacles with ease. The story that some residents made money had become a Second Life selling point – but once again, the reality was less rosy than the dream. Rocky Rutabaga told me he couldn't see how Anshe made her money. The margins are too small, he said. He'd never managed to turn a virtual profit. For most residents, then, Second Life was a way to connect, and to kill time. Outside of the worlds, though, a whole breed of virtual service providers was making a different kind of killing. In 2004, after Sony Online Entertainment petitioned eBay to ban the sale of EverQuest accounts – which were, according to the Terms of Service, Sony's property – a whole raft of third-party websites sprung up to service residents' desire to buy and sell virtual things.

These were the third-party dealers money-making gnome Noah Burn turned to, after raking in virtual platinum from his virtual forgery trick. Noah had explained to me how his experience with some virtual currency dealers taught him a few lessons about trust. On one occasion, he sold $5,000 worth of EverQuest

II currency to a dealer; once the virtual platinum arrived in the dealer's account, the dealer reversed the real-world payment, then claimed their account had been hacked. The next day, though, the same dealer had a large amount of EverQuest II currency for sale. Noah was convinced he had been ripped off, but he had no recourse – and anyway, he was too busy churning out virtual money to worry about one bad deal. But another company, Noah told me, had been honourable and efficient in all its dealings: the largest, IGE.com. Noah was a big fan of the operation. 'They are so fast at handling things, I can't even explain how much of a breeze it was to work with them compared to just selling person to person.'

I'd had some experience with IGE myself. In my days as a resident of Star Wars Galaxies, I'd paid IGE $10, for which I received 10 million Star Wars credits – enough to buy a fast land-speeder, with plenty of change. Then, I'd paid my money by typing in my credit card details to the IGE website, and I'd received my virtual currency in a clandestine virtual meeting, with a fish-faced alien IGE courier, who met me by a virtual bank machine in the city of Coronet, on the far-flung planet of Corellia – where Han Solo was born. After he handed me my credits, I tried to talk with him, without much luck; whoever operated the courier was either too busy to talk, or English wasn't their first language. Noah Burn had told me he suspected many IGE employees worked in China, at so-called 'virtual sweat-shops', where low-wage workers made a better living in virtual worlds than they would have in a real-world factory. (When he contacted them inside the virtual worlds to complete deals, he said, 'they barely spoke English'.) In virtual worlds, these Chinese workers were now an everyday reality. Known as 'gold-farmers', they were recognisable by their broken English, and their tendency to lurk around the most profitable spots, trying to attach themselves to any group that passed. In some circles, their commercially oriented play was discriminated against; Blizzard, the makers of World of Warcraft, had banned tens of thousands of accounts for gold-farming, and, in the West, some groups of players asked all new members to type a few sentences in English before they could join. (Chinese World of Warcraft residents who played for fun had begun to complain about what they saw as racism.) In Korea, Lineage II players teamed up to butcher those players they believed were farming gold.

At the age of 12, Brock Pierce was a child actor. He debuted large, with a starring role as Gordon, the 10-year-old lead of 1992's *The Mighty Ducks*, but by '95 the roles (notably a bit-part in the straight-to-TV *Problem Child 3: Junior in Love*) were less prestigious. As a hobby, he collected trading cards, but he'd always had trouble finding the last one or two he needed. So, in his late teens, to augment his income he set up a business bulk-buying trading cards and selling them individually to people keen to complete their collection. After the bottom fell out of the trading card market, he cast around for another idea. He'd always been a keen online gamer, and, in 2001, after a chance meeting with Alan Debonneville (a Hong Kong-based ex-Warcraft 2 champion), Brock and Alan co-founded Internet Gaming Entertainment (IGE), to help online gamers buy and sell the virtual objects they most desired. (One survey showed one in five virtual world residents had bought gold at a third-party website like IGE, spending an average total of $135 real world each.)

At IGE, residents could even buy and sell their virtual selves. On one day in 2006, you could buy an account which included three characters: a Paladin, a Warrior, and a Priest, 'with excellent gear and skills!', including horses, for $663.99. Once payment was complete, the seller emailed their virtual username and password, and the buyer inherited their virtual self, virtual property, virtual clothes – even their virtual friends, who had no way to tell the transfer has taken place. (There was a glass ceiling in the virtual world, too: on average, one study showed, women selves changed hands for 10 per cent less.)

In January 2004, IGE – already the biggest player in the virtual goods market – bought its closest competitor, Yantis Enterprises, for upwards of $10 million. By August 2004, demand for its non-existent product was so high, IGE hired five new people every week. On a single day in September 2005, for £100 IGE would have sold you virtual currency from one of 14 non-existent places. For Lineage II, your money would have bought you 10 million Adena, which would buy enough swords and armour for any budding elf. Or, in Second Life, you could have bought 20,000 Linden Dollars, to fritter away in a spree at the virtual malls, or invest in 13,000 virtual square metres of riverside land. The homebodies among you might have plumped for 2.5 million Simoleans, to spend in the online version of the bestselling human-simulator game, The Sims. For that, you could fill your virtual house twice over with antique virtual furniture. (At IGE.com, while trading currency, you could also click on the charity banner – 'Virtual Worlds, Virtuous Hearts' – to donate some of your virtual cash to the Mercy Corps, which works to alleviate real-world poverty.)

In October 2004, I spoke with Brock Pierce, then 21, from his office in Dearborn, Michigan. Brock told me his company bought items and currency from suppliers across the real world. Some were American kids who played games at evenings and weekends. Others owned cyber cafes in Europe and the Middle East; they let people play for free, as long as each player donated half their virtual booty to the cafe. IGE also worked with Hong Kong partners who subcontracted the work to mainland Chinese suppliers. There, people were employed to play the games nine to five, hunting virtual beasts, fashioning virtual items from their loot, and selling them on via IGE. I mentioned to Brock the idea of virtual sweatshops. He was quick to interrupt. 'They can earn up to $100 dollars a day,' he said. 'That's a higher wage than almost any career opportunity available in rural China.' (Other sources put earnings at virtual sweatshops between $75 and $250 a month – still a relatively high wage.)

I wasn't earning a virtual wage from virtual worlds, but I was conducting some business there – I invited a few residents in for interviews, a more convenient way to meet than travelling in real life. Plus, I liked having virtual guests. I felt proud of my new virtual office. I wanted to show it to my real-world friends (although, when I asked them to log on and visit, many rolled their eyes and pleaded a prior engagement). My new home was a new place, like the communes my mother and her friends had built – but it didn't replace my old life. I didn't have to move away from my own home to inhabit it. My virtual life was an overlay, like a membrane over the real; it extended my life, but didn't inhibit it. I wondered if I was finding the right balance between the real and virtual after all.

I began to smoke less. The comfort of my virtual home, a kind of security blanket against real-world anxiety, was making my life better. At the same time, in real life, I was settling into a new flat – perhaps the calm that came from being settled helped me to stop smoking. Either way, the real and the virtual were reflecting – and perhaps complementing – each other.

Over time, in the mornings, instead of stepping outside for a cigarette, I would step into my office and log into Second Life. The two addictions had parallels: cigarettes were portable comfort ('You're never alone with a Strand,' as one 1950s British cigarette advertisement read); Second Life was portable companionship.

I found myself longing for my Second Life. Half-way through one dinner party, I abandoned the table to sneak moments at my

PC. I lounged in my virtual office, chatting with my virtual friends, when I should have been in my real apartment, entertaining my real friends. My actual apartment demanded constant attention: the washing up, the floors, the washing up again. My virtual office was free of entropy, and required no maintenance at all. In my real life, I rented my apartment: owning real-world property seemed a faraway dream. In my virtual life, I already owned land, with a beautiful view of the sea. During the day, I began to see as much of my virtual desk as my real one. Often, the virtual world was the more interesting one; my real apartment, which I saw mainly on trips to the kitchen for coffee, began to feel more like a backdrop to my other life.

Inside my virtual home, my real-world worries about rent, the struggle of living in a big city, seemed to fade. Virtual worlds had become wish fulfilment, and I was addicted – as surely as I was addicted to nicotine.

Then, as always, in my paradise, trouble emerged.

Plot 11, the next plot down toward the sea from me, had been sold. My neighbour, Wayne Nohkan, sent me a message saying 'Hi'. The next time I logged in, there he was; we hovered in the air between our properties – the virtual equivalent of chatting over the boundary fence. Someone else had bought the plot behind mine, Wayne said, and they had already erected a sign: 'SL Travels and Tours – office opening soon'.

The next day, a Second Life message from Wayne was forwarded to my email. 'Let me know if my trees block your view out front,' he wrote. 'I'm trying to block out that crap next door.' I logged in to see. The travel agency, which hoped to profit from the growing interest in Second Life by charging for themed tours, was under construction, and it didn't look pretty. As protection against nearby development, I had already bought the lot next to mine, for 3,000 Lindens (about £5); I told Wayne, and he bought the three further down. 'Not sure what I am going to do yet,' he told me, 'but that will give us some buffer from development.'

Then, the next day, our local land baron Rocky Rutabaga sold more property in the area. He'd planned to build an undersea theme park, Wayne told me, but he must have given that up. The whole bay was for sale. In Second Life, you can not only build, but also reshape any land – literally, as they had marketed the feature: 'Now, when you're standing next to a mountain, you really can chop it down with the edge of your hand.' The new buyers of the ocean floor could develop their land any way they liked. Soon my view of the sea might become a view of a building site.

'I've been considering moving to an island and renting,' Wayne told me. 'Someplace with a controlled theme. I don't like zoning in real life, but it's a bit out of control in Second Life.'

In my real life, too, I didn't stay calm for long. During the week I smoked less, but at the weekend I smoked more. On frequent nights out with friends, we searched the urban landscape – in all the wrong places – for the excitement our everyday life lacked. My male friends, in their early thirties – most of whom sat all day at a PC – found few places to find each other and exercise themselves. I remembered going to free parties in the early nineties, and I remember how heavily the government had cracked down on them, beating revellers and confiscating sound systems. The message was clear. Clubbing inside big, expensive buildings was acceptable, but partying in a field was not. Those 'illegal' parties that made us feel so free were modes of release that lay outside the dominant paradigm of consumption, and so they were forbidden. The encouragement of solving our dilemmas with concrete, marketable – and so, profitable – solutions had pushed us apart. Our alternative was to gather in bars, places of consumption, which society understood, and therefore tolerated.

During the week, as I worked alone, my solitude seemed only to increase the tension: my body, like an animal, seemed driven to anxiety by separation from the herd. My mind, eager to ease the pressure, sought distraction. Also, I was a young man. I wanted what young men want. I wanted what cigarettes and alcohol and coffee and nightclubs gave me – but I wanted more. I wanted movement, adrenaline, risk. I wanted to fight.

I wasn't alone.

11

VIRTUAL WAR
Join up and see the imaginary world

In our virtual worlds, we were fighting – but this kind of virtual conflict had a history. People – me included – had been fighting in imaginary places for years.

One afternoon in the winter of 2001, I went with a friend, Chris Lahr, to a gaming cafe, where he'd heard about a new way to kill time. There, in a labyrinthine cellar in the West End of London, kids were gathering to play games, not alone, but with each other. These weren't massive virtual worlds, but more localised computer-generated places, dedicated entirely to armed combat.

I'd played games like these before. In 1996, fresh from university, I ended up working for a new media firm, in a converted old mansion house in Arundel, a long commute from my Brighton home. The office stood alone, among fields, by a run-down dual carriageway; at lunchtime, there was no real-world destination, except the local petrol station, where the sandwiches were wrapped in what looked like medical gauze. Instead, to take a break and to remove ourselves from our workaday surroundings, I and a friend would spend our lunches in a virtual world: we logged into the company network and played 'Quake', a 3D futuristic combat game where we hunted each other through grey, industrial computer-generated corridors, armed with machine guns, grenades, and – if you were lucky and got there first – a rocket launcher.

By 2001, though, Quake was old news. In the West End basement, my friend and I sat at PC consoles, our heads brushing the damp brick ceiling, and we asked the kid running the place what game we should play. 'Counterstrike,' he said, without hesitation.

Counterstrike – as I write, still the most popular online war, game – was a terrorism and counter-terrorism simulation. Played in first-person, as if you were looking through the eyes of your virtual SAS soldier – or terrorist – you bought weapons, then you struggled to kill or save hostages, plant or defuse packages of C-4 explosive at strategic locations. The battlefields of Counterstrike were complex, 3D, convincing. The sounds were real, sampled from real-life gun models. As in real life, one or two shots could kill you, so you were vulnerable; you *needed* your team-mates if you were to survive. Many afternoons, when we should have been elsewhere, we descended into the basement to become warriors: we crouched, our eyes darted into every nook, we inched our way round corners, our fingers poised above the mouse button to fire. Our opponents were real people, their virtual conflict skills honed by many hours inside Counterstrike. They shot us, and we died, and, over time, we learned to shoot them back in turn. We became addicted.

In August 2001, a full month before the 9/11 attacks briefly made 'terrorism' the world's number-one website search term, Counterstrike was by far the world's most popular online war game. Twenty-four hours a day, wherever there was electricity and Internet access, upwards of 2 million people gathered in virtual dust-strewn battlegrounds to shoot terrorists, marines and SAS men – there was never any moral preference for one side

On Sunday 27 June 1976, on board Air France 139 from Tel Aviv via Athens to Paris, two Palestinian members of the Popular Front for the Liberation of Palestine and two members of the radical German militant group Revolutionäre Zellen ('Revolutionary Cells') produced machine pistols and insisted the pilot divert the flight to Africa. After a seven-hour refuel at Banghazi, Libya, the flight landed on an airstrip in Entebbe, Uganda, where Idi Amin had agreed to give them safe haven. There, three more Palestinians joined the hijackers, and all non-Israeli passengers were released. (The entire French crew, also offered freedom, elected to stay on the plane.) 105 Israelis remained on the plane. In exchange for the hostages, the hijackers demanded the release of 40 Palestinian prisoners. In 48 hours, they announced, executions would begin. At midnight on 3 July an Israeli strike force hit the airport. Two Boeing 707s and a C-130 Hercules transport, their cargo bays already open as they landed, unloaded 29 IDF 'Sayeret Matkal' commandos, in Land Rovers and a black Mercedes – an exact replica of Idi Amin's personal limo and escort. Idi Amin's Mercedes had recently been painted silver, but within minutes, the only guards who knew that fact were dead. Just over an hour later, 30 Ugandan troops and all seven hijackers had been killed. To prevent chase, 11 Ugandan Army Air Force fighter jets were destroyed on the ground. The hostages were on a military flight back to Israel. Just one Israeli soldier and three hostages lost their lives.

From the Israeli perspective, 'Operation Thunderbolt' was the most successful hostage rescue strike in human history. The US military was so impressed that they tasked the Defense Advanced Research Projects Agency (DARPA) to develop ways for US soldiers to get the same kind of training. It turned out that Entebbe airport had been built by an Israeli contractor, who produced the plans, and, on Israeli military property in the Negev desert, helped build a full-scale, partial model of the airstrip.

For six days, Israeli commandos practised landing on the airstrip and assaulting the passenger terminal where the hostages were held. When they arrived at the real airport, they'd won the attack a hundred times before.

DARPA was fascinated, but flummoxed. There was no way to build scale models of every possible battlefield and hostage situation. That would mean building a scale model of the whole planet. That year, Nicholas Negroponte, founder of MIT's Media Laboratory, was contracted to the Department of Defense. DARPA approached him for advice, and he proposed a simple solution: a virtual world. They would build technology that simulated various battlefield situations, in which soldiers could practise as if in the real world. At the time, computer technology had barely evolved from room-sized mainframes, so they began with video editing. The project was so successful, the US military began to make video-simulation models of every airport in the Middle East. That programme evolved into the US military's simulation arm, which among other things bought up Atari's futuristic Battlezone tank game en masse, and, in 1996, converted the PC game Doom, which portrayed a futuristic marine hunting demons on Mars, into 'Marine Doom', which showed soldiers with realistic guns.

Nearly 30 years after Israel's Operation Thunderbolt, virtual simulations of battlefield and hostage situations have become a core component of US military training. In June 2003, the US Army commissioned Novalogic, makers of PC war games like Delta Force, to build notoriously complex new equipment – like their 'Land Warrior' technically assisted battle-suit – into new versions of the game, so they could use the game to train their soldiers. The Marine Corp asked Bohemia Interactive, who developed the modern PC war game Operation Flashpoint, to build a custom Marine version. In most ways, because the virtual body could not be harmed, virtual worlds circumvented violence as a route to power. In other ways, though, they began to encourage it.

The man who invented the first machine gun, Hiram Percy Maxim, supposedly did so after a friend told him, 'If you want to pile up gold, invent a killing machine.' Now, the US military had money to fund the most ambitious of virtual worlds. The US Army's Modeling, Virtual Environment and Simulation Institute at the Naval Postgraduate School, with the help of virtual world developers Lucasfilm, spent between $6 million and $8 million to develop 'America's Army' – an online war game like many others, except in this case it was free, and an advert for serving your country. Commissioned in 1999, when Army recruitment was at its lowest in 30 years, America's Army – launched in 2002 – simulated the experience of war, from boot camp to front-line action. What many people didn't know was America Army was also a specific and cost-effective recruiting tool. In 2003, 19 per cent of US Military Academy freshmen had played the game. That year, for the first time in years, the Army met its recruitment quota. ('We want the whole world to know how great the US Army is,' the website declared. 'In elementary school kids learn about the actions of the Continental Army that won our freedoms under George Washington and the Army's role in ending Hitler's oppression. Today they need to know that the Army is engaged around the world to defeat terrorist forces bent on the destruction of America and our freedoms.' To aid the positive message, they sanitised the game; America's Army developers admitted the amount of blood in the game was purposely toned down.)

The value of games in the struggle for cultural dominance hasn't gone unnoticed by those countries America has declared as its enemies. The Syrian-developed game 'Al-Quraysh' shows the history of civilisation from an Arab perspective. 'Under Siege', developed by the same company, portrays the Palestinian struggle from an Arab viewpoint, with Palestinians struggling to protect their villages and olive groves, and also recreates notorious Israeli attacks, like Baruch Goldstein's 1994 machine-gunning of 27 worshippers at a Hebron mosque. (In Under Siege, the hero, Ahmed, must help an ambulance reach the mosque; killing civilians, either Israeli or Arab, leads to in-game penalties.)

As well as cultural propaganda, America's Army also has a more practical recruitment value. A website monitors the statistics of each virtual battle. When a player turns up at a recruitment office, the US Army can access these online records to immediately gauge the recruit's fighting potential.

By 2004, the US Military project that began at Entebbe airport had matured into a plan to rebuild the planet. To aid their stated aims of 'Full Spectrum Dominance', the US Military decided to build a scale model of the whole planet after all. Except, they planned to build it online. Dr Michael Macedonia, a West Point graduate and Gulf War veteran (on 9/11, he was in Corridor 5 of the Pentagon) then headed the US Army's Executive Office for Simulation, Training and Instrumentation, where he oversaw the development of virtual war zones. Macedonia was part of the team which commissioned the developers of 'There', a massive online virtual world, to build an 'Asymmetric Warfare Environment' – a virtual world – to run on the Army's own network, the largest private Internet portal in the world. In AWE – which was the There world, with the Californian beach-hunk and babe outfits changed into military uniforms, and the text chat adapted into voice communication – soldiers would be able to train and re-examine battles in an environment that allowed for social as well as violent interaction.

Beginning with the Army's 101st Airborne Division, soldiers based anywhere in the world could train for warfare in any environment. It wasn't a game – it was a 'tactical decision aid'. Plans were discussed to bring college kids, well-versed in online games, to play the enemy. They started with one square mile of Baghdad – complete with palm trees and Arabic road signs – and, within four years, according to some reports, they planned to model the entire planet, a carbon virtual copy of the real one.

'The reason we started funding the development of these games was to teach soldiers,' Dr Macedonia told the website Gamespot. 'That was our audience – not civilians or kids in high school, but soldiers.' To Macedonia, the AWE wasn't a game at all. 'Our thing is not making people shoot better; it's making people think better.' It was the role-playing, not just the point-and-shoot features, which made the There game engine so appealing to the US Army. 'What's a soldier's experience in Iraq or Afghanistan? Who's the enemy? How do I get these people to not necessarily like me, but to relate to me? How can I keep a riot from starting when the food runs out?' Macedonia said. 'America's Army says it's a first-person shooter. Our games have moved way beyond that. We went from a verbal culture to a written culture, when Homer wrote his stories down. And now we have this medium where we can take people through those experiences. We can do that today in the military, and share those stories, and save lives.

'My particular concern is ensuring that that young sergeant, who's going to go lead soldiers in combat, is not confronted with that situation for the first time while in combat. That's the wrong time to be confronted with that. That's the guy I worry about, not some critic. I don't give a damn. There are guys dying.'

In 2002, There, who made the virtual world of the same name, launched a new company, ForTerra, to handle commercial applications of their virtual world company. In November 2006, I spoke with Robert Gehorsam, President of ForTerra, to see how plans had developed four years down the line. ('One thing I can tell you about working with the Army? It's slower!' he said.)

Robert told me their simulation was never about combat.

'Soldiers have plenty of ways to learn how to fire a weapon. Except in technology like ours, they have no opportunity to learn about the kinds of decisions in different cultures that lead them to decide whether to fire a weapon, or talk. Imagine a typical soldier, in their early or mid-twenties, from the mid-western United States, for whom Iraq is some abstract thing that they are far less familiar about than you and I. How do you build the kind of cultural sensitivity that lets them make the right deci-sion? Realising that you could essentially role-play in this kind of environment was very powerful.

'Obviously the Middle East, especially Iraq, is of particular interest,' Robert told me of ForTerra's continuing work in mili-tary virtual worlds. 'It's ground conflict, it's urban conflict, and it's counter-insurgency. And all of the training work, and all of the simulation, that has been going on in the military for decades, has been about massive tank conflict in East Germany, against the Soviet Union. There haven't been effective simula-tions for the kinds of scenarios where the interaction of the soldiers with the local population becomes really important.'

Robert told me more detail about their first training session, in 2002, with a National Guard group from Illinois. 'They were an artillery unit that was being deployed to Iraq to become mili-tary police,' he said. 'When you're artillery, you're about 10 or 15 miles away from the action. When you're Military Police, you're 10 or 15 *inches* away from the action.'

To help the young artillerymen adapt to close contact with Iraqi people, ForTerra built a virtual checkpoint. They set up 15 PCs in the conference room of a Moline, Illinois, Holiday Inn. Over four days the unit, many of whom were gamers, rehearsed various checkpoint situations, with Army researchers and ForTerra employees playing Iraqi civilians and insurgents. ForTerra varied the scenario each time, with insurgents in different places, and in some cases, no insurgents at all. 'In a typical training scenario, you know exactly how it's going to be scripted,' Robert said. 'In this case, we didn't tell them. So they had to figure out if that family in that car approaching the checkpoint was a bunch of insurgents, or if it was actually just a family. Sometimes they made mistakes – but they weren't real bullets.'

At one point during the training, Robert closed his eyes and listened. 'One guy says, "There's a car approaching." Another guy says, "What's their behaviour? How does it look? What do you think?" And you could hear them gain confidence. We took them through these scenarios, and they said, "Wow. We didn't even know what we didn't know." After being deployed, some soldiers emailed their gratitude. 'They wrote us later after they got to Iraq, and said they really appreciated just those couple of days.'

The 101st Airborne Combat division had a chance to practise in the virtual world only after a tour of duty in Iraq. 'Some of them actually said, "If we'd had a tool like this before we went over, more of us would have come back,"' Gehorsam told me.

ForTerra was building assessment features into its virtual worlds. 'The core of the Army are the sergeants and the captains. They're the junior leaders, so their skill is critical. We've done some leadership training, which is really exciting.' The virtual war world has proved popular with the troops. In 2005, a group of National Guard soldiers were preparing to visit Iraq to liaise with local police to set up security procedures: of their two-week training period for that year, they chose to work with ForTerra for four days.

The advantage of virtual simulation, apart from real-world safety, is the ease of re-running scenarios without mobilising huge real-world forces back to the starting point. Over four years, the Army had invested around $4 million dollars in the AWE.

To Robert Gehorsam, the savings were clear. 'To train one brigade, for three weeks, at Fort Polk, Louisiana, is about $8 million dollars. Of which something like 75 per cent of the cost is getting their equipment there. So what if you didn't have to get their equipment there?'

When we spoke, ForTerra's current, more modest, plans were to extend its virtual world on a slower scale, using the Army's vast databases of real-world terrain data. 'So if you need to populate your scenario with 4,000 civilians, or a couple of old Soviet fighters because that's what Iran has, or something like that, you can now do that.

'The technology can handle any amount of people you want,' Robert told me. 'Once a year, twice a year, the joint forces run exercises that involve ten or fifteen thousand people, that use a whole federation of simulations. We're certainly prepared to do that.'

The technology is adaptable to other fields. ForTerra also working on a commercial project, with a budget of between $1 million and $2 million, funded by the Army Medical Command, to develop a virtual world to train medical first-responders for mass-casualty events – terrorist attacks, hurricanes. ('We work at the extremes of life and death, I guess.') In these virtual worlds, medical workers can practise separating the worst casualties, and treating them in the hospital. They've simulated a sarin gas attack, and are working on dirty bomb scenarios. Those involved can only practise these events for real once a year; it's expensive, and unwieldy. 'This technology allows those people to practise those events as many times as they like, so when the real incident comes, they will be comfortable with each other.'

ForTerra has also customised its virtual world, in partnership with the Federation of American Scientists, and the Fire Department of New York, to train fire chiefs and captains in high-rise fire response. 'High-rise fires are the rarest, and the hardest to train for. And for the commanders they're the hardest, as they typically don't see the fire they are trying to control. They're in a different location.' (The fire chiefs were not as computer-literate as the young soldiers. 'They'd stab at the keyboard with one finger,' Robert told me. 'They're not gamers.')

'There doesn't seem to be any limit to the sorts of situations it's useful for,' Robert says. They're working, for example, on projects which involve the flow of people through proposed building designs, like hospitals, examining whether carts reach the emergency rooms in time.

Previously an editor at Simon & Schuster – after working in its electronic publishing arm, he became the Sony executive overseeing the original EverQuest team – Robert was thrilled by a virtual world that might save lives. 'To come out of the game industry, which is anything but life and death, to something where literally the same code is being applied to the something so vital . . .'

Sometimes, simulations offer another kind of therapeutic hope. In July 2005, ForTerra was asked to demonstrate its virtual world to Dr Fran Harvey, the US Army Secretary. (To show how easy virtual worlds were to navigate, Robert roped in his 10-year-old son, to demonstrate EverQuest.) 'The scenario we did was what's called a "cordon and search". This was an Army squad that was looking for a high-value target, like a lieutenant of Zarqawi's, or someone like that. One of the "playing cards". In the scenario, they had intelligence this person was hiding in a family's house, in a well-to-do neighbourhood of Baghdad. So the scenario played out. With an interpreter, they knock on the door and ask permission to search the house. As they're searching the house, the bad guy takes a hostage, a family member. There's a confrontation; the bad guy happens to be killed, but the hostage is rescued. A soldier is wounded.' They used a cast of 40, including real soldiers, returned from Iraq, who logged on from all over the US, and Iraqi Americans acting as the Iraqi civilians. 'They did angry so great. That sort of angry, Arab, "You insult me!" All of that was captured.'

A retired general, who helped establish the modern army's training programme, witnessed the virtual hostage rescue. In the 10-minute scenario, the general spotted a dozen important – and possibly life-saving – training opportunities. 'Decision points, techniques, things like that,' Robert said. 'How do you stack a patrol along the wall before you enter the house? What's the proper way to ask permission to enter a house in the Middle East? How do you do a hostage rescue?

'We found a Navy Corpsman, which is the Navy's version of a medic,' Robert went on. 'Let me tell you what happened to him. He had been patrolling with the Marines in Fallujah. He had been walking down the street, and a car bomb went off. He came to a second later, and he noticed his leg was lying in the middle of the street. He crawled out from behind shelter, to retrieve his leg, and was shot six more times. He lived. He lost his other leg. He was recuperating six months later when we found him, at Walter Reed Medical Centre. He asked if he could play the role of the medic in the scenario. So now you had a guy who really was there, who could suddenly run around in the virtual world with legs he didn't have in real life.'

The Corpsman corrected ForTerra's simulation, explaining that if the medic entered the house in the way they'd planned, he would have been killed instantly. 'You saw him run in, you saw him call for the medi-vac: he got to live again.'

Ironically, the first anti-war protest in a virtual world took place in the original incarnation of There: on 15 February 2003, as part of a global co-ordinated protest against the imminent inva-sion of Iraq, a group of 100 There residents gathered for the 'Polygons for Peace' demonstration. That day, along with a million others, I marched down Trafalgar square in the middle of a British winter, to register my displeasure at the erosion of international law, and the people who would soon be killed. The There residents did so too, but they marched at sunset, on a perfect beach, under palm trees.

Elsewhere, virtual military conflict was intruding into the real in other ways, too. In World War II, famously, only 10 per cent of soldiers shot to kill; 50 years later, in the first Iraq war, 90 per cent did so. ('When the time came . . . to fire his weapon, he was ready to do that,' David Bartlett, former chief of operations at the Defense Department's Defense Modeling and Simulation Office, told the *Washington Post* of his new recruits. 'His experience leading up to that time, through on-the-ground training and playing Halo and whatever else, enabled him to execute.') It benefits those who construct our strategies of war to desensitise kids to pulling the trigger.

Since America's Army, other commercially available war games have been pressed into military service. The Department of Defense uses 'Tom Clancy's Rainbow Six: Rogue Spear', a PC game, to train personnel in urban combat. The blurring between real-world fact and virtual fantasy brings to mind Baudrillard's famous proclamation, 'The Gulf War did not take place'. In the first Iraq war, the video news piped home to us seemed like footage from a video game; in the more recent Iraq war, the soldiers themselves made the comparison. 'I have seen innocent people being killed. IEDS go off and you just zap any farmer that is close to you . . . hit him with the 50 [heavy machine gun] or the M-16 [rifle],' veteran Jody Casey told 'Iraq Veterans Against the War'. 'Overall there was just the total disregard – they basically jam into your head: "This is Hajji. This is Hajji". You totally take the human being out of it and make them into a video game.'

'All I saw was the street where the RPG came from, and I

just fired in that direction, maybe 20 rounds at most,' 22-year-old Sergeant Sean Crippen told the *Washington Post*, of an Iraq gun battle. 'It felt like I was playing Ghost Recon at home.'

Technology has long bled from the military–industrial complex into entertainment. Talking dolls have their root in 'talking cockpit' projects from the US Air Force, and, in 2004, war-keen children could covet George W. Bush action figures, with a complementary 'Mission Accomplished' banner – or even a 'Talking Uday', a model of Saddam Hussein's son, with a badly wounded face. (When you pull his talking string, the doll yelled, in a mock-Arab accent, 'Someone must help me. I am still alive, only I am very badly burned. Anyone! Can someone call my father? I am in a lot of pain, I am very badly burned so if you could just . . . You shot me! Why did you . . .?' followed by the sound of three final gun shots.) With virtual worlds, the process had turned around: the CIA has an entertainment industry liaison, and Hollywood talent, like *Star Wars* production designer Ron Cobb, consulted on the Army's development of its virtual wars.

Most virtual war games are pure fantasy: there's no pain, no loss, and no 'collateral damage'. (In Counterstrike, you can shoot a hostage, but you can't bomb a wedding.) Even your virtual comrades' dead bodies, after a respectful minute or so, disappear. In response to these games, where meticulously illustrated 3D violence is run-of-the-mill, Joseph DeLappe, Associate Professor at the University of Nevada, Reno, set up the 'dead-in-Iraq' project. Each day, DeLappe logs into the servers of America's Army and broadcasts the names of America's war-dead. He logs in, he types, he gets shot, and he keeps typing.

'I enter the game using as my login name, "dead-in-Iraq", and proceed to type the names,' his website read. 'I am a neutral visitor as I do not participate in the proscribed mayhem. Rather,

I stand in position and type until I am killed. Upon being re-incarnated I continue to type. To date, I have input just over 250 names. I intend to keep doing so until the end of this war.'

'I became interested in memorials soon after the publication online of a website that presented the thousands of proposals for a 9/11 memorial on the World Trade Center site,' DeLappe told me, in May 2006. 'This gave rise to thoughts of a memorial for the thousands of civilian deaths in Iraq.'

DeLappe's words offended some players more than the simulated experience of being shot in the head. Transcripts of his time inside America's Army show the confused and sometimes hostile responses of the virtual soldiers.

>MICHAEL VANN JOHNSON JR. 25, NAVY, MAR 25 2003
>dead in iraq, are you enlisted? reserve? Have you been to iraq?

>ARMONDO ARIEL GONZALEZ, 25, MARINE, APR 14 2003
>dead in iraq, shut the **** up!

Many players ended up banning DeLappe from their servers. 'I am looked upon as an obnoxious interloper bringing real-world content into the magic circle,' he told me. 'Other players get angry, ask me questions, to which I do not reply. I doggedly continue typing the names.'

DeLappe had previously re-enacted presidential debates in the Sims Online and Star Wars Galaxies, and he had also logged into a small-scale Star Trek virtual combat world called Elite Force: Voyager, as 'Allen Ginsberg', and typed out 'Howl' line by line (it took him six hours). 'The other works were for the most part enjoyable to create,' he told me. 'This one is not – it is depressing and weighs heavily upon my conscience.'

DeLappe, who at age 18 had come close to signing up, told

me he found the use of America's Army as a recruiting tool 'problematic in the extreme. If one tries to imagine the US army creating a TV show or a film that purely exists to recruit young, impressionable ones to join up, we might find this questionable, no?'

At the time of writing, 2,853 US service personnel have died in Iraq. As of 12 November 2006, DeLappe had been typing names for a few hours a week, for over seven months; he was still only just over half way through.

In my own real-life quest for stability, virtual war cropped up in the unlikeliest of places. In a meeting about how to handle my mounting debt, my bank manager told me he was a regular player of Vassal Engine, an online medieval war game. I told him hopefully about the book I was working on; he laughed, but refused to give me a loan. Wagner James Au reported on a war veteran who lost a quarter of his kneecap to a mine in Afghanistan, and who used Second Life to help him get over the horrors of war – by establishing a property and gambling empire that earned him $2,000 to $3,000 a week. Au also reported on a US Homeland Security-funded virtual island in Second Life, designed to simulate emergency response in the real world. (Even outside virtual worlds, imaginary selves were being used to support the US war effort. The Maine Army National Guard had issued over 100 full-size cardboard cut-out replicas of service personnel. These virtual soldiers, or 'flat daddies', were intended for families to sit at their kitchen table, take to ballgames, and place in the back seat of their cars, to remind children of their absent fathers.

Cardboard cutouts are no replacement for real family, and virtual worlds are no replacement for real conflict. Both Counterstrike and America's Army offer a limited field in which to relate; you can only shoot each other; teams are limited to

205

20 or so; the battlefields are restricted to an acre of virtual soil. But in our new, larger virtual worlds, the same kind of simulated conflict is also available. In many, like Lineage and EverQuest, there are areas – called PVP zones, short for player versus player – where residents can pit themselves against one another. Usually, all that is at stake is honour, although sometimes the victor is allowed to loot one item from his opponent's virtual corpse.

For most residents, this kind of conflict is nostalgic – they're not training to cast spells in a real war, and, at least in most of Western society, people long ago put down their swords and began to fight each other with property. But I discovered another more personal, more realistic – and more revealing – kind of conflict had crept under the skin of virtual worlds. Virtual property now had a value – and we had started to fight each other that way, too. My own boundary concerns (Wayne's worries about the travel agent; the possibility of new ocean development obscuring my view) were small versions of new arguments, over virtual and moral territory, that had begun to spring up everywhere virtual feet touched virtual soil.

Both Wilde and John Lester had remarked that virtual worlds were a new kind of 'level playing field'. My small local boundary dispute, the fuss over a travel agency and a new water-park, echoed many larger conflicts inside virtual world. I was discovering that in virtual worlds, people do what people always do on playing fields: they compete.

12

us

Together in electric dreams

In August 2004, Derek Jones – in real life Derek LeTellier, then a 19-year-old student teacher from Chicago – had been a Second Life resident for a year and a half. (He'd seen an interview with Philip Rosedale on G4TV, a niche gaming channel, and thought he'd give the budding virtual world a try.) He enjoyed designing interactive scripted objects; he spent time on his virtual dock, tinkering with a virtual sailboat he and a friend had designed. Then, he heard about a competition in the Second Life sandbox, to see who could build the tallest stack of objects. His entry was a full-scale skyscraper, built entirely out of wooden blocks. He didn't win, but after the game Jones stuck around to experiment with the world's physics. He altered the blocks so they would shift, and the tower would collapse. His building experiments became a kind of regular sideshow; each week, a handful of people would gather to watch as he stood on top of his towers, commanded them to fall, and surfed the tumbling blocks to the ground. Then, a friend, James Miller, mentioned the tower reminded him of the World Trade Center. Another friend of Jones, also there, had lost a relative in the real 9/11 attacks. He mentioned he would like to see what it was like to be inside the towers as they fell. So, at his friend's request, Derek Jones built a second tower, alongside the first. The two, along with journalist James Au, and a handful of others, climbed inside.

Derek's intention hadn't originally been to recreate the towers. 'A lot of what looked like symbols for 9/11 mostly were due to practical reasons,' LeTellier told me. 'The shape of the buildings, the size, and the placement of people inside them.' I asked Derek if he was wary of any controversy the collapse might cause. 'A little bit, especially when we put that second tower up,' he said. 'At that point I got a little disturbed about what we were doing. How eerie it looked to have those two towers that looked like the twin towers there, ready to collapse. Before that, it's only an experiment. At that point, it became something more.'

Derek Jones had tired of selecting each block individually to make the tower fall: he had scripted each block to respond to a single, spoken word. Derek shouted his command – 'Die!' – and the two towers fell again.

Then, in response to the falling of the towers, that section of the world ended. The buildings, which had taken Derek Jones just five minutes to build, were among the largest constructions Second Life had ever seen. When they fell, the servers overloaded, and that portion of the world crashed. As if in a rising pall of smoke, the world went black. Every resident was ejected.

After the server restarted, Derek Jones and his friends logged back in to Second Life. By then, the collapse was complete. Like most people who remember the occasion, Derek saw 9/11 on-screen. He had been in the middle of first period, in history class, when his school made an announcement for all teachers to turn on the news. His history teacher turned on the TV, 'and we just sat there the whole period watching and listening.'

After the virtual collapse, standing among the rubble, Derek Jones built a virtual screen, on which he displayed images of his own towers falling. A crowd gathered to watch. Then, the crowd began to argue. Second Life was smaller then – 20 servers, each covering 12 acres, as opposed to over 300 two years later. 'For a while there were only about 100 people who were online at a time,' Derek told me, 'and it wasn't hard to know everyone who was online.' Back then, when a controversy erupted, everyone heard about it. 'Mostly just people who felt that it was offensive to collapse the towers because they had loved ones who had died in the towers and they felt it was disrespectful.'

In real life, Derek Jones was working toward a degree to teach high school history. In his virtual life, Derek was making history. 'I haven't noticed it as much in the much larger Second Life,' he told me, 'but when it's difficult to be in Second Life without seeing things like the towers collapsing, then there's always bound to be people who are offended. It's that type of event in history where a lot of people remember exactly where they were when the towers fell,' he said. 'And watching what we did in the sandbox brought back those memories for people. People had interpreted it as kind of a recreation.'

Later, on the Second Life bulletin boards, the sandbox argument raged on. 'Damiana Domino' called the project 'really tasteless . . .' She argued painful memories should be left out of Second Life. 'It's unfortunate that in a place where no physical harm can come to us, we still find ways to hurt each other,' wrote 'Ananda Sandgrain', a Manhattan resident in her first life. The event was tasteless, 'David Cartier' thought, and James Au's coverage was 'sensationalist and exploitative'.

Others disagreed. 'It was closure for me,' Derek Jones's friend, who had lost a relative in the real-world collapse, told James Au. 'I wanted to know just what he went through. How it would have felt for him. Second Life allows me to do that and live to tell the tale.'

'If you didn't like what was going on then you could just go elsewhere,' 'RisingShadow' wrote.

We share a multi-cultural world of diverse ideas, added 'kohne Kato'. 'For our own sanity, we must be tolerant.'

This is just a game, said 'Brad Lupis'.

'Yet another one who just doesn't get it,' 'Grim Lupis' (no relation) replied. 'This is just a game to you. To others, it's something completely different.'

In October 2006, Derek Jones visited my virtual office, to talk about the fall of his towers, and the subsequent controversy. Dressed as his usual virtual self – a short, cartoon-monkey-headed man, in an Imperial Stormtrooper uniform, with a single pearl earring – he told me how it felt to be inside a collapsing building.

'When the building begins to fall underneath you, the floor starts going down, columns collapse all around you,' Jones told me. 'It was quite a sensation even though it obviously wasn't real. All that could be heard was the constant clanking of the blocks hitting each other. For me at least, it just made me wonder how terrifying it would be if this was actually happening, with the floors falling from underneath, watching pieces of the building scatter away.'

As we spoke, the sun set. It was a foggy night, and outside my office, snow was falling. I asked if he wanted to recreate the second falling of the twin towers. He said yes. Derek Jones winked out of existence, and I accepted his offer of a teleport. In the sandbox, I watched as he pulled a skyscraper, floor by floor, from his pocket. And there it was. A tower of wooden blocks, like the one he'd built two years before.

When the tower was built, we stood inside, near the top floor. The walls were open to the virtual elements; the noise of the wind was louder up here. We stood, up in the clouds, lit from the side by the last rays of the virtual sun. I looked down to the ground, far below, and for a moment felt dizzy. 'Die!' Derek said, and the towers fell for a third time.

As we fell, the air filled with the sound of building blocks collapsing around us. In the two years since he'd first knocked the tower down, Second Life technology had improved; this time, the server managed to stay online.

In Second Life you could build what you like, be what you like, say what you like, as long as you didn't offend others. And that's where the problems really start. 'In football, everything is complicated by the presence of the other team,' Sartre wrote. We had developed our perfect worlds, and what attracted us was that other people lived there too. But the problem was, other people lived there too.

One by one, Derek Jones picked up the blocks, which now covered the plain, and I flew off. I looked down, and he waved at me from among the rubble.

After September 11, EverQuest II players held an in-world candle-lit vigil, but in the years following Derek Jones's re-enactment, Second Life responses to the attacks were varied – and still controversial.

In 2005, Second Life residents constructed hundreds of 9/11 memorials. Most avoided controversy: they built virtual memorial gardens, or virtual memorial plaques, or virtual memorial statues of NY firemen raising the American flag. One man, Rusty Vindaloo, listed the names of all who had died that day. But another resident, 'Sexy Casanova', bit the bullet, and constructed a much more detailed replica of the World Trade Center. Perhaps crucially for his popularity ratings, he didn't knock them down. Even so, many residents took a while to accept it. 'At first I thought it was morbid,' 'Olympia Reebus' said about the Towers' third incarnation. 'But now I realise it's a way to "never forget".'

Throughout millennia, mankind dreamed alone. Now, suddenly, in our virtual worlds, we were able to share and inhabit each other's dreams. But wherever human beings share things, fights break out. Our virtual worlds were no exception. In moments like the second World Trade Center crash, what should be a virtual utopia descended into yet another struggle over right and wrong.

'I have a question,' 'Emericus Phaeton' wrote, in the final comment on a Second Life website's coverage of the event. 'When does Third Life come out so we can escape our second one?'

The new virtual conflicts weren't just between residents. Sometimes the residents themselves gathered together, to register their displeasure with the world's makers. Consumers don't usually rally against changes in products. When The Coca-Cola Company introduced 'New Coke', no one campaigned in the supermarket aisles. They just didn't tend to buy the cans. But if Coca-Cola owned your whole world, and it wasn't just the taste of the drink they altered: it was your job, your house, or even your ability to walk – you might complain.

In virtual worlds, there is a history of protest against the ruling classes. In 1999, residents of the fantasy virtual world Ultima Online, angry at software problems that had lost them valuable virtual items, protested in a suitably medieval fashion: they stormed the castle, and murdered the king. (Their victim, 'Lord British', was the online self of Richard Bartle, the man who had created the world.)

In January 2005, World of Warcraft's developers Blizzard made some changes to the Warrior character class. Many warriors felt their virtual lives had been unfairly restricted. To highlight their plight, the players decided to hold an in-world demonstration. A hundred gnome warriors gathered en masse in the Dwarven city Ironforge, and stripped naked. It took some time for a game GM to notice the bare gnomes, but when they did, the totalitarian boot came down. 'ATTENTION: Gathering in a realm with intent to hinder game play is considered griefing, and will not be tolerated,' the GM announced. 'We appreciate your opinion, but protesting in-game is not a valid way to give us feedback.' There were no water cannons in World of Warcraft for the GMs to turn on the crowd, but gnomes who persisted with their naked frolics (as well as a few innocent bystanders) had their accounts temporarily suspended.

The attendant joy of virtual worlds – the narcotic virtual world companies profit from – is that, by removing our selves from our bodies, they ease our suffering. The attendant sorrow of virtual worlds is that, of course, we don't leave our problems behind: they simply re-emerge in another form. In the real world, democracy didn't have an easy birth, and elsewhere, in other virtual worlds, the struggle of the people to be heard seemed to be mirroring our social struggle for representation.

In April 2000, when Sony Online Entertainment negotiated with eBay to prevent EverQuest players selling accounts or EverQuest items, eBay's press release declared that Sony had applied to their 'Verified Rights Owners Program', designed to stop people selling items for which they do not own the copyright. That meant, in effect, if you identified primarily with your virtual self – as 20 per cent of EverQuest players declared they did – then Sony owned you. In this light, worlds like EverQuest were totalitarian regimes, and virtual residents lived in a new kind of bonded slavery.

To Sony Online Entertainment, this was a selling point. 'You're in Our World Now', they told every resident, every time they entered the world. In these virtual worlds, society wasn't a democracy; the relationship was more like that between citizens and an occupying power – as was illustrated in August 2004, inside the virtual world Star Wars Galaxies. A group of players discovered a credit 'dupe', like Noah Burns's forgery shortcut, with which they could generate as much virtual cash as they liked.

The developers, understandably unhappy with this threat to the game balance – and their real-world revenue – decided to clamp down hard. They traced everyone who had come into contact with the hacked credits – 44,800 residents – and, whether they knew about the dupe or not, the residents were banned. The wrath of SOE rained on the just and the unjust alike.

Although many successfully appealed the ban, those players who felt they had been banned unfairly decided to protest. They created new virtual selves, and gathered together in a prearranged spot inside Star Wars Galaxies – outside the Theed Starport on Naboo, the home of Jar Jar Binks – to protest their innocence. Sony broadcast warnings to local residents to leave the area. Those who ignored the warnings found themselves scattered randomly across the Star Wars galaxy. (The online cartoon website Penny Arcade satirised Sony's attitude; 'Sir. We have reports of player protests on Naboo,' a lieutenant reported. 'I recommend we resolve this in a way that shows we respect our customers.' In response, the Emperor held up a crooked finger. 'Teleport them into space.')

From Sony's perspective, the protesting residents were ruining the fun. From the residents' perspective, Sony was abusing its power over their virtual lives. 'Somebody saying something in the game and being witnessed by somebody else can reflect not just on the game but on Lucasfilm and George Lucas,' Ralph Koster, a lead designer on Star Wars Galaxies, told *Canadian Press*. 'If someone started walking around in the San Diego Zoo screaming profanity or handing out Nazi leaflets, the park would remove them from the premises. We need to be able to do that also.' But the Naboo protestors were also at the front line of an underlying moral struggle. In 2000, an EverQuest resident called Mystere, who played EverQuest around 20 hours a week, published EverQuest fan fiction online, which included the (fictional) story of a virtual rape of a 14-year-old girl. Mystere was banned from EverQuest. 'If we determine that one person's actions make EverQuest a game that other people do not want to play, based upon those actions, we will exercise our right to refuse service,' Gordon Wrinn, EverQuest's Internet Relations Manager, explained. 'The laws governing the use of copyrighted material . . . give us the exclusive right to permit or disallow the outside use of our intellectual property so that we can properly manage our business and nurture the EverQuest brand.'

In the meantime, the more personal struggles near my virtual home had taken on a new edge. Someone else had moved into the area; our new neighbour had a larger, more palatial home – on his roof were two huge military helicopters and an Israeli flag. Further down the hill, my other neighbour, Wayne Nohkan, had decided to build around his virtual home, to preserve his view. He had constructed a Japanese garden, complete with a shower of snow, which drifted sideways and somehow through the wall of my house; now, when I sprawled on my chaise longue to watch virtual TV, a cloud of snow fell around me.

Virtual snow doesn't make you cold, and I didn't mind. It was a small hint, though, of the virtual boundary disputes that had sprung up all across Second Life. Residents who didn't get along sometimes descended into a war of ugly structures and billboards, a symbolic struggle over territory that mirrored the ideological banner exchanges that erupted between the US in Guantanamo Bay and those across the fence in Cuba. Then, after Wayne's bugbear, the Travel Agency, was complete – the finished structure looked a lot prettier than the building site had done – on the hillside above my office, a new structure sprung up. Two stacks of cubes, each with a different theme, hung unsupported in the air. One stack was plastered with GI-Joe-style poseable dolls made into gay pin-up poses. On each face of the other set of cubes were anti-Bush jokes: a

Connecticut road sign, 'Birthplace of George W. Bush', customised to include ' – We Apologise', and a photo of George W. and Dick Cheney photo-shopped to look like Beavis and Butt-head, with the caption 'Huh huh, you said Bush!' 'Huh huh, you said Dick!'.

These posters echoed an earlier virtual conflict that had spread across Second Life. In December 2005, one resident, Lazarus Divine, bought up small plots of virtual land all across the world. These kinds of small parcels were common: a search of 'land for sale' inside Second Life showed hundreds of small plots, a few metres square, for sale – sometimes literally for pennies – billed as 'Excellent Ad Lot'. On each of his plots Lazarus placed a giant blue billboard that read: 'Support Our Troops – end the illegal war in Iraq. Restore US credibility – impeach Bush.'

Many Second Life residents were unhappy at the real-world intrusion. (Some erected their own billboards: 'Impeach Lazarus Divine'.) In a straw poll conducted by Wagner James Au, over 70 per cent of the world's residents had a strong opinion on the posters. Linden Lab brought up the issue in its weekly newsletter. 'Over the past many months the Second Life landscape has been dotted with signs calling for the impeachment of President Bush. The ensuing debate has people on one side calling for the suspension of the sign creator for spamming the landscape, and on the other side championing his right to free speech . . . Second Life is built on the twin values of tolerance and free expression: tolerance of other people's views and the right to follow one's own path. We believe that these two values combine to allow for the fullest emergence of innovative new experiences. Sometimes those experiences will be amazing and sometimes less so, but on balance the community gains when its Residents have the widest freedom possible.'

*   *   *

There were hints, though, that some of those posting anti-Bush posters had ulterior motives. The plot of land behind my office where the Bush cartoons hovered had a label attached to the land: 'Got ugly neighbours? Buy the neighbourhood!'. The implication was that those who posted the pictures did so to encourage local residents to pay above the odds, just to clear the view.

The anti-Bush posters didn't bother me – in fact, I agreed with them – and I wasn't tempted to buy the land to remove them. But, without meaning to, I had entered into another kind of conflict that hit closer to home.

Wagner James Au wrote to me. He had heard I was working on a book about virtual worlds, and he was working on one too. He wanted to clarify the stories I would be covering. He asked for a broad outline of my book, which he could forward to his agent, to reassure publishers our material wouldn't overlap. We met, in a Dr Seuss candy land, to talk it over. I told him I would be writing about a range of virtual worlds, not just Second Life. He seemed pleased. He seemed proprietary about Second Life; he said he 'didn't mind' me writing about Wilde, as if he in some way owned the Second Life narrative. The next day, though, he forwarded me an email to his agent, in which he explained – contrary to what I had said – that I would be covering Second Life only in a chapter or two.

Every writer knows the feeling that someone else is working the same story. You can sense them out there, mapping out the same territory, stalking the same narrative prey. It encourages a kind of friendly enmity; every writer wishes other writers well, but there's always the hope that you'll get your story told first. In virtual worlds, I was discovering, as you walked the exotic landscape, feeling like a virtual pioneer, you could sometimes actually see the competition strolling by. Still, Wagner James Au had made an effort to be courteous about our potential territorial conflict, and I was grateful to him, as a guide to my early Second Life years. Others, though, weren't so polite.

When I first travelled to meet Wilde, June-Marie told me she met someone who was working on a book with me. It was news to me. 'Robbie something,' she said.

I knew who it was. A month or so before, I'd met up with a photographer, whose current project was taking portraits of real-world people, then exhibiting them alongside images of their virtual selves. (A boy with multiple sclerosis, whose oxygen face-mask strangely echoed his Star Wars Galaxies bounty hunter's boxy helmet; a fat player with a thin virtual self; a mother who, through the electronic looking glass, became a punk.) We'd exchanged stories, and I left confident that we could cooperate without competing.

After my visit to Wilde, I emailed the photographer, asking him to stop using my name in his book pitch without my permission. A few months later, I wrote a column about the photographer, and I emailed him to ask for some details on a story he'd told me about. He told me he wasn't sure that would work for him. Instead, he suggested I write a longer piece about him. (I resisted the temptation.) A year later, after the publication of another piece I wrote which mentioned a story he had pointed out, he emailed me again. I called him, made some polite chat about his own book, and thought nothing of it. A week later, he sent me another email. I was using him to further my own agenda, he told me. I should have pitched to use him as the photographer for the piece. (I had, but the editor chose to run his own photos.) He was angry I had used the story, and suspicious about my call. He accused me of showing a 'lack of character'. 'Now you have contacted me again, ostensibly to meet up, but actually to fish for more information, this time about publishing dates, etc.,' he wrote. 'Be careful how much you take,' he wrote. 'I'm not your mother,' he added, in case there was any doubt. This last remark was an accusation that I had already used people in my previous book, and also a claim to know more about me than I knew about myself.

The email shook me. Was it true? Did I take too much? Was it time I gave something back to virtual worlds? Was I lazy, using others to further my own agenda? Had I forgotten life was hard? Then, I settled down. The reality was that I had been drawn into a different kind of territorial conflict, no less real than Wayne's anxieties about the encroaching travel agency. Cultural commentators are occupiers, too – we invade the story, tell it our way – and, in our new virtual gold-rush, everything, even the story of the world itself, was up for grabs. As a chronicler of virtual worlds, I too was claiming a kind of territory, and other people wanted to claim it too – or, if they felt I would stake my claim first, they might try to ruin it for me. We were bound to clash.

I had experienced the same kind of animosity after my last book. Some disciples of my mother's guru, angered at my irreverent portrayal, wrote online diatribes and sent me angry, moralising emails. They felt the guru belonged to them, and they were angry with me for presenting a different story. The same seemed to be happening here. People felt virtual worlds belonged to them, and, where our viewpoints crossed, I had become an intruder in their domain.

That night, aggrieved by the emails, fighting the urge to respond, I couldn't sleep. I lay in bed, staring at the ceiling, until an old childhood dream, which used to help ease me into sleep, returned. I imagined myself able to fly, to become invisible, and to pass through walls. I left my body, got out of my bed, walked to the window. Liberated from my self, from gravity, and from the gaze of those who would harm me, I drifted off above the streets of London, under the stars.

13

VIRTUAL SEX

Boys who are girls who like boys who are girls

As it turned out, the time I'd slipped out of a real-world dinner party to hang out in my virtual office hadn't gone unnoticed. The next day, my girlfriend asked me, 'Do *you* have a virtual girlfriend?'

Since their origin, virtual worlds have turned our heads away from our real-world relationships and toward the TV screen. Women who lose their boyfriends to video consoles had coined a name for themselves, 'PlayStation Widows' – later customised by an online support group, who called themselves 'EverQuest Widows'. But, as well as pulling us apart, virtual worlds were also bringing couples together.

Games company Verant began building EverQuest in 1996; by 1999, when EverQuest launched, their expectations were modest. 'When I joined the project, EQ was just an idea,' senior game designer Bill Trost told me. 'They wanted to create a graphical MUD, and had some idea about how it would look, but not many specifics.'

'We came at the right time, with the right weirdly addictive design,' the Sony executive in charge of EverQuest, Robert

Gehorsam, told me. They'd expected a fantasy-themed game, but they found they'd built a world.

During development, they'd had to fight their corner against Sony Consumer Electronics, who, intent on the upcoming PlayStation 2 launch, didn't see how an online PC game fitted their gaming strategy. They won their internal battle, and, at the world's launch, Trost and his colleagues planned for a few thousand subscribers. Within a year, they had half a million residents. Despite the explosive growth, it took the first EverQuest wedding to drive home the fact that what they'd built was an entire world, rather than just a game. They heard about the wedding from a resident, and logged on to watch characters exchange rings and vows, in a world they had made. It was nothing they could have predicted. 'There was a GM, me, Brad McQuaid [EverQuest's Executive Producer] . . . and we saw a wedding in the game. It was awesome,' John Smedley, who originally conceived EverQuest, told me in 2002.

It wasn't just the law that was struggling to catch up with the new possibilities inside virtual worlds. The fault-lines were being redrawn in every area of human experience. Virtual worlds had become a place where people could act out their fantasies, and, in some cases, the relationships were as 'out there' as the costumes.

One of the first stories to attract me to Second Life was a column by Wagner James Au, about the virtual love affair of a Second Life resident named Torley Torgeson. I had met Torley Torgeson, briefly, in my early days inside Second Life, and it was Torley's upset over an article I had written that had led to my trouble at Linden Lab. Torley, real name Torley Wong, used to wear a neon-pink monk's robe, with bright green gloves, to match his pink and green speedboat. Torley had Asperger's syndrome, and liked extreme colours. He took to virtual worlds quickly, moving into a custom-made dumpster, like a bright, energetic version of Oscar the Grouch. 'For the first time, Torley believed he'd found somewhere he could truly call home,' he wrote on his website, of his entry into Second Life. Linden Lab later hired Torley to work on bug testing and user interface; he was renamed Torley Linden. By the time I met Torley, he wore a black dress, and he had breasts. Torley had become a woman. Sometime in November 2004, his male character, Torley wrote on his website, had 'vanished into the space-time rift.'

Meanwhile, somewhere across the virtual continent of Second Life, Jade Lily was born. Jade's owner was a man, but he chose to join Second Life as a woman, just to see what it felt like. (In 2006, a study showed, as many British women as men spent time in virtual worlds. Another study, by Stanford University PhD Nick Yee, showed men across all virtual worlds chose to inhabit virtual worlds as virtual woman around a third of the time.) Jade's creator originally joined Second Life to have an online relationship with an ex-girlfriend, who now lived far away. The girlfriend joined as a man, and they tried a few virtual dates. 'I thought it would be interesting to have a relationship with a guy in Second Life who was actually a girl in real life,' Jade explained to Au. 'It didn't work out.' But Jade kept playing as a woman, and soon Jade and Torley met. 'Jade's the type of person who I felt I "knew" early on,' Torley said. The two hit it off, and are now an inseparable virtual couple – even after they both confessed their real-world sexes. 'I am in love with Jade,' Torley said. 'Simply put, I am happy when I am with her.'

'I'm not attracted to guys physically,' Lily insisted. 'In real life, I'm clearly attracted to women. In Second Life, it gets shady. I see my avatar, Jade, and I'm compelled to play a female role . . . because it's what she's supposed to do, I guess. Second Life has either taught me a lot about myself, or created more questions. Maybe both.'

Torley and Jade, overwhelmed by their feelings for each other, even told James Au they hoped to meet in person. Their love was so pure, they thought, that perhaps their lack of homosexual feelings wouldn't matter. 'Do I want to meet Jade in real life?' Torley told Au. 'ABSOLUTELY, YES! She's such an exceptional person. Simple as that. There are certain things that can be faked online, but real personality shines through. And she shines so brightly.'

I approached Torley to talk about his relationship, but, although I apologised for the trouble I'd caused, he didn't want to talk. I was discovering, though, that not all relationships through the electronic looking glass took such a hysteric shape. Virtual worlds were a way of making more concrete a relationship that would otherwise be fragile and distant. A relationship with a far-away partner once meant occasional awkward chats on the phone; now those distant connections could take a more convincing shape. And, in some cases, virtual relationships had stepped out of the screen to become real.

A few weeks after Alayne Wartell had told me about her virtual fashion business, she dropped by on another visit to my virtual office, to tell me how she met her husband, Eddie Escher.

Two years before I met Alayne, her younger brother, who had joined Second Life, persuade her to become a resident. 'He kept bugging me to try it,' she said. 'I was sceptical. I'd never been interested in MMORPGS' – by which she meant Massively Multiplayer Online Role-Playing Games, a hackneyed term for fantasy virtual worlds like EverQuest. 'But I tried Second Life, and the building hooked me, and I made good friends and had fun with them. And, of course, not long after I joined, I met my husband.'

Alayne, newly reborn as Fallingwater, had flown across the Second Life landscape searching for a place to settle. She spotted a building she liked, 'a futuristic bubbly really nice pod thing.' The nearby land was for sale, so she bought a plot, and began to build her own home.

After a few weeks, as neighbours do, Fallingwater and Eddie said hello. The pair began to socialise. (He had built a brain in a jar, which he had scripted to respond to nearby conversation. She would greet Eddie, then say hello to the brain.) Soon, she found she felt shy when other Second Life residents were around; she looked forward to meeting Eddie alone. 'I remember spending time chatting with him and maybe a couple of other people in there, and I remember starting to hope I'd see him over there. And it turns out he felt the same – he'd hope to see me, and if I had visitors, he'd feel shy.

'You probably know or have heard how fast things can go here,' Alayne told me. (I had noticed. In another survey by Nick Yee, one in five female EverQuest players said they'd had a crush on or fallen in love with another player.) 'It's like life intensified. It was maybe a couple or a few weeks later that he asked me out on a "date".'

For their first date, Eddie took Fallingwater, or really Alayne, to what was then that world's only private island. Linden Lab had given the island away as a prize in a contest, and the owner had turned it into a romantic getaway; he charged residents to bring dates to his island paradise. 'They set a table with dinner for us,' Fallingwater said, 'which we both laughed about, because we think Second Life food is so dumb. And there was a little room with a fireplace and stuff, and it was all very sweet and nice. The funny part is, he was offered it when we, and our friend Maggie, were hanging out. So he had to invite me *and* Maggie, to not be rude. But Maggie knew the score and backed out.'

Across the private island, Eddie had set up a trail of roses, each one with a clue to find the next. 'How could I go wrong with a guy like that?'

I asked if they had fallen in love.

'We did!' Alayne said. 'And it didn't feel weird.'

The lack of physical reality, according to Alayne, made their romance smooth. 'I think the distancing in a way lets us be more ourselves. You don't have any physical stuff getting in the way. It doesn't confuse things. You're getting to know the person, not the body.

'I was less nervous, the distancing of typing to each other, and not having to make real eye contact is very freeing. I was more nervous about our first phone call.'

Eddie Escher – real name Chris Edwards – lived in Harrogate, North Yorkshire; Alayne lived on the outskirts of Philadelphia. But they spoke on the phone, and they enjoyed each other's virtual company. Two months later, over Christmas and New Year, Eddie flew out to visit Fallingwater. Chris and Alayne met for the first time. 'I tried to keep in mind the fact that meeting face to face can be very different,' Alayne told me. 'But it didn't change how I felt, and I was very confident that we'd get along in real life.

'I met him at the airport gate. I wasn't even nervous until about an hour beforehand, when I was getting ready to drive to the airport. And then, I started hyperventilating.

'I was waiting outside the gate, pacing and shaking. I saw him coming out and he has this bouncy walk. It's kinda funny. Then he walked up to me, and we kissed, and the world around us disappeared.'

I asked if Chris resembled Eddie. 'Well, he's an android, so, no!' Still, their time together was a real success. 'We had a great time and my family loved him too,' Fallingwater said. 'It was really hard to part.

'I started getting teary about it a couple days in advance. We both did.'

A few days later, on the phone, they got engaged.

At least once, inside Second Life, the pair argued – still, they visited each other in the real world twice, and decided to live together. Chris ran his own games company, which seemed on the brink of bankruptcy. Alayne had a secure job. 'I was working for Towers-Perrin [a professional services firm], the biggest and most corporate place I'd ever worked. The corporate atmosphere sucked, but for a while the work was really fun.' Chris made plans to move to Philadelphia. Then, Alayne lost her job. 'It was due to a total fuckup on my part. I think I really wasn't happy there, and was dealing with it in a passive way.'

After missing a lot of work, Alayne was made redundant; at the same time, Chris was hired by a successful games company, Rockstar Games. So they switched; Alayne got on a plane to England. For Alayne, it was a relief. 'I'm glad [our plans] reversed. I've gotten a new start, and it's terrible what's happening with US politics these days.' Within a month of her move, in a Yorkshire registry office, they married.

The couple never bothered with a Second Life wedding. 'That wasn't important to us. Though we did have an engagement party that a friend really wanted to have for us.'

After a few months of struggle with work-visa bureaucracy, Alayne began to design her virtual fashion label. 'I love my job, I love my husband, and I'm enjoying living here.

'Second Life has improved my life vastly,' she said.

At the time of writing, there have been an estimated 5,000 virtual weddings in EverQuest. By the summer of 2006, according to Sony, 20 couples had married in the real world after meeting inside EverQuest; Funcom, the developers of the science fiction world Anarchy Online, claimed the same number of real-world marital successes.

Elsewhere in virtual worlds, romance had become part of the virtual money machine. For Valentine's Day, 2004, Chinese virtual world developer GinSoft sold special edition games vouchers, which entitled residents to playing time, as well as a one-time-only extra: a shower of virtual flowers, to help romance their virtual date.

Not all virtual worlds are as open as Second Life to online sexual experimentation. In Star Wars Galaxies, tame fan events like the 'Mrs Galaxies contest', a beauty pageant for residents' virtual selves, have been permitted, but in some virtual worlds, those who have tried to express their sexuality online have been punished. In January 2006, Blizzard, the makers of World of Warcraft, banned guilds – groups of residents with similar interests – mentioning homosexuality. (Their reasoning, in reference to their 'Sexual Orientation Harassment Policy', was that such an advertisement would incite others to harass the members of gay guilds. In this virtual world, being openly gay was forbidden, because it might incite people to openly dislike gays.)

Virtual worlds have a history of a more permissive attitude to sexual experimentation. In 2000, Richard Bartle spent a long year as Head of Online Games for a start-up company. With a team of six and a budget of almost zero, Bartle decided to try to revive text-only worlds, by giving them sex appeal. He developed a sex-focussed text-only virtual world, with some radically new features never seen in games before (room descriptions that were sense-specific, which, for example, would be described in terms of sound or heat as if you were blindfolded – 'hmm, that feels like the heat from a branding iron' – and actions that were limited by, for example, being tied to the bed). Nonetheless, after eight months, the game was cancelled.

The success of virtual worlds has led to smaller, sex-focussed worlds, dedicated to meeting niche needs. In 'Sociolotron', residents can drug and rape one another; and 'Naughty America', scheduled for launch in late 2006, planned to offer a range of sex-focussed virtual environments: public and private sex areas, cowboy rooms, make-your-own-porn rooms. SeduCity, by Stratagem Corp, is a 2D sex world that launched in 2001 and has 1,500 residents. Red Light Center, in Beta testing at the time of writing, allows people having virtual sex to talk to each other with headsets. Rapture Online, set to launch in 2007, is a 3D sex world designed to be anatomically correct. Developer Kelly Rued hopes couples will use the world to connect when they are apart. It's big business, to the extent that in March 2006, Californian porn company Digital Playground trademarked the term 'Virtual Sex'.

Games have been compared to pornography, and there are parallels: appearance without substance; experience without risk. In October 2006, an Oklahoma judge issued a preliminary injunction against a bill, passed the previous June, that would have made video games and pornography parallel in the eyes of the law. (In September 2005, one porn company, Top of the Food Chain, cashed in on the parallel, releasing a series of videos, with porn stars dressed up in face-paint and pointy ears, called 'Whores of Warcraft'.) In the US, the porn industry grosses between $10 billion and $14 billion a year – about on a par with the video games industry. In the Western world, sex is more and more part of our monetised transactions, demonstrating both how isolated we are – how desperate we have become for phys-ical company, even in imaginary form – but it also highlights how sex has become a refuge, the one place marketeers have steered all our future hopes. We live in a sexualised culture, where we drive ourselves wild with desire and call it advertising, but our fear of the sex urge incites us to look at sex publicly only sideways, through reality TV shows and adverts for shower gel. But within virtual worlds, where the morality police have yet to catch up with us, the virtual pioneers are letting it all hang out. There, many people have online sexual relationships with people they've never met, and every other Second Life resident I met had a naked avatar or a BDSM animation in their virtual back pocket. In virtual worlds, where we are liberated from the restrictions of our bodies, sexuality is often the first area with which people experiment. Many residents see in virtual worlds the seeds of a new kind of utopia: a world free from the dangers of contraception and disease, which recaptures a post-war, pre-AIDS innocence, where gender politics and sexual morality no longer apply. (There are as yet no laws against online bigamy.) Once again, virtual worlds reminded me of the communal experiment I was born into. In virtual worlds, like in communes, there is a different sense of morality; and, like in communes, nothing is truly private. In many virtual worlds, it seemed, we were living a whole new liberated summer of love.

The sexual freedom of my mother's guru's communes had a dark side. 'In a better world, mothers would initiate their sons into sex, fathers their daughters,' my mother's guru Bhagwan once said. In my childhood communes, the occasional girl under 16 would be paired with an adult or a visiting group leader, 'so they could have a good first experience of sex.' There was dark side, I discovered, to virtual sexuality too. In late 2003, Peter Ludlow, professor of philosophy and linguistics at the University of Michigan, journeyed into the seedier side of Alphaville, The Sims Online's capital city. There, among that world's 80,000 residents, he found scammers, a whole Sims neighbourhood devoted to sadomasochism, and 'Evangeline', a virtual madam who managed a stable of virtual prostitutes, exchanging cyber-sex for 'Simoleans' (the Sims virtual currency).

Evangeline was openly racist: Ludlow once walked in on her virtual property to see a dark-skinned avatar trapped with fences, and Evangeline announced she had 'a monkey for sale'. She claimed to have set up the first Sims brothel, in October 2002, and that she earned up to $50 per trick. 'My girls worked hard,'

Evangeline told Ludlow. 'I only hired real cyber sex girls who talked dirty.' Evangeline's girls charged 20,000 Simoleans (then around $4.50) for a virtual blow-job. Richer clients were catered for by Evangeline herself – who, she claimed, charged the equivalent of $40 or $50 per customer. Evangeline sneered at those who worked in the usual ways – known as 'skilling' – to develop their Sims Online fortune. 'Why skill when you can suck dick to keep food on the plate?' she said.

After publishing the interview, Professor Ludlow put in some detective work and published the cyber-madam's true name on his website. 'Evangeline', it turned out, was a 17-year-old boy from Florida, and some of his 'girls' really were underage girls. His work as a virtual prostitute and madam was arguably a major felony. At the virtual frontier, though, real-world law has yet to catch up. Even after Ludlow's article, no prosecutions were brought. Still, his mother did reportedly cancel his Sims account. (Electronic Arts also cancelled Ludlow's account, claiming he had advertised his website in-world; Ludlow insisted his ban was because he had embarrassed the company.)

Electronic Arts didn't like the seedy under-belly of its virtual world being exposed, but in the 'Mature' areas of Second Life, I discovered, as long as it didn't break real-world laws, anything was permitted. There, an ongoing rivalry simmered between two fetish groups: the 'Goreans', who favoured master–slave relationships and sadomasochism (for a world without physical pain, S&M seemed oddly popular); and the 'Furries', who dressed up as animals for fun and sexual kicks. ('I hate the furries,' Philip Rosedale had told me. 'What's up with these people who want to dress up like animals?')

In the PG areas, though, Linden Lab kept a tight control. One virtual sculptor, 'Stormy Roentgen', was upset after copies of one statue – a woman breast-feeding a baby – was removed from PG areas for revealing a nipple.

Virtual worlds seemed to mirror the origins of cinema, in delivering images of bank robberies and porn: for much of Second Life's development, the 20 most popular places in that virtual world were almost all strip clubs. There, in clubs modelled on their real-world equivalents, naked avatars gyrated around chrome poles, and gaping men sat on barstools to watch. Virtual strip-clubs occasionally departed from real-world standards; the naked virtual dancers would sometimes break-dance; virtual men and women on the dance floor would wave virtual dildos. Some strippers had signs above their heads: 'Want sex? IM me.' Many clubs had upstairs rooms, where virtual sex was bought and sold. Prices for virtual sex varied between 500 ($1.60) and 3,000 ($10) Linden Dollars an hour; typically, the club took 20 per cent for every virtual trick. (In one posting on 'The Second Life Herald', a virtual bouncer complained he received a tenth of the wage of the escorts who worked in his club.)

Second Life escorts could also be hired privately, through the virtual classified ads. In October 2006, a search for 'Escorts' in Second Life's directory of users and places brought up 383 results. Each listing came with an image and a description; 'Broken Hearts' was apparently 'a dark, smoky strip club, the kind where the dancers break the rules'; the girls at 'Moist Escorts' were 'hotter than you!' Some were ludicrous: 'Specialty pubes! Stop by to see my awesome collection of specialty pubic hair designs!'; 'Free sex, free cocks, free clothes!'. Some were barely literate: 'Group of sexy horny women hear to pelase you!'. Some escorts offered 'anthro' services, a niche word implying virtual sex with a virtual animal (one escort traded under the name 'Giant Horsefly'). Still more escort services were mafia connected: Carducci's Escorts was partnered with Carducci's Guns,

Employment and Jobs, and Carducci's Horse Track. Would-be punters didn't have to fly blind; at websites like SLescorts.com, residents could read reviews of virtual hookers.

After Ludlow's investigation, 'Evangeline' disappeared. So – purely in the spirit of the story – I decided to rent myself a different virtual escort. I chose Second Life, because that virtual world is only accessible by adults, so there was no risk of a minor at the other end. Nonetheless, I still felt awkward about my first encounter with paid sex (not least because my girlfriend was asleep in the upstairs room). So I roped in a real-world friend to keep me company.

In virtual worlds, we don't have to worry about disease, but there are other dangers. One Second Life resident, wronged in some way by another virtual self – with whom they'd had a virtual relationship that had spread offline, to the extent of exchanging photos – had wreaked a uniquely virtual kind of revenge. They'd built a scripted object, designed to look like a desirable accessory: a red pair of wings, given away free to anyone who clicked on them. These wings, though, had a secret purpose: any time any resident put them on, they broadcast a compromising picture – an image of the victim's real-world self masturbating – to everyone nearby. The outbreak was small, but it was perhaps the first virtual analogue of sexually transmitted diseases.

In my case, I hadn't angered anyone that much – but embarrassment was still a possibility. The real person behind the virtual escort might also be any of the people I'd already met. The chances were slim, but, afraid for my virtual reputation, I created a new virtual self, and logged in under a different name.

There were certain elements of Second Life's sex trade I wanted to steer well clear of. In September 2004, one Second Life resident, 'Sasami Wishbringer', offered her services, through a group called 'The Edge Escorts', as a virtual eight-year old sex slave. ('Small, petite appearance,' her profile read, 'though perky and in the blossom of physical maturity.') She also offered cartoon child porn, although Linden Lab quickly removed it. A year later, one scantily clad World of Warcraft Night Elf called 'Jailbait_15' tried to sell one hour of her sexual services on eBay. 'I have several sexy outfits I can wear for you and getting new ones every day. I love to dress up. You are welcome to take screenshots and make movies of our time together. I am very photogenic!' she wrote in the ad. In the end, no one met the minimum $10 bid.

On the Second Life forums, Robin Harper, Linden Lab's VP of Community Development and Support, posted Linden Lab's response to the Sasami outcry. 'There are people who are role-playing children engaged in sexual activities,' Harper wrote. 'While not a terms-of-service violation – no illegal activity – it could be argued that this behavior is broadly offensive and there-fore violates the community standards.' If they had evidence of any real-world child abuse, she wrote, they would notify the authorities, and close associated Second Life accounts. If resi-dents engaged in inappropriate sexual activity in public areas, they would face similar consequences. There was little more Linden Lab could do. In the US, an actual child has to be involved for child pornography charges to be brought; the Supreme Court has ruled computer-generated images depicting a fictitious 'computer-generated' minor are constitutionally protected. In the UK, even computer-generated sexual images of children were illegal. If Sasami Wishbringer was British, she – and her clients – risked jail-time.

In Second Life I sent an instant message to a madam, and within a minute received a reply: there were two escorts online. The price was 1,000 Linden Dollars (about £1.50) for an hour. I picked an escort at random, and within a minute I received a teleport invite.

I accepted, and re-materialised in what seemed to be upstairs from one of Second Life's many virtual strip-clubs: in a 'VIP' room, decked out in virtual tiger-print wallpaper. Various odd items were dotted around the place: a ball, a bench, wall-shackles. And there, in front of me, was my virtual lady of the night. I made my avatar gulp nervously. She laughed. Then she took off all her clothes.

As far as I knew, my new nubile sex-worker employee could have been, in the real world, a middle-aged man from Texas. (The real world selves behind Second Life residents are approximately 40 per cent female; but, according to Linden Lab, female Second Life residents play for longer, so each virtual self you met was as likely to be a real-world, woman as a real-world man.) 'She' took me through a variety of poses. Following her directions, I clicked on button after button ('Male BJ'; 'Male wall push-up'; 'Male doggy'), and she did the same.

In the Sims Online, there were no sexual animations. Evangeline's girls offered simply dirty-talk in a hot-tub. In Second Life, I discovered, much more was on display. Some of Second Life's most profitable businesses revolved around avatar customisation: dances, hugs, costumes, and avatars in various stages of undress. The default Second Life avatars have no genitalia, but my companion had clearly invested in an avatar 'skin' – Second Life outfits that change your body shape, in this case, to a long-haired, buxom, beautiful blonde – with all the detail filled in. She invited me to kiss her (which meant, basically, walking up close and her typing 'mmm' and '*kiss*'). Then she lay down on the floor and opened her legs.

In Second Life, for more anatomically accurate virtual sex, you had to visit shops like 'The Black Room Genital Shop' to buy gynaecologically realistic selves, and add-on genitalia. I hadn't bothered. She had genitals, but I didn't. My first virtual sexual experience looked oddly like an Action Man getting it on with a red-light girl.

Back in 1678, the first famous British actress, Nell Gwyn, found herself outside a London theatre, sheltering from the rain, next to a young prostitute who'd sought the same refuge. A carriage went past with a young couple messily necking in the back. Gwyn turned to the prostitute. 'Another profession ruined by amateurs,' she said. The escort I had hired didn't want to talk about her virtual life on the record so I searched the classified listings again. (This time, I really was only after conversation, although I wondered how often the girls had heard that line.) During the search, I spotted an ad for 'Femme Fatale'. 'New Zealand's no.1 gentlemen's club has come to Second Life!' it read. The real professionals, it seemed, had stepped in for a cut of the virtual action.

Perhaps understandably, Aurora Walcott, manager of the virtual Femme Fatale, was the one virtual resident I met who was reluctant to give their real-world name. 'I live close to Cleveland, Ohio,' was all she would tell me. There was no way to confirm her story, and there was also a theatrical feel to Aurora's language ('I must say your message ignites my curiosity. When are you typically available here in-world?') that caused me to doubt her story. Still, a month later, when we traded emails, she left her real-world name on by mistake; it was a woman's name. And, even if her story were exaggerated, it might still inform about the way we reinvented ourselves in virtual worlds. I invited her to talk in my virtual office.

Her real identity may have been cloudy; her virtual self was laid bare. When Aurora teleported into space a few feet above my desk, there was something wrong with her dress; all I could see was her body shape, with the word 'Missing' written across it (an occasional Second Life bug). She nipped behind my couch to change outfits, into a tight red boots, a red top, and a short black skirt. I invited her to take a seat wherever she felt comfortable. She perched on my desk, her virtual skirt hiked up, and I could see she had no underwear. I wondered what my neighbours would think. In the virtual world, I could see, my neighbours were out. In the real world, my neighbour's kitchen light was on. I closed my curtains.

This was the story Aurora told me about how she came to work as an escort in Second Life. She had been born with a hole in her heart, she told me. 'I also have leaky valves – like a car,' she said, and laughed. As her virtual self bowed forward, her skirt hiked further up her thighs. A year before she visited my office, when she was 30 years old, she was forced to convalesce for a long period after another heart operation; that was when she first logged on to Second Life. Within a month, she decided to become a madam.

She advertised in the Second Life classifieds for a few weeks, and built up a roster of eight employees. She schooled her 'girls' in dirty talk, and gave them sexy 'skins'. Unlike many virtual escort agency owners, she let her girls keep the money they made. 'I felt that if they were doing the work, they deserved the cash and the returning clients,' she told me. 'I had my own rates.' I saw her rate card: 'Exhibitionism', outdoor or in private, cost 1,000 Linden Dollars (about $3) an hour; 'couple-sharing', a foursome, cost 4,000 Linden Dollars (about $12) for the same amount of time. There were some services she did not offer, including 'Bestiality'. ('Sorry, I love my "bitches",' her rate-card read, 'but not in *that* way.') Payment was always up front. Working new johns alongside regulars, she earned the equivalent of $10 a day, although she put most of the money back into her club.

'Aurora' sounded like it could have been a Kiwi name – but, it turned out, the woman behind the virtual self had never left the US. She'd stumbled on the Femme Fatale club's website, and liked what she saw. 'Although I have yet to even visit New Zealand, I found the club stunning,' she said. 'I also wanted a classy atmosphere for myself here.'

In her real life, Aurora told me, she'd had only one sexual partner. ('Many of my Second Life clients were shocked to learn of my inexperience,' she told me. 'I tend to have lived more erotically in Second Life than in real life.') She came from a strict Catholic background, and her virtual sex work had helped her come to terms with her own real-world lack of experience and confidence. Also, she felt it was safer than real-world experimentation. 'This was a learning experience for me,' she said. 'I never willingly had anal sex. Now, I ask for it.'

Aurora's real-world partner didn't know about her online escort work; he too lived a virtual life, but he preferred World of Warcraft. Although she said he would laugh if he heard, she preferred not to tell him. She was careful to keep her virtual life and real life separate – apart from one early slip. 'I only allowed one person to see me on web cam,' she said. 'That became a nightmare. It was early in my online life, so to speak. We had even exchanged phone numbers. I haven't thought about this since it happened. He would call numerous times each day, for months.'

Aurora blanked his calls. 'Then, I read he had committed suicide. He wrote me a letter the night before, asking why I wouldn't talk to him anymore.'

Once again, I wondered how much of her story was true. There was another reason to mistrust her words: Aurora, it turned out, was a writer, of as yet unpublished suspense novels. ('I have my own filing cabinets of rejections,' she said.) She saw her escort work as a mode of fiction, which gave her 'the experience taking on a new genre as a writer'. 'The "art" in escorting in Second Life is in the written form,' she said.

According to Aurora, the bad experience in the real world planted the seeds of the end of her life as an escort. Also, she had met another man, another Second Life resident; they had feelings for each other, and had considered meeting in real life.

It was time to leave 'the life' behind. Also, she had other plans. Sex workers have ambitions, and it seemed this was true in the virtual world too. After six months, Aurora had closed her escort agency to go into business, a natural progression from her work as a madam. Like the call-girls in *LA Confidential*, cut to look like movie stars, Aurora and her girls – taking advantage of their new virtual flexibility – once offered virtual sex in the guise of a whole range of female stars. The girl might model for an hour, trying on different celebrity skins, until the client decided whom he wanted. (I asked who was the most popular. 'I'd say Pamela Anderson and Angelina Jolie are tied,' she said. One client asked for 'a transgender', and another asked for Jack Nicholson. She obliged both. Aurora found it remarkable – a sign of our times – when some clients wanted something other than a celebrity. 'Interestingly enough, there were often clients who preferred the "girl next door" look,' she said.)

Now, along with one of her employees, she had left sex work behind. She now made a better virtual living selling her hand-sculpted celebrity selves to other residents. Business, she said, was booming. She showed me round her store, a three-levelled complex, with a virtual porn theatre and a picture of the porn star Jenna Jameson (with a caption, 'Going Down?') in the lift. On the walls were pictures of her celebrities (*Buffy* star Sarah Michelle Gellar, Janet Jackson, J-Lo) next to images of their real-world selves. Some looked more life-like than others. (I couldn't resist; for 500 Linden Dollars, about £1, I picked up a copy of Drew Barrymore. Aurora, delighted at my custom, offered me a free Vin Diesel; I turned her down.) I asked what was included in the price; apparently, not everything. 'Unfortunately, cocks are purchased separately,' she said.

Like Alayne, Aurora told me her second life had improved her first one. 'It's connected me with a new sense of myself,' she said. 'I've crossed paths I once was too fearful to cross even in my own imagination.' I asked what kinds of paths. 'Being sexually adventurous,' she said. 'Learning what pleases me. How to reciprocate.'

Reciprocation was what Kyle Machulis, aka Second Life resident qDot Bunnyhug, had in mind when he built a vibrator that could be scripted to activate in time to Second Life virtual sex. In October 2006, Kyle, who a year and a half before built a homebrew dildo attachment for Microsoft's Xbox console (the 'SeXBox'), released his vibrator script to the Second Life public. (Kyle told me he had even made a sex toy controller for text-worlds.) His field, he said, was 'teledildonics': computer-controlled sex toys, linked together across the Internet. In a talk at Second Life Community Convention, a real-life gathering in San Francisco, Kyle told the crowd he saw no surprise in the surge of virtual fetishism. He mentioned 'pony play', a sexual fetish where one or both partners halters up and acts like a pony. In the real world, the harness and equipment would cost over $5,000; in Second Life, it cost $2. In a presentation at the convention, Kyle demonstrated his vibrator. He pulled up an example avatar, a blue cube – 'an ordinary cube. But if you *are* a cube, it's kind of hot,' he said – and, in the real world, pulled out a 'Rez Trance' vibrator, a customised add-on for an innocent PlayStation 2 game, Rez, which was originally intended to augment that game's synaesthetic gameplay by vibrating in the player's pocket. In 2004, Jane Pritchard of the website Game Girl advance, wrote an article about having sex with the Rez Trance vibrator, and a thriving secondary market arose in Rez Trance vibrators, which at the time fetched $30 on eBay (although, after Kyle launched his Second Life plug-in, he joked, the eBay asking price for Rez Trance vibrators doubled). At the conference, Kyle demonstrated his Second Life script; when the cube moved up, the vibrator moved up; when the cube moved down, the vibrator moved down. It was a proof of concept, which enabled Second Life designers, using the Rez Trance vibrator, to build any sex toy they wanted.

'While this was mainly interesting to me from an engineering standpoint – the same technology could be used for things like driving or flying games in-world or something, I just happened to deal with sex toys – the actual need soon became much more apparent,' Kyle told me. 'There are quite a few people that use SL for sex. They might feel uncomfortable using a web cam or audio setup, or they might have certain needs that cannot be fulfilled through that medium. So, the augmentation of being able to do damn near anything you can think of, and some things you can't, and some things you don't want to . . . in Second Life, *combined* with the physical interaction, made the world much more immersive.'

Devices like Kyle's vibrator further blur the line between real and imaginary connection. Does virtual sex with someone who is not your real-world partner count as cheating? The dilemma has been with us, in a simpler form, for millennia. Thinking about sex with someone other than your wife – 'lusting in your heart' – is infidelity, apparently Jesus said. Many would disagree. But talking dirty with a virtual self while having sex with a machine? I'm sure my girlfriend wouldn't be happy if she walked in on that. (Although I suspect no one would.)

Had my girlfriend been serious about her virtual two-timing worries, there were people who could help. Inside Second Life, for 100 Linden Dollars an hour – plus virtual expenses – you could hire Marki Macdonald, a virtual PI, to set up a 'honey-trap' and tempt your partner into virtual infidelity. Similar services were available in other virtual worlds too. I found an advert on eBay: 'Introducing: Sim Spies, at your service.'

'Sure it seems innocent enough playing The Sims Online, but a person not necessarily looking for an affair can be drawn into the flirtatious world of chat and become a cheater. Beware! If your mate frequently stays up after you've gone to bed and they are doing more typing then clicking, it could be a warning sign.

'You do not need to spend another night lying awake in bed waiting for them to come to bed. You do not need to go weeks on end without making love or endure the gut-wrenching pain of longing for them to "touch you like they used to". If you're sick and tired of not being able to eat, not being able to sleep, and struggling every day with sadness and uncertainty . . . then we are here for you.

'This auction includes our team of Sim investigators going undercover to dig up all the dirt and expose those cheating Sims. We have a team of undercover Sim Divas that can try and initiate contact to see if they deny being in a relationship, or if they are looking for any fun on the side. You will receive screenshots of all chat and private messages and actions. You can finally have the proof you need to confront them and see the shock on their face when they know that they are busted and have been caught up in their web of lies.'

Like all good marketeers, the Sim Spies sowed anxiety to reap a profit. 'Can you trust them? Find The Truth Out Now!'

14

MY VIRTUAL SISTER
Beyond the nuclear family

In real life, sex builds families. In the virtual world, people are born whole. Second Life is over-18 only, and residents discovered to be under-age are immediately banned. (In the early days of Second Life, some well-known virtual designers were ejected in this way.) There is another, separate Second Life, called the Teen Grid, open only to minors, but no connection is permitted between the worlds. When residents of the Teen Grid turn 18, Linden Lab transfers them to the main Second Life universe. They have to leave their younger friends behind, so Teen Grid residents have developed their own tradition: a 'REZuation' party, to say goodbye, and to commemorate their graduation from the smaller pond into the larger ocean of virtual adulthood.

In my strolls around virtual shopping malls, I had seen virtual animated babies, which cried and demanded attention. Residents who acquired these babies could even go through a simulated 'birthing' process, with virtual doctors and midwives – and some women had claimed the process had helped them come to terms with miscarried or stillborn children. Some residents, I knew, role-played as children, for their virtual 'adoptive' parents – but in any real sense, virtual selves couldn't have virtual offspring.

In one survey, 80 per cent of virtual world residents had no real-world children; it could be that the demands of real-world children preclude the spare time to live another life. But virtual worlds, with their ability to conquer distance, were intersecting with our newly separated family lives too.

In my own life, my virtual lives had made my family life easier. My father, with whom I had connected through early computer games, still lived in another country – and we still connected occasionally through computers. After I moved into my real-world flat, we played a game of Risk online, and, once I'd set up my virtual office, I invited him to come for a visit.

After my father had logged on to Second Life – he chose one of the default body shapes, a kind of futuristic cyber-Goth that looked a bit like an evil clown – I showed him round my office. (He hadn't finished the process of customising his character into his own unique virtual self, and the bug that had made Aurora Walcott's dress disappear had infected his eyes; when I looked closely at his new face, each eye had 'missing' written across the iris.) We sat down for a minute and watched a short film. Wanting to show him around, I took him to the spaceport, which modelled the history of space travel; my father and I swooped among the history of rocketry, between scale-models of Russian Vostok and American Apollo orbital launch rockets.

I wondered aloud what else he might want to see. 'It's alright,' he said. 'I think I've seen enough.' I felt sad. I'd visited him in person two months before, but this was the first time we'd spoken since then. The 'missing' tag across his eyes seemed ironic; since I was two, we'd lived apart, and I'd often missed his presence in my life. We'd always had difficulty reaching each other, and even here, in Second Life, it wasn't easy to connect.

The oddness of my father's virtual appearance – especially the spiky leather wristbands – reminded me of the few times he and I had met in another virtual world, World of Warcraft. Some virtual worlds, like Second Life, offer you the chance to change almost every aspect of your virtual self. In others, like the phenomenally successful World of Warcraft (with, as I write, 7.5 million residents), there is less room to choose. You can elect to belong to one of six races (including elves, dwarves, and humans), and you can alter a few other small details, like eye or hair colour. Later, as you progress, you acquire new clothes and armour that help you on your way, but the overall effect is a world of near-identical residents, like a residential theme park, where all the employees and visitors wore the same costumes. In World of Warcraft, tasks (hunt goblins, deliver this letter to the king) are set for your virtual character right from your virtual birth, so the world is full of people running back and forth on the same quests, like people repeating rides at Disneyland. My father had played World of Warcraft for over a year, so his character was far more powerful than mine; when I logged on to visit him, he agreed to meet me back near the beginner's town to take a look around.

My father lives in Germany, and played on a German server; for fun, I gave my new virtual self a German-sounding name, 'Günter the Hunter'. When I arrived – I flew down to land on the back of a griffin – he was waiting on the dock for me. 'Hi,' I said.

'Sorry, I can't talk,' he said. 'I'm waiting to meet my son.'

After I persuaded him it was really me, we hung out in World of Warcraft for an hour or so. There was little to do apart from complete quests, so we ran around killing ghosts to collect gold. After a while, the tasks were so similar, all sense of our identities seemed to disappear. I realised, my virtual father could have been anyone.

Now that video games were not just for kids – at the time of writing, half of US households own a dedicated games-playing machine, and, in those households, 20 per cent of gamers are over 50, and more American 18–49 year olds than under-18s indulge – virtual worlds had also become a place where generations connect. Despite my mixed success in connecting with my father that way, the same was true for me, too.

My half-sister, in her early teens, also plays World of Warcraft. In May 2006, for her birthday, I bought her some virtual gold. I logged on to IGE.com, selected the World of Warcraft European Server, Onyxia, paid $36.90 from my credit card, and the next day – her birthday – she received 500 virtual gold pieces. (Technically, the transaction was against the laws of the world. I did worry I might get her banned, separate herself from her beloved virtual life – but nearly a year later, she was still online.) With the character our father had helped her create, she went on a virtual shopping spree. A few days later I logged on again, and she came to meet me on the same dock where I'd met my father. She had virtual friends, she said, but none were around, so she suggested instead that we take a walk. Her character, an elf called Anela, took me for a stroll through the deserts and jungles of Azeroth. My sister lived with my father in Germany; this was the first time we'd hung out in six months.

She took me on a tour of her world, pausing considerately every few minutes to let me catch up, as I walked the long distance from the nearest graveyard after being munched by every passing scarecrow or T rex. (Her character was level 40; mine was level 1.) She showed me the new clothes she'd bought with my virtual gift (her favourite was a new pointy hat), and her virtual horse, called 'Horse'. She led me carefully through the rainforests of Stranglewood. The local fauna, scenting easy prey, pounced at every turn. A nearby 'Murkgill Warrior', aiming for me, saw my sister and attempted to run away in fear; she killed him and stole his fish oil. She slayed and skinned a passing wolf.

She showed me a village, populated by enemy players, where she liked to hide and jump out to attack. One enemy, a dwarf named Grimbat, did pass by, but my sister was in a generous mood; she waved, and the nervous passer-by waved back. 'I don't kill him,' she said.

'Ah,' I said. 'Very nice of you.'

Another three enemies passed by, chased by a pack of dinosaurs. My sister stepped in to help; the others escaped, but my sister was killed. In the meantime, as she strolled back from the graveyard, a passing enemy player strolled up and knifed me in the back, killing me instantly. My sister wanted revenge, but I hadn't had time to get his name.

Our father's birthday present to her had been a new PC. Up to then, she'd had to borrow our dad's PC to play. Now, she could play from her room, and the two of them could play online together.

I was born in the seventies, in the decade where people – and especially families – drifted apart. (The seventies are the only decade in which Richard Dreyfuss's character Roy Neary, in *Close Encounters of the Third Kind*, would believably trade his family for the company of some passing aliens.) Like many children of the seventies, I, too, experienced the agonies of separation. When I was four, my mother and I moved into the communes of her guru – a bearded man-god who promised ecstasy and delivered mainly absence. I was supposed to be the child of the commune, not of my mother. (My father already lived elsewhere.) In the communes that bore Bhagwan's name, she and her friends danced, rolled their heads, swayed their arms, beat cushions, broke down their social conditioning and set themselves free. Meanwhile, we children filled our lives as best we could with the things we found around us.

I filled the space with my imagination. Bhagwan had already

stripped away our past and our Lego; then he began to predict the end of the world, through nuclear war and disease. I began to imagine this had already happened. In my daytime reveries, hidden behind a commune sofa with a doorstop Marmite sandwich, I clambered over the rubble of civilisation. By chance, I had uncovered the purpose of the imagination: to conquer absence. Our dreams give us a lens through which to examine what we lack – just as virtual worlds do.

Through the electronic looking glass, relationships within families, the heart of so much conflict, can be eased, too. In January 2006, a survey showed that 30 per cent of parents play games with their children, and two-thirds of those felt those games had brought their families closer. Now even estranged families can use online worlds to stay close. As one father, Clay Thompson, explained to *Computer Games Magazine*, he had arranged for a specific clause in his divorce decree to allow for three hours of online contact per week; they lived apart, but he could spend time with his children online. 'My son loves it when I make him invulnerable and spawn dragon after dragon in Neverwinter Nights,' he said, of their time together in one virtual world. 'My daughters and I hit the shopping block in ToonTown and then go back to their virtual home to try them on together. It was the most fun I've ever had online, just hearing them giggle.' In World of Warcraft, Thompson found he enjoyed the role of a healer; casting spells to keep his children alive felt good.

(Virtual worlds don't always bring families together. In April 2006, in Dunedin, Florida, father Joseph Langenderfer burst into his son's room after an argument, waving a pistol. Joseph thought his son spent too much time playing online games instead of doing the laundry. His plan was to shoot his son's computer. The bullet hit the wall instead, and Langenderfer Snr was held for attempted murder.)

My own mother's addiction, to her guru, took her away from me for nearly 10 years. I found her again, but that discovery delivered its own kind of trouble. It turns out we can leave our families, or we can stay, but they break our hearts either way.

Perhaps, though, we can now enact our stretched-out family heartbreak through virtual worlds, as we have examined them through the lens of cinema. 'My son and I have become much closer through gaming,' Clay Thompson continued. 'It offers quality time I wouldn't get otherwise. I'm taking care of my kids online like I would if I was there.'

Thompson was careful, though, to try to avoid his children's enjoyment of virtual worlds slipping into a full-blown addiction. 'I've seen kids addicted to everything from TV to Gameboy Advances to MMORPGs to card games like Pokemon – and so much more,' he told the website Gamer Dad. 'When I see my son throw a tantrum about playing, or he misses dinner, or refuses to go to bed on time, or wants to play online versus with his guest he invited over – well, it's time for a talk, and in some cases, a grounding of a couple of days off the PC.' (Clay wasn't averse, either, to making himself invisible and following his son around the virtual world, to make sure he was OK.)

My father had worked with computers his whole career, so he was comfortable with his daughter playing World of Warcraft, although he did limit her time online. But virtual worlds, with their capacity to distract children from the real world, made some parents anxious. Links between computer games and violence among children have been argued for decades. In December 2006, the German Minister of the Interior backed a law that, if passed, would criminalise the development, publishing, and playing of violent games. Under the law, my own time inside Counterstrike, shooting virtual terrorists, would have been punishable by jail time. The concerns are perhaps understandable, given that, in Europe, 60 per cent of children play video games every day – but the facts don't seem to support a moral crusade. US video game sales doubled between 1996 and 2004; in the same period, violent crime halved. Some studies have shown that children with computers at home perform slightly less well at school – and other studies have shown that constant use of email can dull our thinking as much as smoking weed. But there's an argument, too, that video games make us less repressed, by giving us a risk-free outlet for basic violent impulses that society cannot condone. Video games are perhaps, as a games store I once saw advertised, 'Beyond Therapy'. In early 2006, Edinburgh police began a scheme to combat anti-social behaviour: they hosted weekly video game contests, between trouble-makers and police. (The police tended to win at the driving games; the kids tended to win at virtual football.) Since the scheme began, the number of youth-related crimes in the area has fallen by half.

Virtual worlds offer children other kinds of refuges, too. A Portuguese organisation called the Assocciacao Recreativa para a Computacao e Informatica uses Second Life as a virtual refuge for abused children in Portuguese safe houses. They invite children into the game, then help them with social and technical skills inside the virtual world.

Unarguably, video games do reduce the time we spend in our bodies. At the time of writing, an American child is six times more likely to play a video game than ride a bike. But new, mechanised forms of imagination have long been seen as threats to our children. Public cinema began in 1894; by 1896, in the French short *Le Coucher de la Marie*, actress Louise Willy was naked on film. Early cinema 'coin-up parlours' were seen as a moral threat, and laws banning them were debated in the US senate – even early novels were regarded by some as a threat to the young, in case they distracted devout children from religious texts. In each case, with the introduction of a new form of expression, the younger generation had helped us bring those shared illusions into the culture. Through play, it seems, kids teach us each new media's opportunities and limits.

All play is a way to create a small, safe environment in which to act ourselves out, without fear of harmful consequence. As children, we make our world, and inhabit it to discover ourselves. Mindful of the crucial role the young would play in determining how virtual worlds affect our lives, I decided to talk with someone from the next generation who was at home in virtual worlds.

In November 2006, Linden Lab announced its plans to open up its server software in the foreseeable future, allowing others to set up and manage their own virtual worlds. But, driven by the political pressure of inhabiting someone else's world – and by the real-world financial pressure of virtual world subscription fees – smaller, homebrew universes had already sprung up elsewhere.

Years before, I'd read the work of Dr Henry Jenkins, Director of the Comparative Media Studies Program at MIT, who called computer games 'virtual play spaces': areas where young adults, in an urbanised world with scarce empty land, can find 'complete freedom of movement' to explore themselves outside society's moral gaze. I'd never seen as literal example, though, as 17-year-old Todd Robertson. He and his friends, landlocked in the urban sprawl of north London, hadn't built a clubhouse, or colonised a corner of a favourite pub; they built their own virtual world.

In July 2004, an NCsoft employee leaked the official Lineage II server files – the data which enabled them to run a world. Soon, enterprising players realised that, with some time and money, they could set up private versions of Lineage II, and run their own universes. Two years later, private virtual worlds were a booming business. (In China, where broadband prices are low but game subscriptions relatively high, one private server had 50,000 residents. In 2006, Chinese publishing company Shanda sued Actoz, the developers of their virtual world Legend of Mir II, after the source files were leaked onto the Internet; fewer players would pay for the 'authentic' virtual world, Shanda argued, when they could play in the same world for free elsewhere.)

The most successful private universe – L2Extreme, a version of Lineage II with five different server-worlds – had tens of thousands of residents online at a time. Websites like Gamers 200 listed the top 200 Lineage II servers, each advertised with basic travel-brochure copy, designed to encourage you to visit their world: 'Shops!'; 'Sympathetic ambience!'; 'Fishing!'.

Todd's partners started their journey into virtual worlds as a core of three north London school friends. At first, they played online war games like Counterstrike, but they soon discovered Lineage II. After only a few months, they moved to private servers, because there they had more fun; they could advance their virtual selves faster, because the world was tweaked to help them along; there seemed to be more events, a feeling of community and exclusivity, which kept them playing. They moved from server to server, conquering and growing bored with each in turn, all the while talking about how they could do it better themselves. For a long time, it was just talk, until one evening another player – whom they'd fought alongside in Lineage II, but never met in real life – liked their ideas and offered to bankroll their own server. They made plans, and another Swedish friend offered a high-end PC as a test bed. With some basic knowledge of C++, a programming language, and a lot of time, they chose a section of the Lineage II universe, and sculpted it to their desires.

Then their shadowy financier pulled out. Still, it seemed a shame to waste the work, so they raised the money themselves, rented a server box, christened their new world L2Supremacy, and moved in.

When I first met with Todd to discuss his private universe, his server was a month old; he and his friends already had a stable peak-time population of a hundred or so players. As the tasks of managing a universe grew, Todd became is the Event Manager. In a custom area they christened 'The Coliseum', he organised virtual tournaments, where players competed for virtual prizes.

According to Henry Jenkins, the purpose of our new virtual wastelands was to escape the prying eyes and order of society. In homebrew virtual worlds like Todd's, rule-breaking, or attempted rule-breaking, came with the territory. To help prevent trouble makers, Todd and his friends used a series of tricks they picked up on their travels through different private Lineage II servers. They added a delay to the login screen, to plug one popular loophole where people could log in twice and gain a virtual advantage. Also, they added a series of invisible, name-less creatures, hidden in inaccessible areas below the surface of their world, which would crash the client when they are clicked on; this stopped automated software, with names like 'L2Walker', which were designed to advance your virtual self's skills auto-matically while you were away from your PC. Todd even had rivals. A group of their online friends, who had been part of the same clan until Todd's group split to build their server, set up their own server, L2Frenzy. 'The day after we announced ours,' Todd told me, 'they coincidentally announced they were doing it too.' The other group has attempted to sabotage L2Supremacy; overloading their website, and hacking into their world with GM privileges to wreak havoc. Todd insisted they didn't retaliate. 'We're doing better than them,' he told me, referring to their higher rank in the Gamers 200. 'As long as we're on top, I don't mind,' Todd told me with a grin.

Todd's older sister told me she worried about the time he spent in virtual worlds; about the lack of real social interaction, and the possibility that Todd would meet strange men on the Internet. I told her I wasn't worried. He was at the forefront of a new movement that seemed only set to continue. (In August 2006, the latest Lineage II update, Chronicle 5, was also leaked. The rumour Todd heard was an NCsoft insider received $10,000; the site which bought the server files sold it on for $5,000 – and soon the files were everywhere online.) Todd and his friends were learning to manage their own finances, as well as the economy of their whole world. Server space and bandwidth cost money, so most private servers offered their players the chance to 'donate'. In practice, most donations were rewarded with gifts of powerful items. (The ratio of effort to reward was greatly improved. L2Extreme sold weapons for between $50 and $130, and a level 80 character, fully powered up, for $150. For comparison, at Team VIP, a third-party broker for virtual items, a level 63 character on a US commercial Lineage II server would have cost you $408.49.) The donation process was very popular – and cheap compared to playing the retail game. Some servers made serious money. On one week, L2Extreme reportedly pulled in $24,000; they regularly closed their donation process, Todd told me, so they could catch up on delivering the freebie items. One of Todd's motivations for setting up his own server was his egalitarian ideal. Much like in real-world politics, those running these private virtual worlds shone favour on their friends, and those who donated money. 'On those other servers, there's a lot of favouritism,' Todd told me. 'In L2Supremacy, we're very fair.' If virtual worlds were the new Wild West, they wanted to depose the corrupt sheriff, and put the people in charge.

Todd and his friends had worked hard to build their world, and now they could enjoy their god-like powers. They could create anything, be anything, kill anyone. 'We can make ourselves invisible,' he told me. 'I can turn myself into a tree, and watch people wander by.' But it wasn't all fun. With his friends, through hard work and strong political ideals, Todd had built an entire world. Now he had to manage it. Because they hoped for as many residents as possible, they realised they needed to slow the supply of powerful items, so new players don't begin at a total disadvantage. To reduce demand, they raised their prices.

Todd was learning to manage people, too. Their world was growing faster than they could cope; they were forced to take on staff, and it fell to Todd to interview prospective new gods. I asked what kind of questions you ask a potential employee, who'll help you run a world. He thought for a moment. 'One question I asked,' he said, was, 'If you told someone to stop doing something disruptive, and immediately, right in front of you, they did it again, what would you do?'

'Ban them?' I guessed.

Todd shook his head. 'We want people to stay on our server.' The correct answer, he said, was 'Turn them to stone for two hours, to think about what they'd done.'

When I first met John Lester inside Second Life, he showed me Brigadoon, the island refuge he'd built for BrainTalk's Asperger's sufferers. We met on top of the island's single hill, in a structure he'd placed before any residents moved into Brigadoon: a Greek temple, modelled on a real-world Temple of Zeus, overlaid with photos of original mosaics. 'I remember I was telling someone about this Greek temple I had made,' he told me, of the unique relationship with even colossal objects in virtual worlds. 'And I said, wait, here let me pull it out. You can store anything in your inventory, and so I pulled this Greek temple basically out of my pocket. I said, let's sit in the temple and talk.' (Brigadoon wasn't all so serious; later, John showed me the beach hot-tub, meant to encourage a more relaxed kind of interaction.)

John's prototype amphitheatre seemed appropriate, a metaphor for what many people hoped virtual worlds would deliver: a new kind of public-spirited, civic society, where residents could still have a direct effect on the shape and function of their world. There, high on the virtual mountain air, amid the inspirational scenery, we loftily discussed the importance of fantasy life to the proper evolution of young souls.

I mentioned a book I had read not long before, Bruno Bettelheim's *The Uses of Enchantment*. 'He talks about the importance of fairy tales, culture's dream-life, in the proper development of moral and psychic strength in children,' I told him.

'I will have to check it out,' John said.

'He talks about how fairy tales speak to children's unconscious, and give them clues to life's essential, difficult dilemmas, in a way that an adult could never simply explain,' I said.

'We watch other people's dreams on TV, in movies, and even in video games now,' John said. 'Our culture isn't growing the way it used to, from the people up. Nobody shares or makes up stories much anymore. That's what television is for.'

'Yes,' I said. My virtual self nodded earnestly.

'But in virtual worlds – well, in Second Life – everything here is created by people. There's no Disney,' John said.

That was true – but not for long.

15

CORPORATIONS
Branding virtual dreams

When I missed my first appointment with Rivers Run Red, Second Life's leading British virtual branding agency, I expected a rain check to be straightforward. A few days later, I received a reply from a company: Blackberry. 'Finally out of the woods – scratched to bits and beetles in my hair!' The company clearly wasn't an everyday branding agency.

In fact, when I finally met Justin Bovington, co-founder with his wife Louise of Rivers Run Red, at their east London offices – painted entirely white, like their Second Life island – I realised we'd met before. When I arrived, the pair handed me their business cards: on the one side were their real world details, and on the other, their full-colour Second Life selves. Justin's virtual self, in a blue and black chequered shirt, looked like a groovy dad; Louise's other self, Jordie, looked like a stripper. Although this was the first time we had sat side-by-side in real life, Justin's Second Life avatar, Fizik Baskerville, had met mine, Errol Mysterio, in early 2004, over a chat with Wagner James Au (at the time, I think, we were hovering over a Dr Seuss wonderland complete with giant purple spiral candy sticks).

For a long time, corporations were surprisingly uninventive

about how to extend their brands into virtual worlds. In July 2006, an in-game advertising company, Massive Inc., launched a kind of virtual billboard they called, snappily, 'interactive advertisement technology' (essentially a 3D model of a Toyota Yaris). In September 2005, the US bank Wells Fargo had dipped its toe a little deeper into virtual worlds, with Second Life's Stagecoach Island: an invite-only corner of the virtual world designed to teach financial literacy to young people (while also promoting Wells Fargo bank). It would seem, though, that companies who wanted a successful presence in virtual worlds had to try harder. People are attracted to virtual worlds because they want to take part; ads that tried to press a message didn't seem likely to grab their attention. 'You don't walk into someone's house and demand they look at something,' Justin told me. 'So we don't do that in Second Life. What we do is corral it. We can set up areas where people can come and take part, enjoy themselves; they can opt in, or opt out.'

In the early days of virtual worlds, brands ran free. When I joined Second Life, you could buy a virtual Adidas T-shirt for a hundredth of the price of a real one, and none of the money went to Adidas. Any virtual world developer would, when issued take-down notices, remove any trademarked material – but back then, no one seemed to notice. By the time I met with Rivers Run Red, that had begun to change. Over the summer of 2006, after a rush of publicity about virtual worlds, and Second Life in particular – with the early tipping point perhaps the May 2006 appearance of Second Life on the cover of *Business Week* – corporations had begun to pay attention. (In one meeting of a multinational entertainment company, Justin told me, someone from top management, discussing their billion-dollar budget, turned to his Creative Director and said: 'What's our Second Life strategy?' The Creative Director had no idea what he meant, but he found out fast.) When we met, Rivers Run Red's clients included the BBC and Disney; they had created a virtual premiere of *X-Men 3* from within Second Life, with a live camera feed from the red carpet in Cannes. (After this event, so many virtual snapshots of the event were uploaded onto the picture-sharing website Flickr, that the Flickr management decided to ban virtual images from their site completely.) To help promote the film *The Hitchhiker's Guide to the Galaxy*, they built a virtual Marvin the Paranoid Android. Since the *Business Week* article, Justin said, 'everything has changed. Last year, 80 per cent of our business was real-world business. Now, 80 per cent of our business is virtual-world business.'

'Advertisers love Second Life,' Justin said. 'Second Life is fluid and quick enough to measure the results immediately. You can create something that's immediately relevant for that moment.'

For many, it seemed, taking up any kind of place in a virtual world meant upsetting those who are already there. As Justin reminded me, Rivers Run Red had its own difficult virtual birth. In December 2003, they bought the first Second Life virtual island at auction, for $1,250 – many times what residents expected it to cost. The residents, defensive at the best of times, were outraged – even more so when they discovered Rivers Run Red were a corporate agency. There were protests: Second Life residents held banners with crossed out Disney and Gap logos, and some conducted mock-terrorist attacks on their island, Avalon. Over time, though, the company's commitment to working with residents became clear. They employed a whole group of full-time, virtual employees, spread across the real world, who, Justin told me, they felt they knew, even though they had never met in real life. By the time of my visit, their concern to respect the existing Second Life culture had calmed their detractors. 'We've turned down a lot of work that wasn't right for the community,' Justin told me. 'One of the largest PR projects that has happened in there, we felt, was counterproductive to the creative' aspirations of the residents. You can't just dump stuff in here and expect people to take an interest.'

Their growing influence in the Second Life community was mirrored in their geographic location: Avalon, their 16-acre island, was directly in the centre of the Second Life map. After they spoke at the 2006 Second Life Community Convention in New York, where virtual friends could meet the real selves behind them, their importance to the community, and to Linden Lab, was set. (Justin confessed he had even been given a few Linden Lab Second Life logo pendants.) 'We made a promise to the community, Justin told me. 'We would never ever do billboard advertising, nothing traditional. We would always develop our ideas with the community.' They work hard, he explained, to create something that gives both ways, so they are 'engaging consumers in a conversation by permission.' Their ethos was to make sure consumers wanted to interact with the brands, as distinct from what Justin referred to as the 'interruption culture' of the TV commercial. 'People I talk to think young consumers are apathetic,' Justin told me. 'They're not apathetic. They're just very well defended against advertising. They're too busy living their own lives.'

Once again, it seemed virtual worlds had the capacity to help reverse the order of things. In the real world, corporations used people; in virtual worlds, perhaps, people could begin to earn back some control. Rivers Run Red was commissioned by Reebok to help build its virtual brand value. Keen to add value over existing virtual sneakers, they designed a store in which residents could customise Reebok shoes to their own desires. In the first month, Justin told me, the store sold 18,000 pairs. Their ultimate aim was to take the most popular virtual design and market it in real life. In May 2006, Rivers Run Red organised a virtual festival, inside Second Life, to coincide with a real-world BBC Radio 1 music event at Camperdown, Dundee. In total, 6,000 people attended the virtual event, which was also projected onto screens in Dundee. 'We watched it happening,' Justin told me. 'Every hour, a new time zone came online. As the Americans went to bed, the Koreans were getting up. People were wandering around Second Life, telling other people to come and see.' They'd planned the Second Life festival to last four hours; after two days, they needed some sleep; they shut the festival down. The next afternoon, Justin logged back on; even without the music, the party was still gong. 'Some guy arrived with his helicopter and got out with his posse. There was a guy with a wheelchair who was dancing with someone else dressed as Bertie Basset. Then there was a bee craze; someone came dressed as a bee, then everyone left to get bee costumes. We didn't have to do too much; the avatars themselves became the theatre.'

Rivers Run Red made a living in the corporate world, and something of that world's awkward language occasionally leaked into their conversation. At a conference talk I attended, Justin broke humankind into marketing categories: passive recipients, active interpreters, engaged participants, and soon, apparently, we would all be 'monetising'. Rivers Run Red was doing some monetising of its own; *Business Week* reported the company charged between $5,000 and $1 million per campaign (although Justin insisted most of the accounts were in the lower end of the range).

Justin told me he saw Second Life as broadband's 'killer app'. ('Shopping on the Internet turned out to be just catalogues online,' he told me. 'Second Life has the capacity to be so much more.') To Justin, virtual worlds were a place in which all our previously distinct modes of art and expression came together. This was true for companies, he said – 'We are a games company, a film production company and a design company, all at the same time' – but also for people, including himself. 'Second

Life has enabled me be the painter I've always wanted to be,' he told me. 'I can be a painter, a filmmaker, a writer and a designer all in one place. I love it.'

When I spoke with Bill Trost, lead designer of EverQuest, in 2002, he told me he thought virtual worlds could become the dominant mass media. 'The more people play these types of games, the more variety we will see in the types of experiences they offer,' he said. 'I really believe that the variety and quality of content offered in MMORPGs will soon rival that currently being offered on cable TV. I think Sony Online Entertainment is in a good position to become the HBO of the Internet.'

When I visited the Rivers Run Red offices, the company was planning to explore these possibilities in depth. With Rob Marchant, a young TV director, they were setting up a virtual TV studio, to film avatars in the same way as in a real studio. They planned to launch the first fully virtual TV channel, 'VirtualLife.TV', and make Second Life avatars virtual TV stars within the world. They were in discussion with major TV networks, and planned to launch, 24 hours a day, with an additional 1,000 hours of original programming, including many films made inside Second Life.

Talking about their upcoming projects, Justin's face lit up. His fascination with virtual worlds was clear. He adhered so closely to his virtual self, he told me, that his staff have nicknamed him 'Howard Hughes' – 'I never leave the island,' he said.

No wonder his employees needed some time in the woods. They'd been there, it turned out, for a survival course with the British television naturalist Ray Mears. It seemed like the perfect antidote to a virtual life, but even in their time off, they found they had Second Life on the brain. Justin told me how he held up a stick, twisted it at Ray Mears' instructions for making kindling, and he had joked that it looked like virtual hair. 'It reminded me of Second Life,' he told me. 'What people remember about Second Life, the most memorable thing they do at first, is to grab a texture, and bring something from the real world – a photo of themselves, their partner or their cat – into the virtual world. They've projected a level of personality into their virtual surroundings. People automatically get it. It's like making things, even at the most basic level, out of twigs. Out in the woods, we were playing with fire, and we felt like we were reliving a key moment in human evolution.'

I asked if he saw the emergence of Second Life as a parallel moment in evolution. 'Absolutely,' Justin said.

As virtual worlds like Second Life began to make headlines in corporate publications like *Business Week*, big business had begun to take note. A week after I visited Rivers Run Red, I received an email from Rory Caren, a Media Relations Manager at IBM UK. IBM's global Vice President of Technology, Irving Wladawsky Berger, was visiting the UK on a whistle-stop tour, promoting the possibilities of virtual worlds.

In 1911, the Computing-Tabulating-Recording Company was incorporated in New York City. By 1985, the company – then known as IBM – was the largest computer company in the world. Within a decade, though, IBM's losses were so high – $8 billion in 1993 alone – that the board considered breaking up the company. The world had shifted from centrally purchased, integrated solutions, to bit-by-bit solutions that focussed on individual productivity. IBM was nearly left behind.

Berger, born in Cuba, joined IBM in 1970. By the mid-nineties, Berger had become crucial to IBM's survival. He led IBM's efforts to move into supercomputing, and to help clients achieve the business benefits of the Internet. IBM's 'e-business on demand' efforts, which he headed, were central in dragging the company back from the edge of bankruptcy. Now,

Irving Berger had decided virtual worlds would form the next level of the Internet, and – perhaps driven by a determination never to go back to the difficult times – he wanted his company to be there: to ride the next wave, of what he called 'the leap from e-business to v-business'.

The email invite I received to meet Irving Berger stressed how serious IBM was about virtual worlds. 'IBM's chief technology strategist, Irving Wladawsky Berger, is going virtual,' the email read. Irving saw virtual worlds as 'signalling the next profound shift in how people use technology', I was informed; virtual worlds were 'the next frontier'. If that hadn't made things clear, the number of people at the meeting did. When I arrived at the meeting room, at an IBM building on London's South Bank, I was told it was 'a global meeting'. There were five others in the meeting room; listening in on a conference call were ten more. Even greater numbers were there, it turned out, although it took me a moment to notice: projected on the wall was IBM's virtual island inside Second Life, with at least 15 people in virtual attendance, from real-world locations as far away as India and Australia. (One resident had silver skin, and a wide pair of fairy wings. 'I see you've gone native,' I said. She laughed. 'Yep.')

Irving Berger turned out to look friendlier than I'd pictured him: tidy grey hair, and a round, cheery face. I asked why IBM was so interested in virtual worlds. In his marked Cuban accent, Berger told me he was the chairman of the Board of Governors of the IBM Academy, 'a group of the top technical people around the world'. A colleague, Chris Sharp, had approached Berger to talk about virtual worlds. 'At the time that took me a little by surprise,' he said. 'But I'd been around smart people enough that when you get advice like that, you listen very, very carefully.' The Academy study led to a more operational study by IBM's technology team, which led to a strong recommendation:

virtual worlds were something to which IBM needed to pay close attention.

Berger said he thought the crucial point of virtual worlds was that they shifted the role of the user: from being controlled by the interface (be it by a visual desktop analogy, or the command line interface) to the user being in charge. He thought of virtual worlds as the 'immersive web', with the potential for change 'bigger than any before'. Virtual worlds now reminded him of the Internet in 1994, he told me, 'because around that time, the number of people using the then fledgling world wide web was growing very rapidly, but business had not yet discovered it. And it seems like right now we are at the point of a massive initiative.' Berger was convinced that along with the benefits of ubiquitous computing, there was a new kind of danger. How do we organise computing when computing is everywhere? 'If you look at what's going on in IT, I don't need to tell you performance is going up in leaps and bounds, prices are dropping like crazy. IT is becoming embedded in everything, from medical technology, to cars, to RFID tags in consumer goods. This stuff is exploding.

'But I believe that the Achilles heel of this wonderful world is the complexity,' Berger said. 'If you make what's going on complex enough, people won't be able to figure out how to use it. One of our biggest challenges is to make IT systems and applications far, far more usable to human beings. IT systems in business, government, healthcare, education, everything.' Virtual worlds, he thought, were a way to integrate in this new era of distributed computing; a new metaphor, to unify networks like the desktop metaphor – the one we use on our PCs every day – unified the file system. 'I think that a lot of the complexity in IT is because systems and applications have really grown from the machine up,' he said. 'We do our machines, we do middleware, we do applications, then we put in a thin layer of human interface. We need to turn around our metaphor for design. The metaphor now has to be, if you are going to design a hospital management system, the question is, how do human beings think about hospitals? What is a hospital? There are very few human beings in a hospital that worry about XML, and stuff like that. There are patients, and doctors.'

I asked what specifically they were hoping to achieve inside virtual worlds. Berger's early thoughts were that certain key areas would benefit immediately: customer service, telemedicine, prototyping and education. (In India, where IBM is hiring thousands of new employees, the training procedure for new recruits will include time spent in virtual worlds). They hoped to 'salami-slice' the marketplace, another IBM employee, Ian Hughes told me: charge money for providing business services, like interactive book-selling, that would apply to any virtual world. But the overall impression I had was more one of excitement that had yet to clarify into a concrete goal. A seismic shift was taking place, they felt, and IBM was determined not to be nearly left behind this time.

IBM is a large organisation, and, like all large organisations, it has learned to talk while saying nothing. 'This next generation web will be a global consortium which means partnering within this grand experiment of technology is fundamental to the success of the "immersive Web" and future business,' my invite read, which is another way of saying how nice it is to work with other people. At one point Irving used an acronym – 'ERP Applications' – I didn't understand. I asked him to explain, and he faltered. 'ERP applications,' he said. 'Enterprise Resource . . . Enterprise Resource . . . What's ERP?' ('Enterprise Resource Planning,' a disembodied woman's voice chipped in drily from the telephone.) Berger had never actually spent time inside a virtual world, but that didn't seem to matter. Irving was a visionary, not in the trenches. His presence and enthusiasm had driven

IBM's efforts to 'dip their toe in virtual waters', as he described it. When we talked on a more general level, his ability to grasp the over-arching implications was clear. 'People understand virtual stores much more clearly as a metaphor than, say, a catalogue, which is how most e-business websites operate,' Berger told me. In the same way, he said, 'virtual worlds feel real. If we don't worry about managing the complexity, we may have all this technology that frustrates people. The virtual forces you to humanise.'

I asked Irving about the geographic limitations of virtual worlds. Websites are, in one direction, perfectly scalable: one person or a million people can see the same page. Virtual worlds, on the other hand, can only pack as many people in a certain area as will fit. Berger's perspective was that this would force corporations back into a focus on people. Virtual worlds are inherently democratic; first because, relative to the real world, everything is so easily accomplished, so the competitive advantage of corporations is reduced. Virtual worlds are a more level playing field. This is true for the disabled, whose limitations are transcended inside virtual worlds, but it's true for us too, against the might of incorporated groups. Second, though – and it was something I hadn't seen before – Irving pointed out you can only make use of the vastly expanded mode of communication when others are nearby. 'You're forced to think on a more personal level,' he told me; and, in a world straining to keep our corporations on a leash, this can only be a good thing.

'This is going to have a huge impact in business and in society,' Berger told me, 'in ways we do not yet understand at all.'

Among the people in real and virtual attendance were members of IBM's Eight Bar group – scientists, consultants and executives who held meetings and conducted experiments in Second Life. After we met in the real world, I met with Ian Hughes, an

IBM consulting IT specialist for 16 years, member of Eight Bar, and official full-time 'Metaverse Evangelist', at the IBM Second Life island 'Hursley'. Ian's Second Life self, ePredator Potato, looked like a predator – a human-hunter copied from the film of the same name – although his fearsome aspect was undermined by what appeared to be a pair of fishnet tights. Hursley was like an IT department from the future. Ian showed me experiments with links to websites outside Second Life. A man stood in a field and, via a link to Amazon, called up his search results in the air in front of him; he could move them, like Tom Cruise's character in the futuristic thriller *Minority Report*, to find the book he was looking for. I followed ePredator to a virtual tennis court. IBM managed the Wimbledon website, he told me. On this virtual court, they transferred live ball location data, recorded on custom keyboards by professional players; this virtual court replicated each shot. Virtual spectators could watch the match accurately modelled inside Second Life with only a slight delay. (To accompany the virtual Wimbledon, Ian had built a copy of the best-selling real-world Wimbledon merchandise: a Wimbledon towel. It was a 'virtual banner-ad', Ian said, a kind of 'avatar-based marketing'. People advertised Wimbledon, and paid for the pleasure. In the virtual world, though, the Wimbledon towel had an unadvertised feature; you could throw it in the air, and ride it as a flying carpet.)

Ian Hughes explained the day-to-day work of a Metaverse Evangelist. He mostly met other IBM employees to explain virtual worlds like Second Life (apparently, over 200 'IBMers' were Second Life residents), and there were also some meetings with IBM customers, 'to understand how they could use it too,' he told me. 'So it's a lot of time showing and explaining to people to help them "get it". And random crazy meetings helping people understand why IBM even cares.'

The Eight Bar group formed in February 2006 with two

members; when Ian and I met, in August 2006, there were over 100, all having virtual meetings and experimenting in Second Life. 'Everyone wants to sit down in a virtual world, for some reason. It's natural,' ePredator/Ian told me. He pulled out something called a 'multi-gadget', by another Second Life resident, Timeless Prototype. 'This gadget creates chairs as you need them,' he said. 'The more people who sit down, the more chairs appear. It's a very useful tool to indicate to other people around you're having a meeting. But it's not private; you haven't put walls and a roof around it. We can gather together and discuss things, and other people can join if they want to.'

Meetings inside Second Life, he said, were more playful. In the real world, he said, after meetings were over, everyone left; after Second Life meetings, people milled around to experiment. 'That's when much of the creative stuff happens,' he said. (Earlier, Irving Berger had explained why these kinds of virtual tools were so important. 'In IBM, we have meetings around the world on every imaginable subject all the time,' he said. 'Today the bulk of the meetings are just conference calls. All of a sudden, we have a much richer environment, that can make our meetings far more productive.' Also, he said, they had to keep up with the competition. 'One of our major software organisations is collaborative software – and we are now designing the next generations of collaborative software, so we want to make sure we build into our next generation the right mechanism, so our clients have access to this kind of cutting edge.')

'We're not playing, we're doing research,' Irving Berger had told me; but they were playing too. I'd seen pictures of Eight Bar members who had lined up a row of the recently launched Second Life Toyota Scions, placed a ramp on either end, then jumped the cars in virtual motorcycles. The next time ePredator and I met, inside Second Life a week or so later with no senior IBM staff around, ePredator materialised a larger-than-life version of the classic video game Space Invaders. The army of invading aliens, rendered in 3D, began to wage war on a nearby Wimbledon billboard. Then it was time for him to go. In front of my eyes, ePredator morphed from a stockinged space-hunter into a man wearing a casual suit. Next to him, a Harley Davidson motorbike appeared, and he rode off.

Later, at a real-world conference focussing on Second Life, I met another IBM Metaverse Evangelist: Roo Reynolds, young, clean shaven, wearing a similar suit to his online self. Despite his occasional adoption of large corporations' sexless jargon (in IBM, a 'global innovation 3D Jam' was their idea of a party), Roo's enthusiasm for virtual worlds was clear. 'In Second Life,' Roo said, 'designing and creating something becomes the same thing.'

At the time of writing, IBM was already holding virtual meetings inside virtual worlds with more then 20 major clients, including a telecommunications company, an aerospace firm, a petroleum giant, and 'a major UK grocer' that, according to one Reuters report, 'wants to build a virtual storefront that will allow consumers to buy real-world groceries online.'

Both Ian and Roo told me IBM had some concerns about the company's entry into Second Life. Inside Second Life, sensitive IBM topics like patents, for which secrecy is paramount, were forbidden. Conscious that the world runs on Linden Lab's servers, they were wary of discussing anything that would harm IBM if leaked; they hoped eventually to have an internal virtual world, maintained on servers they controlled, and accessible inside the company, for such secret work.

Robert Gehorsam, President of the virtual world developer ForTerra, told me he had been approached by corporations who weren't comfortable operating inside Second Life, because of that world's shaky response to its sudden growth. Robert was generous about Second Life's versatility, but had doubts about how robust that world was. 'Ultimately, Second Life is a great consumer application,' he said. 'But it's not oriented to supporting what an organisation needs. Security, reliability, highly defined applications, things like that.'

Robert Gehorsam had spoken with IBM, who showed ForTerra what they were doing in Second Life. 'I don't think they understand the difference between Second Life and an industrial strength system,' Gehorsam said. 'How many times a week does Second Life go down? These are built-in problems. I will say that people are coming to us with prototypes they'd built in Second Life, and saying, "We can't deploy with this".'

Ian Hughes had told me the same thing. 'That's something we're having to explore, access control in this environment,' he said. 'All companies who move into this environment will have to think, what happens if somebody sits on top of your logo, strips off and takes a picture of themselves? On normal web pages, that doesn't happen. You don't get someone wandering around your space, causing problems.' Second Life resident Biscuit Carrol, who ran a start-up business giving Second Life tours and holding virtual conferences, also told me that for his corporate customers, security was paramount. 'For example,' he told me, 'people can fly around the windows and eavesdrop.' His solution to that problem was to build his Second Life conference rooms so high, no one could fly to them; you had to be invited to teleport in. 'Even so,' he told me, 'someone could just strap on a jetpack.'

Other businesses were moving into virtual worlds. In June 2006, American Apparel, the US clothes brand with a turnover of $80 million, set up shop in Second Life. The virtual American Apparel outlet was designed to look just like a real-world venue except on a beach-front instead of a high street. When I visited, it was clear that virtual worlds were a trap for corporations, as well as for people. Virtual versions of real-world companies revealed not just how brands wanted us to see them, but also how they saw themselves. The American Apparel store was on a tropical island, the glass-fronted store surrounded by casual, ethnic-looking benches made out of wooden logs. Inside, cheesy pop blared in an empty store. Wood veneer flooring was overlaid with rainbow racks of their trademark coloured T-shirts. The brand's outré sexuality had bled into the virtual world too: on the upper floor back wall were stills from 'Beautiful Agony', a series of videos of real people's faces as they reached orgasm. For the first time, though, the corporate presence in virtual worlds led to real-world consequences; virtual T-shirts cost just $1, but – for a limited time only – each virtual purchase came with a $15 voucher to spend in a real American Apparel store.

However, the launch of American Apparel inside Second Life was widely seen as a failure, or rather, solely a PR success, aimed not at the virtual community, but at the front page. There were no store-keepers. In the first 10 days they sold a reported 2,000 virtual items, which earned them $2,000: less than a day's trade in a single store. (Prices for virtual construction vary, but according to the *Wall Street Journal*, building a corporate Second Life presence costs around $20,000.) One resident, Dave Lime, part of a group called the 'Second Life Liberation Army', used a scripted object to push virtual residents out of the store, in protest at the lack of residents' rights. A month later, the store was deserted. For two days, I lounged around the virtual shopfloor, waiting to speak with a customer. Not a single soul walked in.

Around the same time, other multinationals began to latch on to the potential of virtual worlds. By October 2006, MTV, Coca-Cola, Sun Microsystems, Intel, and Warner Brothers all had a Second Life presence. In some ways, these businesses were following the money: 2006 was the first year in which UK online advertising revenues overtook print media, and more British money was spent advertising on Google than on Channel 4. A whole range of virtual businesses had sprung up to service the new corporate presence; one tour guide charged Aus $10 an hour.

Once again, in the rush to occupy the new territory, the rules of engagement had yet to be established. Residents worried, as I did, that corporations might take control of the virtual landscape, in the same way they had taken control over the real. The early signs, though, seemed to indicate that inside virtual worlds, the balance between corporations and consumers would be a little more even. In the real world, corporations battle, through advertising and isolation, to shape our surroundings to suit themselves. Virtual worlds were a new battleground, a clean slate where both forces – self-determination and corporate control – continued the struggle. But American Apparel's relative failure inside Second Life seemed to point to a new, healthier balance between people and corporations, yet another levelling of the playing field. Inside virtual worlds, at least at first, brands seemed less equipped to convince us they were the gatekeepers of the media that connected us. As Irving Berger had told me, the corporations that would succeed in virtual worlds would be those who focussed on people – which could only be a good thing.

At that time, almost all the real-world reporting that came back through the electronic looking glass into mainstream media was about the money: the scale of the economies, the virtual, 'non-existent' objects that could be bought and sold for real cash. This reporting simplified the revelatory capacity of virtual worlds, but there was a reason for this, too. It's not just that capitalism bribes every innovation to its own purpose, like an oil baron buying up politicians. It's also that the figures themselves did beggar belief. In 2005, residents of Second Life traded $1.47 million worth of virtual property in May alone. In 2006, the yearly market across all virtual worlds was estimated at $1 billion. These are huge numbers. To put them into perspective, *Titanic*, the biggest-budget film of all time, earned total domestic gross of $402.6 million. World of Warcraft made Blizzard Entertainment $300 million in 2005 alone.

It was no surprise, then, to discover that other big business entertainment firms had joined in the exodus. For the 'reality' show *Laguna Beach*, MTV had commissioned a modified version of the virtual world There – the same world ForTerra had modified for the US military – to create 'Virtual Laguna Beach'. Billed with the strap line 'Live It', that world was a chance for viewers to move into a world modelled on the show, 'alongside friends and fans', based on the show's real-world locations: 'the whole Laguna experience in a parallel online universe.' MTV were even premiering the shows inside Virtual Laguna Beach, before they aired on live TV.

In June 2005, *Titanic* director James Cameron announced his new film, *Project 880*: a 'completely crazy, balls-out sci-fi flick', according to Cameron. The film would be accompanied by a virtual world to be launched months beforehand, to allow people to inhabit the story's universe before the film ever reached cinemas. Films, dreams, worlds: Cameron clearly believed, as I did, that the three constructs were related. 'I create worlds, too, though mine are narrative-oriented,' he said.

In an interview with *Business Online*, Cameron expounded on his desire to see players create their own worlds. 'I want to see developers create games in which players can add to the worlds as they go along, so you can see what hundreds of thousands of people in this game environment can create. It's like each is being handed a tool set ... Instead of creating a $50 million game, you're creating $2 million games and letting them grow themselves.'

Cameron saw parallels between our new virtual worlds and

literature, specifically science fiction. 'So much of literary sci-fi is about creating worlds that are rich and detailed and make sense at a social level,' he says. 'They force people to be more imaginative.'

After business, more media followed into virtual worlds. BBC reporter Paul Mason persuaded his company's flagship current affairs show *Newsnight* to shoot a segment inside Second Life, broadcast on 5 January 2006, with presenters' voices dubbed over the animations. And, in October 2006, the press agency Reuters announced a full-time Second Life reporter, whose sole mission was to bring virtual news to the attention of the wider world. I met with Adam Reuters (in the real world, 30-year-old London-based Adam Pasick), to talk about his virtual beat. Adam had already worked for Reuters, he told me, and the management approached him with the job offer. 'I cover Second Life exclusively,' he told me, 'with a focus on business and economy stories.'

Then, a group of odd-looking passers-by – including a snappily-dressed man with puppet-hands, and a Grim Reaper – landed nearby. In another levelling act, this time between the press and the people, they encircled Adam Reuters, and began to taunt him.

16

VIRTUAL ART
Creating ourselves anew

Justin Bovington had called the Second Life residents' role in the virtual Radio 1 festival 'theatre', and that seemed to me exactly right. Just as had happened when I met with Adam Reuters, the people inside virtual worlds had begun to take a more active role in the life around them. It seemed a new expression of the same drive that produced cave paintings and ritual dances, and later cinema and theatre: the desire to enact ourselves.

Our basic sense of self first arose from our instinct to create. The word 'person' comes from either the Greek 'prosopa', or the Latin 'personae' – from per (through) and sonare (sound) – both names for masks used in theatre. At the beginning of my journey into virtual worlds, I hoped I would discover not only what they revealed about our selves, but also how they shaped them. Theatre helped evolve our sense of the self; would virtual worlds help re-evolve our sense of the other?

What matters, becomes matter. At the same time Freud pointed out the significance of dreams, Lumière brightened those dreams with a light bulb, so others could see them. Now, as our collective unconscious found material existence in a global digital network, we could lay out our dreams for others to inhabit. Our fantasies had always been real, in the sense that they drove and inhabited our lives; but now they could be measured, and, in virtual worlds, co-habited.

Most creative work is an attempt to make these worlds real: to reach into a world of solace and bring something back. In the past, we imagined our heavens through prayers and song. Fiction gave us each a more intimate, personal holiday from our selves. Then, with cinema and later television – whose power to shape our consciousness both entranced and terrified us – we could sit together in rooms and gaze directly into these other worlds. Now, we can inhabit our dreams – which changes both us, and our dreams.

Virtual worlds seemed part of a natural progression, from mass enactments of ourselves, which most of us witnessed passively, to more personal participation. Philip Rosedale had told me he saw virtual worlds as a remedy for what he called the 'Faustian bargain' of one way, non-interactive media like television. 'We all got TV, and it enabled us to see and learn many things, but unfortunately those things had to be centrally authored, without our participation, by a very small number of people,' he told me.

Philip saw Second Life, built and managed by the residents, as a natural correction to our early, disempowering media – a better place, owned by us all. Perhaps that was why the Second Life community seemed to thrive on drama: virtual worlds were helping us reclaim control, from soap operas, cinema and news-papers, of the dramas of our own lives.

'A man must choose,' Isaiah Berlin wrote. 'One can save one's soul, or one can found or maintain or serve a great and glorious state; but not always both at once.' I had seen there were many virtual residents who wished to establish a great virtual nation state – the makers of the games, the builders of the societies, buildings

276

and worlds within those games. But people were also working in virtual worlds to save their souls.

Only through imagination can we address absence: art and cinema give us a lens through which to examine what we lack, and now virtual worlds provided us with a new perspective. Virtual worlds could be a place where we remembered ourselves, too. Wagner James Au reported on one Second Life resident, Duuya Herbst, who was among the last 15 surviving members of the Deeni people, a small tribe living in Oregon, USA. In a war with gold miners and the US government in the late 1800s, the Deeni tribe was almost wiped out. Now, Duuya had built a virtual replica of the dance hall that was host to his tribe's 'Nadosh' feather dance, a solstice celebration of renewal. With just a handful of surviving pure-blood tribe members, he was trying to salvage the spirit of his ancestors and save their language by recreating their tribal rituals online.

There is a long tradition of writers and artists working with virtual spaces. In 1981, Robert Pinsky, one-time US poet laureate, wrote about the close parallels – rhythm, metre, intensity of meaning – between poetry and computer code. *Mindwheel*, Pinsky's work in a text-only genre of collaborative prose-writing games now known as 'interactive fiction', was an attempt to introduce surrealism to games. The late Douglas Adams, in partnership with Infocom developer Steve Meretzky, wrote some work exclusively as interactive fiction.

In the rush of excitement after the Lumière brothers' first films, cinema made us wonder what could be seen; now virtual worlds, with their capacity to let us feel what it is like to do impossible things, make us wonder what can be done. The new possibilities can both enlighten and confound us.

But virtual worlds cannot be measured directly against cinema and literature. The open-ended journey that characterises virtual worlds might make for terrible, say, theatre. (As games theorist Espen Aarseth has pointed out, no one wants to play *Hamlet: The Game* – 'Fail – time and time again: – to avenge your father's death!'.) Virtual worlds are not just interactive cinema, they are something new. David Mamet wrote, of the beauty of movies, 'they are actual records of the light which shone on us.' If so, then virtual worlds are actual records of the light we wish might shine.

Actors already earn a living from video game voiceovers – to the extent that, in May 2005, two Hollywood unions threatened a strike over actors' shares in game royalties. (Of the top 10 selling games in 2004 nine were made with members of actors' unions – including James Caan and Samuel L. Jackson.) But now virtual selves were so readily available, others were making films entirely in the virtual world.

Machinima, the virtually generated films I'd been watching on my Second Life TV, were so popular that world makers like Linden Lab include features to help residents record their antics for later editing. The StrangerHood, the show I'd first watched on my own virtual TV, I discovered had been commissioned by Electronic Arts as a promotional tool. Elsewhere, there were machinima about love affairs inside World of Warcraft, and characters from the futuristic war game Halo, musing existentially on the plight of being trapped in a world of eternal war. There were even live versions of machinima, more akin to theatre than cinema. In August 2006, US-based marketing company Millions of Us – 'Virtual Worlds. Real Brands.' – organised Second Life's first theatre: virtual actors performed 'From the Shadows', by Enjah Mysterio (no relation to my own virtual self), in a virtual version of a modernised London's Globe Theatre, as re-imagined by the architect Norman Foster. (I had thoughts myself about staging *The Tempest*. At the end, for Prospero's farewell, the scenery, the Globe theatre – even the surroundings, the earth and the sky – would fade to nothing 'Our revels are now ended,' our virtual players would say, as everything around them slowly disappeared. 'These our actors / As I foretold you, were all spirits, and / Are melted into air, into thin air / And like the baseless fabric of this vision . . .')

When I visited Rivers Run Red, they mentioned they were working with Penguin books inside Second Life. I asked for an introduction, and within a few days I had invited Jeremy Ettinghausen, a Digital Publisher at Penguin, aka Second Life's Jeremy Neumann, to meet me in my virtual office. There, Jeremy told me how Penguin planned to bring the first cyber-punk novels – the works of art that first envisioned shared virtual spaces – into the very worlds they had predicted. They began with Neal Stephenson, whose *Snow Crash* – the book that Philip Rosedale had used as a recruiting tool – was now available inside Second Life, as a virtual book. Or at least, as part of a book: the virtual edition included the first chapter, with an audio link, and another link to buy the book at a discount from the Penguin website. Scheduled for a virtual appearance in early 2007 was William Gibson, the science fiction author who coined the word 'cyber-space' after watching kids gaze, as I had done, into the blinking screen of a early coin-op arcade game. Plans were being laid to recreate Blue Ant, the advertising agency from his bestselling novel *Pattern Recognition*. When Jeremy and I met, months before Gibson's scheduled appearance, Gibson, or his agent, was emailing Jeremy about Second Life daily.

'Because we publish *Snow Crash*, it seemed a really easy entry point to do something with that book,' said Ettinghausen. 'Though if I worked for Mills & Boon, I'd definitely be setting up a 'romance novel' simulation in Second Life.' Jeremy had been inside Second Life from March, and, he told me, he had never been gripped by anything so strongly. He'd rented a small spot of virtual land inside an area of Second Life called 'The Future', 'just so I can invite people to "join me in the future"!' In April 2006, Jeremy began promoting Second Life inside Penguin, betting his enthusiasm would spread; by the time we met, in October, his bet had paid off. 'Over the last three or four months the UK press has gone mad for Second Life, making me look prescient,' he told me.

I asked Jeremy if Second Life was a place where thought was less important than action. 'I don't think it is less thoughtful – I go to quite a few discussions in SL and hear a high calibre of thought. But I think "reading" is under threat generally as people increasingly go online for entertainment. Now that you can watch TV on your mobile phone while downloading music and firing off emails, reading old-fashioned linear text is a tough sell. And this is also why it is important that we establish a presence in here.'

Jeremy took me to his land. The Future, it turned out, was high above the clouds, so to help get around, Jeremy gave me a jetpack. He showed me a crooked house, where floors twisted to become ceilings. Then, he had to leave.

I strolled around Second Life, looking for other examples of in-world publishing. In one corner of the mainland, I came across a store called Pamela's Books, where Second Life self-publishers put up their books for sale. Browsing the store was a little different from a stroll around Borders: as I clicked on each book – a science fiction horror called *Dobbit Do*; a 'Dallas-type tale' called *Cigar Box* – a larger version of the book, taller than the virtual me, appeared against the far wall. Elsewhere, I strolled into a meticulous copy of Paris's famous Shakespeare and Company bookshop, complete with worn sofas, and the shop's motto – 'Be not inhospitable to strangers / lest they be angels in disguise' – written over an inside archway. Every wall was stacked high with virtual books. The store was more theatre than commercial venture. It had been built by a woman from Pennsylvania, Sharon Ritter, who had never visited the real place. The books weren't readable, but it wouldn't be long, I thought, before our virtual selves would be able to stroll through an Amazon store itself. (The Amazon founder, Jeff Bezos, was an early Linden Lab investor.) My American agent's UK partner, Greene & Heaton, had established a virtual office in Second Life. For an hour a week, Will Francis fielded questions from virtual residents, and searched for new clients inside Second Life.

Other authors had appeared inside Second Life, to promote and discuss their real-world books. Richard Bartle, the inventor of MUD, and Stanford Law Professor Lawrence Lessig, had sat on a virtual podium, inhabiting avatars crafted to resemble their real-world selves, to give virtual book readings and answer questions. The editor of the futurist magazine *Wired*, Chris Anderson, had appeared as his virtual self to read from his bestselling book *The Long Tail*. One author, science fiction writer and technology activist Cory Doctorow, made the entire text of his book, *Someone Comes to Town, Someone Leaves Town*, available as a free Second Life edition. Elsewhere, visual art, too, was being virtually explored. A few real-world galleries had built virtual Second Life equivalents, and, in February 2006, Linden Lab offered a $4,000 scholarship to an art student willing to spend a term exploring art in Second Life.

In the meantime, the Rivers Run Red film festival had moved closer to a reality; they'd built a giant, floating blimp for the festival, which they planned to hold in conjunction with the charity Cancer Research. A celebrity patron, rumoured to be Ray Winstone, would appear in virtual form. I flew up to take a look at the blimp, which floated hundreds of feet above their island. On the blimp's upper storey was a dance-floor, where, on squares of flashing lights, a group of people were dancing in sync. I asked if they were waiting for the film festival. 'No,' one said. 'We're waiting for Duran Duran.'

In early 2006, Peter Wells-Thorpe, who worked with Duran Duran to develop their online and technology strategy, approached Linden Lab about creating a Duran Duran presence inside Second Life. Linden Lab referred the band to Rivers Run Red, who began talks about creating a whole new Duran Duran section of Second Life. In the meantime, word had leaked; groups of these fans, 'Duranies', (a total of up to 5,000, Justin told me) had heard the band was coming; they logged in, and they waited. One 'Duranie', JoJa Dhara from Holland, told me she had been a fan 'from teenage to housewifeyears.' They had heard about it after the band's co-founder and keyboardist Nick Rhodes did some interviews, she explained, and news of their virtual plans spread across the Internet. Now, JoJa and her friends logged in every day, to lounge around Avalon and wait for Duran Duran, staying awake sometimes until 5 a.m. to talk with other fans. When I visited, the fans had accumulated furniture: a candle, three deck-chairs, a fish-bowl and a fax machine. The fish was a gift from Justin Bovington, to keep them entertained; they named the fish Nick, after Rhodes. 'Nick is a holy fish to us,' JoJa Dhara told me. 'NickFish is ours.'

The fans were certainly dedicated. Brim Iredell, another fan – a tall blonde in a long green ball gown, who already ran a gallery in Second Life – was 30 years old; she'd been a fan of Duran Duran since the age of seven, when her mother took her to a concert. 'I cried tears of joy and rapture through the whole show,' she told me. She seemed to know all about the plan for an island, and how Fizik was working on it. Nick was her favourite, she said, 'although I named my son Simon.'

*   *   *

The band wouldn't be the first internationally renowned musicians to appear in Second Life – Suzanne Vega had already performed a virtual concert – but they would be the first band to embrace whole-heartedly the possibilities of the new place. They planned to build a huge destination, Duran Duran's new virtual home, which would spread across four whole islands, to re-create themselves, and to meet their fans. In November 2006, over lunch at an Italian restaurant near his West London home, Nick Rhodes told me about the band's vision.

Nick had first stepped into Second Life six months before. Peter Wells-Thorpe gave him a tour, starting at Rivers Run Red's white-themed futuristic island. 'The first thing that struck me was how fabulous it looked,' Nick said. 'I'd seen "The Sims" before, but this was a new level. Things had moved on.

'Then I saw a person take off and just start flying around. Then, I learned about teleporting. *Then*, I saw there was a search engine, where you could just type in whatever you like.' Nick typed 'Goth', and teleported to a Goth club. 'There were great looking Goth chicks, dancing around.' Nick clicked on a danceball. 'I never dance. But I found myself dancing around. I have to say it was a pleasurable experience – knowing that I'd managed to do it with a mouse.'

Nick left the club, and flew over a field. 'Then we went into a flower. And that sold me on the entire experience. Because inside this beautiful flower, there was a bee. I loved this bee. I am an absolute obsessive about detail, to a painful degree. That's what keeps me awake at night. When I saw the bee, I was completely sold. Anyone who's gone to enough trouble – this flower was tiny, and miles away, just there on the grass, on some plain. We were going over it, and we came down, and went into the flower, and there was the bee. And I knew the place was for me. First, we thought, let's build a stadium. But then we thought: why not build a world?'

Nick and the rest of the band quickly decided they wanted to build virtual versions of their real selves, to inhabit the new world. The avatars would have the same names as the band. Nick – in the real world, louche, smart, with dyed blond hair – watched Rivers Run Red create the virtual version of himself. He delighted at their attention to detail: 'They photographed our eyes, to get the eyes right.'

Duran Duran has worked with Vivienne Westwood, and more recently, Giorgio Armani; to Nick, style was very important. 'When we set out for this project, one of the questions we raised was, what are we going to be wearing?' Nick said. To style the band's virtual look, Nick spoke with a friend, the designer Antony Price. 'Antony is an amazing British designer,' Nick told me. 'He designed a lot of the clothes for the artists we liked in the seventies, for Roxy Music and David Bowie. He did all of the outfits for our "Rio" video. Antony is another real maverick. He's incredibly clever, technically. He's one of the few designers I have met who can draw something, and go and cut the pattern himself, and he can go and make it, and it will look exactly the same as the drawing. Very few people, even some of the major designers, have that skill on their own. Knowing how technical he is, I knew he would like this concept. In fact, we've asked him if he will open a boutique on our island.'

Nick didn't like his Second Life version's round shoulders; he wanted a square cut. 'Of course, that's not the way things normally work. Your clothes stick to your body. We found ways around that, by using building blocks to create straight lines.' (Rivers Run Red added blocks of virtual wood to each shoulder, and sprayed them to match the suit.)

Duran Duran planned to launch their Second Life presence with virtual gigs by their virtual avatars, which they would include in their real-world tour listings. They would pre-prepare some elements, and play some elements live. 'We will be able to improvise, and interact with the audience,' Nick said. They were working with the American film company Giant Studios to use their motion camera equipment, used in the *Lord of the Rings* and *King Kong* films, so Simon, Nick and the band would have their familiar dance moves.

Although the band's virtual selves would share their real names, they would, Nick said, be different people. They were other selves, not the band members, with dreams and hopes, and some unknown connection with these people, outside the world, who the virtual band could sense but not see. 'The avatars are going to stay in their personality from day one,' Nick told me. 'They won't be able to answer questions about "Girls On Film", because they don't know about it. Of course, once we play the song live in-world, they can then answer a question about playing it in-world.

'I rather like the idea if you're going into this bizarre fantasy, that you keep it bizarre,' Nick said said. 'I'd rather be talking about a 20 foot eggshell that's just cracked open, than talking about something I did 20 years ago. Much more interesting to me at this time in my life.'

The band had even written a song, produced by Timbaland and provisionally titled 'Zooming In', from their avatars' perspective. 'It's literally in-character. We thought OK, what's it like to be living in-world? What's the weather like? What do they feel like every day? Who do they fancy? What is their world about? I'd like to play it live in there. We could say, "This one's for you!"'

In the meantime, the band was inhabiting Second Life anonymously. Andy Taylor, the drummer, became a virtual woman. 'I think he's been rather enjoying it actually,' Nick told me. 'Especially when he says "No" to guys. There's something going on there. I haven't asked yet. I know one of the other guys went in as a really short, big guy, and nobody would talk to him. Eventually somebody walked past, a big, tall skinny guy, who said, "Hey there, little dude. How is it down there?" No one would talk to him. I quite like going in as an outcast. I think that'll be my next project.'

Named after an evil doctor (Dr Durand Durand) in Roger Vadim's cult film *Barbarella: Queen of the Galaxy*, Duran Duran have played with identity throughout their career. Nick traced the band's willingness to adopt new personas from the time they were forming their identity. 'We grew up in the seventies. And for music alone, the seventies were about as inspiring as you can possibly get. You had glam-rock, which was at the centre of our universe, which had David Bowie, and Roxy Music, Sparks, Cockney Rebel – all these really interesting acts, that all had their own personality, that all were fairly outlandish. And they were reinventing themselves, and particularly Bowie, with every record. That was pretty exciting, to go on that journey with them.'

Nick cited a long list of seventies genres as inspiration. 'At various times throughout the decade, disco music, punk rock, heavy rock, pomp-rock, if you like – Pink Floyd, Yes, all those "goblin" people – electronic music; people like Kraftwerk were a huge influence on me. So there was such variation in rock and pop music. And then this huge variation even within genres. That sort of set the parameters on our vision. And they were pretty broad. We decided that we could be a rock band. We could also be an electronic band. We could also play punky if we wanted to. We could play disco grooves and funk, and we could make really beautiful ballads, or we could make fast, raunchy rock tracks. And we could also do incredibly esoteric ambient things. I think a lot of bands find a sound and stick with it. We were fortunate enough in that Simon has a very distinctive voice, so as long as we stick that on top of whatever we're doing, we can go where we like. Because of that, in everything we look at, we try to find something new, something exciting.'

Formed by Nick, along with John Taylor in Birmingham in 1978, the group has sold over 70 million records; they've had 18 singles in the Billboard Hot 100, and 30 in the UK Top 40. Since their first album, 'Duran Duran', in 1981, the band has accumulated followers worldwide: when I met Nick, their fan club had over 150,000 dedicated members. Although considered by some an eighties band, they sold more records in the nineties than the eighties. Throughout their career, they had ridden the early waves of new technology. In the eighties, they were among the earliest bands to issue extended remixes, 'night versions' for club play. In 1984, they were the first act to build video screens into their tour shows. They were also among the first bands to embrace the Internet. 'The first Duran Duran site was up in '96 or '97,' Nick told me. The technology had yet to catch up with his vision. 'The ideas I had, we did a lot of them, but nobody could operate them. We were doing these things in Flash, and creating these animations, but everyone was on dialup. Nobody had a computer. And so it was an absolute catastrophe. But I liked it! Because I could play with the demos.'

Duran Duran were the first band to offer paid music downloads. Through the online service Liquid Audio, they sold their 1997 single, 'Electric Barbarella', for 99 cents. 'When people were cursing Napster for ruining the music industry, I have to say, I thought completely the opposite,' Nick said, of the time. 'I didn't like our songs being taken free. I still don't particularly, I'd rather people paid for them. But I saw what would happen. It was like the Wild West at the time, but inevitably police come along, and sheriffs, and they sort the thing out. But the labels didn't see that. It took them a long, long time to catch up. I'm glad we did it, even though it sold so few copies.'

That album, 'Medazzaland', was hit by pressure from stores, who were threatened by the new distribution – in the same way Wal-Mart recently declared they might stock fewer DVD copies of movies offered for download on Apple's iTunes Store. 'If that record ever had a chance to be a hit,' Nick said, 'it was completely destroyed by the fact that the main chain-stores in America, some of them refused to stock our record, because we were selling direct. And they were afraid they were being cut out.'

In more recent years, the band has overlaid animation on live footage of concert crowds; the audience reached up to touch the non-existent figure they could see walking across their heads.

Duran Duran's Second Life selves were an extension of this digital curiosity. They were already working on the technology to use their avatars projected on the back walls of real-world gigs, a technology tested in October 2006, at the British Academy Video Games Awards. Projected on the back wall, in a clear, soft-edged white room, adorned with pop-art, which I knew to be Rivers Run Red's Avalon, Nick's avatar opened a virtual envelope and read out the nominations. 'What a great pleasure it is to be here this evening, in your world,' Nick's avatar said, his voice modulated as if to come from some other, digital place. As the virtual Nick was about to announce the winner, Nick's real self walked on the stage. Waving a remote control, he pressed a button to freeze his virtual self. 'I'm sorry,' the real Nick said, pointing to the screen, 'But he's not to be trusted. The winner is . . .'

In a way, I had discovered, all virtual lives were a kind of theatre. Jeremy Chase had played the mafia role with an almost camp commitment; Aurora Walcott's story could have been real, or it could have been imagined, but the tale interested me either way. People were inventing themselves; at times, they seemed to take that reinvention too seriously. It was a relief to talk with Nick, who approached virtual worlds from a much more playful angle.

'The one thing that I guard rigorously is naivety,' he told me. 'I think if you lose that as an artist entirely, you're sunk. And so every time I see something new, I feel almost like a child with a new toy. I feel as though there's some beautiful thing to explore there.'

Nick envisioned the Duran Duran island complex as a self-contained world within Second Life: 'A complete vision of a town, conceived by one person or one organisation, and done purely on a creative basis, to see what happened in that area,' Nick said. 'Like having a bubble, with people living in it. Almost like people study ants, and watch what happens in their community, who does what, how it builds and how it spreads.

'We're always looking for a new way to do something creatively, using the tools that we have available to us,' Nick told me. 'Being part of a band, you're looking at ways to reinvent. But it has to be something that is appealing, and intriguing. And often I look at technologies and ideas people have, and you just think, no, it's not for us, it's not going to impact what we do, I've seen something like that before, let somebody try it out first. But with Second Life, it was rather different. The instant that I saw it, I just knew. I understood.

'You'd have to be a cynical and somewhat miserable human to not be fascinated by the idea of having a character that you can make whatever you like – maybe a giant potato, if you like – to go and live in this whole community.'

Nick was clearly delighted by the endless possibilities to build and play. He wanted to build a store, and open a hotel, 'with everything. You check in, someone gets your baggage, something gets lost, you have to call the bellman, then you get room service because it's too late. You watch a movie, then the maid comes in, because you forgot to lock the door.

'I could get addicted to it, if I allowed myself,' Nick told me. In fact, Second Life had already invaded Nick's consciousness. 'I've had a lot less sleep,' he said. 'Not from being in the world, but from thinking about it. That's why I don't sleep at night.

They keep knocking around my brain.' (I asked if Nick kept a notepad by his bed. 'I have pads listing my pads,' he said.)

'I love technology,' Nick told me. 'I like any opportunity that is a challenge. And when I first saw this, it was like walking into *Alice in Wonderland*. I thought, OK, now we can have some fun. This really is a blank canvas and we can paint whatever we like all over it.'

The Duran Duran area of Second Life would consist of four islands, themed so visitors could start in a city, then stroll from the urban to the rural to the pastoral – somewhere between a surreal theme park and an interactive Duran Duran version of *Yellow Submarine*. One area, Sanhedralite, was named after an early Duran b-side ('Simon invented the word,' Nick told me, 'and because we were inventing a world, I thought it would be quite poetic to use that.') Azizi, the main city, was Duran Duran's vision of 'our sort of downtown New York, with our lofts and our tall buildings. That's where it all happens.' Another area, Tlön, was named after the world from Borges's story 'Tlön, Uqbar, Orbis Tertius', about a lost country, known only through the single surviving copy of its encyclopaedia. 'In deference to him, somebody else who had created a world, I thought it would be nice to have that name too,' Nick said.

Justin at Rivers Run Red gave me access to the Duran Duran island, a work-in-progress, and I took a brief flight around their vision. I flew into a towering lipstick skyscraper, to visit the as-yet eerily empty Japanese restaurant at the top. Around me ran conveyor belts of virtual sushi. Through the windows, I could see the clouds drift over the rest of the Duran Duran world. On the floor below, in a ghostly bridal suite, a wraith leapt at me from a mirror, and, when I lay on a virtual bed, I rose flailing into the air as if possessed. Lower still was the 'Barbarella Apartment', a pink and purple hotel room with pop-art above the bed. In the more remote, wilder areas of the Duran Duran world, a cherry-red ray-gun spouted water into a pool, where oil paints leaked from flattened tubes into the sea. Above the pool, a 3D Dalí painting wriggled disconcertingly, as if distorted by the heat. Towering above the world was a Mount Rushmore-style monument to the band, the face of each band-member carved in virtual stone. Around the cliff flew Nick Rhodes' origami birds.

Nick told me they'd planned their islands as a reflection of both the band's past and their future. 'Whilst I never look backwards, one is only ever a sum of all one's experiences,' he said. 'And I am very much that. If I have certain references that I have always liked, I tend to be loyal to them. Elements of that are within our world without a doubt. It's very easy to cite films like *Blade Runner* and *Brazil*, to say how fantastic they were, to say how much they influenced the world, visually. So we have nods to those: we have a blimp with a winking girl. It just happens to be the Rio girl that's winking.

'Maybe there are little clues in there somewhere to where the world came from, because they are things that have meant something to me in some way.'

To honour their influences, the band planned to include a walk of fame, with people – Jean Cocteau, Liberace, Orson Wells, William Blake – important to the band. Elsewhere, there were mirrors that reflected unusual things out of the corner of your eye, black swans and panthers, and a haunted house. There was an underwater nightclub. ('Of course!' Nick said.) There were flowers that, when picked, had a psychedelic effect on your virtual self's view. On their website, the band had an agony aunt email, Ask Katy. Fans emailed personal questions and the band answered posing as her. They planned to install a virtual version of Katy on their island, in a fortune teller's tent, to act as a guide for new visitors.

Nick was paying close attention to everything in the island, from the tiny to the huge. 'I'm ready to build the virtual bees,' Nick said. 'I'm ready to build the virtual subway line.' Both Nick and Justin Bovington had planned the island to a meticulous level. ('I thought I was obsessive,' Nick said. 'I've met my match in him'.)

'I've spent days making noises in the studio, for what the jelly-fish will sound like as you swim past them. And the noises the cable cars will make as they go through the mountains, and when they stop.' In the end, for the cable car, Nick ran a coin slowly down the length of a guitar string.

In general, Nick told me, he tried to create sounds, rather than record them. For the island's virtual cars, he'd tried at first to sample a real car, but he eventually decided the artificially generated sounds worked better: virtual sounds for a virtual world. There were things he just couldn't record. 'What should a cold winter sound like?' Nick said. 'I've been trying to work it out.'

For fun, Nick Rhodes had also recorded himself, modulated into his avatar's voice, reading a series of oddly phrased voice messages, made for the Duran area of Avalon, to enliven the virtual fax machine. ('The voice makes me in trance,' 'Duranie' JoJa Dhara had told me, when I visited.) 'Hello: Where am I?' the voice asks, when you press the 'messages' button. 'Who are you? Why are you talking to me? What am I doing here? I need to know the answers.' 'I have no idea where I am. If I did, then I would tell you.' 'I think I'm almost ready. I'll be there, with you, soon.' 'All the dreams I have ever had have all come true – here, with you, in this place.'

'They think I'm the fish,' Nick said. 'They think it's me. So one day, I'll go in as the fish.'

Nick hadn't yet visited his virtual fans, but when he did, he wasn't going to hold back. He planned to attend Duran Duran's own concerts. 'I could be one of the audience, too. I could be three of the audience.' Even when they weren't performing, Nick planned to play in his new world. 'One thing I want to do is plague the island with 50 or so Nick Rhodes,' he said. 'One sitting in a cable-car, one meditating, one having a conversation with a 12-foot alien. It'd be like Village of the Damned.

'In a way, it's like playing god,' he said. 'You are creating your own world, and you can make what you like in that world.'

A month before I met Nick, mid-way through the US tour, Andy Taylor left the band again. On their website, the band announced an 'unworkable gulf' between the rest of the group and Andy, and stated they could 'no longer effectively function together'.

'Just like everybody else, I encounter problems, and difficult people, and things I don't want to do,' Nick told me. 'Sometimes I have a headache in the morning. Still, I do actually love life. I like the experience of it, and I think that it is precious. And therefore this mirroring of what we have, but being rather more perfect, and a lot less dangerous, I think suits a lot of people.'

In my journeys through virtual worlds, each resident I'd met had been attracted to virtual worlds for their own particular reason. I'd expected those I found to be the disenfranchised, the ostracised, the loners. They were, I discovered – but no more than the rest of us. I began with the belief that people were so eager to rush into these new ideal spaces, to leave their real-world sorrows behind – but, I discovered, that was my own particular plight. Each person I met was caught in a different struggle; in each case, virtual worlds offered them ease. In a world where music magazines were closing, and the remaining press had written them off as an eighties phenomenon, Duran Duran seemed to hope for renewed attention. The nine souls of Wilde Cunningham moved into virtual worlds not to escape sorrow – at least, not directly; they emigrated to escape their physical restrictions. Todd Robertson moved into virtual worlds because the rough area of north London he lived in was a dangerous place. A young man of his age who ventured out into the streets of east London – where, in November 2006, a boy was sent home from school for wearing a stab-proof vest – risked a mugging or worse, a struggle I remembered from my own teenage years on the London streets. Virtual worlds offered Todd a place, free from attack, where he and his friends could switch his real-world vulnerability for virtual omnipotence, and discover themselves. Jeremy Chase seemed to have found, not respite from sorrow, but an escape from anonymity; in virtual worlds, he found some of the notoriety he craved. Even the virtual criminals were escaping something: crime, an attempt to shortcut life's long ratio of effort to reward, is just another refusal to suffer. Some virtual residents I met seemed to be trying to journey too far away from themselves. At the real-world launch party for a new super-villain-themed virtual world, *City of Villains*, I met an immense, rotund French man, who declared seemingly without irony that he was known in the game as 'Mr Musculator'. We spoke for a while, in broken English. He said for the last two days his computer had stopped working. 'Life without a computer is not worse living,' he said. If there was a particular group that seemed over-represented in the people I'd met in virtual worlds, it was the stay-at-home, those not necessarily poor, or shy, but isolated: housewives like Anshe Chung, those let down by their bodies, like Wilde and Patrick Sapinski; and those like me, isolated by choice: the idle, the depressed, the daydreamers.

Virtual worlds offered us what we lacked. Unlike other addictions, which seemed to insert themselves as replacements for particular difficult hopes – heroin in place of peace, gambling in place of success, pornography in place of intimacy – virtual worlds are a catch-all, a panacea that extends beyond the psychic even to the physical. Like our imagination, they offer us a chance to re-create – and thus relate to – whatever is missing.

It seemed I was under the same illusion. The illusion that had seduced my mother, and the illusion that drove people in their millions to seek out other possibilities online – the idea that life should be easier than it is.

But the illusion of safety isn't always a retreat from life; sometimes it's a medicine. In her book, *In Sickness and in Play: Children Coping with Chronic Illness*, Cindy Dell Clark, professor of human development and family studies at Penn State, talks about the ways children with chronic illnesses use what she calls 'Imaginal Coping' – narrative games that weave their pain into play. One asthmatic boy pretended his breathing machine was a toy plane; another diabetic child re-imagined his needle as a zebra, giving him a kiss. All play is a way to create a small, safe environment in which to act ourselves out, without fear of harmful consequence. As children, we make our world, and inhabit it to discover ourselves.

As adults, much of our entertainments are attempts to recreate this earlier innocence. We gather around all kinds of ritualised confrontation, where anxiety and loss are lessened and what remains is structured play. Baseball fans who obsess over statistics; or those who build medieval armour and weapons, and re-enact historical conflicts, free from the real blood that marred those times: these people inhabit, for a while, a safer, more formalised place, where conflict and struggle can be neutralised.

Artists create to express their wound, and pain drives us to narrate. Like art, virtual worlds seemed to offer a universal solution – an overly seductive one, perhaps, a medicine that could be mistaken for a cure – but in each case, virtual worlds offer a chance to experience the opposite of the difficulties inherent in the real world. The pursuit of virtual dreams was an anaesthetic for our troubled present; but also, it turned out, an anaesthetic for our troubled bodies. Virtual worlds had the capacity to ease not just our emotional pain, but also our physical pain.

For Wilde Cunningham, the step into virtual worlds helped ease their real-world physical troubles of disability and shame. But there was also another group of people, who arguably have even more reason to emigrate from the real world; another group for whom the journey through the electronic looking glass meant a journey to a world with less agony. Those with a condition which is acknowledged to be the most painful known to medicine: burns victims.

Dr Hunter Hoffman's interest in virtual reality began as an interest in how people remembered what was real, and what was imaginary. Using early nineties virtual reality equipment, he discovered that a combination of visual and tactile information produced the greatest immersion in digitally created worlds – he simulated eating a chocolate bar, and, as the subject ate the digital bar, he put a real chocolate bar into their mouth. What he noticed was that the combination of virtual and real totally absorbed the patients; they would ignore everything else going on around them. He began to consider who would best benefit from this absence from reality. A chance encounter with David Patterson, a psychologist who had been using hypnosis to ease pain for medical patients, led to a decision to collaborate. At first they worked together for free, in their spare time, until, after some early and remarkable results, Paul Allen, the co-founder of Microsoft, stepped in to support their research.

They decided to work with burns patients, because they suffer the most. Serious burns need to be redressed every day, an agonising process that takes up to an hour. Damaged pain receptors report constant pain, and most pain receptors are in the skin. Dr Hoffman began each study by asking each patient how much they enjoyed having their burn bandages changed. They used to ask if he was crazy. Some even grew furious with the question. A few weeks later, after hanging out in Dr Hoffman's Snow World – they donned virtual reality helmets to throw virtual snowballs at virtual snowmen while the bandages were changed – most patients reported a six or seven on a scale of enjoyment from one to 10. It was the most painful part of their treatment, and they were starting to enjoy it.

Dr Hoffman told me he saw virtual worlds as just another technique for easing people's pain. 'It's like a normal dose response: someone in more pain needs more morphine,' Dr Hoffman told me, on the phone from his mother's house in San Diego. 'When you're trying to treat burn pain, you're treating someone who's *really* in pain. To help them, you need a really good virtual world.' After his success with burns patients, Hoffman began work with other psychologists to extend his virtual-reality cognitive therapy to other areas of treatment. Working with Dr JoAnn Difede, Assistant Professor of Psychiatry at New York-Presbyterian Hospital, Hoffman developed a simulation to help Manhattan residents traumatised by the 9/11 World Trade Center attacks. 'They start by looking up at the World Trade Center, completely intact, on a beautiful blue-sky morning,' Hoffman told me. 'A lot of times, that alone is enough to elicit an emotional reaction. But after an hour or so, when they're comfortable with the buildings, we cause a plane to fly by. It doesn't crash, but it really upsets them. The difference between doing this on a computer screen, and doing it with a tracking VR helmet like we do, is that the illusion of going back, of actually being there, is infinitely increased. They're not just watching: it's September 11th again. Then we move on to a plane which crashes, but with no sound, no explosion. We do it over and over, for hours, until they're at a point where they're upset but not desperate to leave the room. Then we add sound effects. A booming explosion, people screaming, more special effects, a second plane crashes, then the towers collapse: smoke, sirens, people, confusion. It's very effective.' Of seven 9/11 patients Hoffman had treated, six improved dramatically. All six had failed to respond to any other psychological treatment.

The success with post-traumatic stress has inspired more applications. Dr Hoffman was working with the US Army to develop a treatment for soldiers recently returned from war zones with post-traumatic stress syndrome. With more funding from Paul Allen, Hoffman was working with a therapist from Haifa University in Israel, to treat survivors of suicide bombings.

I asked about the technology behind his virtual scenarios. 'Right before I started using VR, a good VR computer was $175,000. Soon after I started, a new one came out, which cost $90,000. By '96, when I started working with burn patients, a really good machine was $45,000. Now, you can buy a computer for $3,000, which is just as good as any of those old ones. You can use a laptop.' I asked Dr Hoffman about the software they used. 'Well, we're using custom software at the moment, developed by the US military at great expense. I'm looking at new software, though, at the moment. It looks fantastic. State of the art.'

'Really?' I asked. 'Which one?'

'Unreal Tournament,' he said, referring to an off-the-shelf futuristic combat game, which costs $39.99.

In the work of Dr Hoffman virtual worlds healed the physical pains of burns patients, and in the work of Dr JoAnn Difede, they healed our fear of the past. In the case of the millions of virtual émigrés, refugees from a difficult world, they healed a different kind of pain: our yearning to belong. Virtual worlds were medicine for a broken world, and, as with all medicines, sometimes people took too much. In the summer of 2005, in his favourite all-night games cafe in Kangju, near Seoul, 24-year-old Kim Kyung-Jae decided to play his virtual character for as long as he could. He told his mother he was going camping with his friends, and settled in at a cafe. He ate noodles from a vending machine, drank complimentary cups of instant coffee, and played games. Eighty-six hours later, still inhabiting his virtual self, deep-vein thrombosis set in. A blood-clot formed, and moved to his heart, and Kyung-Jae died in his chair.

Virtual worlds seemed to ease some basic modern discomfort. But was the medicine worse than the disease? Were these new virtual émigrés holding themselves back from the suffering of the world too? Or were they plunging into a new mode of being, one that would deliver a new perspective on our plight? I decided to travel to Korea, where the mania for virtual worlds, and their capacity to generate both pleasure and pain, had reached its peak. In 2005, more people visited Korean-made virtual worlds than visited Korea. I would do both.

17

KOREA
King of the world

Until I met the king of the world, I had become convinced the trip had been a waste of time.

Our flight from London to Seoul had been long. My girl-friend popped a Valium; I didn't. She slept; I didn't. On the plane, I read my *Rough Guide*. South Korea is a place of contra-dictions, I read. Koreans are proud of their country, but readily adopt other cultures (50 per cent of South Koreans declare they are Christian). South Korea is a successful, affluent nation – the fourth largest lending nation in the world – but under constant threat. I mentioned to the young Korean in the next seat that I was from London. South Korea is about the same size and popu-lation as the UK, he told me, but Seoul has the second largest metropolitan population in the world. He took my map of Seoul and carefully described each region: the business centre, City Hall, the student areas near the national universities, the rowdier area near the US army base. He smiled at me. 'Seoul is a very friendly place,' he said. 'Also, very near North Korea. One nuclear weapon . . . Boom!' He grinned and swept his hands across the map.

At Seoul Incheon airport, after 18 hours of travelling, my

girlfriend and I argued. For half an hour we dragged our bags through the ranks of expensive black 'luxury' cabs, shouting the whole time, to find a stand with normal priced taxis. From the window, we watched as we crossed the reclaimed land around Incheon airport and Seoul drifted into view.

I'd been expecting the bright LED towers of Tokyo or Hong Kong; Seoul looked more like Birmingham. There were no steel high-rises, no hectic snake-vending street markets. Thanks to the government's vision of Seoul as a 'hub of Asia', even the road signs were in English as well as Korean. There were blocks of flats, rickety houses, and cars. Then more cars. Then we were stuck in traffic. The cab driver pointed out the window and spoke in heavily accented English. In our delirium, we thought he was agreeing with us. 'Shitty Hole!' he said. Our despair took on an edge of hysteria. (He meant, we later realised, 'City Hall'.) My girlfriend had wanted to go to Hong Kong, but at the last minute I persuaded her to come to Seoul 'for the experience'. In the cab, she gave me a look that told me I was going to have trouble keeping her happy for the whole week. Or even for the first day. I slumped lower in my seat.

On the subway, we read the English language *Seoul Times*. The South Korean government had recently decided to move the capital from Seoul to the area of Yeongi-Kongju. The new capital, scheduled to begin construction in 2007, was controversial. On the subway were government-sponsored adverts supporting the move, pointing out all the problems with life in Seoul. My girlfriend pointed out one of the ads, above her head. 'Look,' she said. 'Just as we arrive, everyone else wants to leave.' Seoul, it seemed, was a place where people found disappointment.

In our hotel room – which consisted of a bed, a small gap, and the wall – the Internet wasn't working. The room's only distinctive feature, mounted in the centre of the far wall, was a short orange cord wrapped in bright emergency-red plastic, labelled 'Escape Rope'. We were on the seventeenth floor.

And so it went on. Our hotel room had a remote control that affected the television but also, according to no apparent logic, the lights and other room features; one button turned off the ceiling lamp, but turned on the television and the bathroom fan. Another turned off the fan but switched on the bedside light. Each night we had to play our own version of the cryptic gameshow *The Crystal Maze* just to get to sleep. In Korea, as more than one helpful vendor informed me, they didn't sell English power adaptors; to get one, apparently, you had to pop over to Hong Kong. I finally lied through my teeth to get hold of just one from the Seoul Westin Chosun Hotel. So each night, in addition to the jet lag and the light show, I set my alarm to wake me every two hours to charge my laptop, minidisc recorder, camera and phone in shifts.

Halfway through my trip, the day before I visited NCsoft, over a sorrowful, solitary 'surf-n-turf' salad plate at an empty Sizzler – the only open restaurant I could find – I chastised myself for coming at all. Instead I should have just written about the games themselves. Or gotten another job entirely. Builder. Taxi driver. Elsewhere, at exactly the same time, my girlfriend was by the hotel pool with two English teachers from New Zealand. When she said she was in Seoul for a holiday, they choked on their drinks and told her to get out while she still could.

As my journey went on, and I made my appointments to see games professionals, it became clear that the BBC had arrived in Seoul weeks earlier, and had spoken with some of the same people. Were they scooping me? Did they ask better questions? As the days went by, it grew worse. I bought an expensive digital camera, but forgot to take photos. I forgot to call that guy back. I'm a bad person. I should have been a musician. I'm lazy compared to these lean-looking Koreans. I have no stamina. In the hotel mirror, I stared at my slack physique. I seemed to be in even worse shape here than I was back in London.

That night, back at the hotel, I flipped between channels dedicated to mysterious cartoons, shopping channels, and computer-games tournaments. On these last channels, indecipherable armies of space-tanks attacked one another, insectoid shapes scuttling and scuffling over an alien landscape, the players surrounded by dry ice. Sports-style commentators sat behind a desk, apparently discussing timing, reactions, and tactics. At the end of each match, it seemed, the loser was nearly crying; although the winner too seemed close to tears, and it was hard to tell whether their eyes were red from emotion, or from years of staring at a video screen. Further up the dial, there were channels and channels of Koreans fucking like crazy. My girlfriend and I were getting none. I was taking pills for exhaustion, given to me by a Chinese doctor in England: small balls apparently made of iron, which bruised my throat as they went down. Not long before, there had been SARS outbreaks across Asia. Was it me, or had a lot of people back at the airport been *sneezing*?

In Seoul, the line between dream and disappointment seemed paper-thin. I arranged to spend some time with a team of professional gamers, who turned out to be a group of Canadian kids who shared a cramped flat. They played Starcraft, Korea's most popular spectator game: a futuristic military strategy game, where two players controlled opposing armies of space-tanks with frenetic mouse clicks and flicks of the wrist. The Canadian gamers showed me replays of famous matches, mistakes made under pressure, tactics never seen before. 'More people in Korea know the rules of Starcraft than know the rules of chess,' one told me, although I had no way to check this.

These people lived off savings, shared bunkbeds, and argued over whether they could afford take-out pizza. In Korea, it seemed, the disappointment and the dream offered by virtual worlds almost precisely balanced out.

Then, when I finally reached the headquarters of NCsoft, makers of Lineage II, I spent almost the whole day discussing the financial end of massive online worlds. I kept trying to steer the conversation to something salacious or even surprising, but they only wanted to talk business.

I had been told in advance that the NCsoft server room was the most secure non-military installation in South Korea. Every teenage hacker in the nation dreamed of penetrating their vaults. It was, I had been told, protected by guards, steel doors and fingerprint scanners, like the Bellagio vault in *Ocean's Eleven*. The reality, I discovered, was more like *Being John Malkovich*: a hidden lift button, an unlabelled second floor. We pulled on antistatic slippers and strolled around the server room: racks of silver boxes, lit by halogen lamps, cooled by a frigid breeze. It could have been the heart of the data-management strategy of any multinational business. Back in the meeting room, under the watchful eye of NCsoft's Head of International PR, one of their Games Masters, powerful characters who hang out in the game and field player's problems (a cross between the headmaster of a wizard school and your local MP), read a prepared statement welcoming me to 'the exciting world of Lineage II'. We toured the call centre, which looked just like a call centre. I listened in on a few calls. I had hoped to overhear inane queries like, 'I've teleported myself into a tree, how do I get out?' or, 'this elf is stalking me . . .' but I heard just standard business issues: bounced payments, missing passwords. Everything was business-focussed. I knew the stories, but the reality seemed more prosaic. I began to think that this was a dead-end, a business that suckered millions into paying regular fees . . . not a shared dream-world but a racket, a knowing illusion peddled on children by businessmen. I didn't know whether there were really any stories to be told. I'd met my movie star in the street, and they'd turned out to be just a regular guy. I was still not convinced there was a story.

Then, in came Kyu Nam Choi. He plugged in his laptop and logged on, and the transformation happened in front of my eyes: the owner of a struggling hamburger restaurant became the king of the world.

When I met the king of the world, he ran a restaurant in northern Seoul. He woke up around 9 a.m., showered, pulled on sweat-pants, sandals and a T-shirt, and walked to his restaurant to open up. If you saw him on the street – a stocky, black-haired, 32-year-old South Korean, with a weary face, which he hid behind a wide, black fringe, pulling up his restaurant's shutters – you might have thought he was down on his luck. His shoulders were slumped. He looked tired. Sometimes, as he opened up, he couldn't help but look over his shoulder. There is always someone who wants to kill a king.

No wonder he looked tired. Like any world leader, he found it hard to get enough sleep. Most days, along with his brother, he ruled his kingdom for 20 hours out of 24; and that was not including the time it takes to run his restaurant. Since he had been crowned, his other business, the restaurant, had suffered. He found it hard to keep up with the paperwork. On top of running a restaurant – and ruling the world – he made ends meet with a range of odd jobs. He had no wife to make additional demands on his time, but even so, there were never enough hours in the day. He barely had time to manage his staff, and lately there had been fewer customers for the staff to serve. By about 10.30, the restaurant was usually still empty. He walked upstairs to his office, sat down on his padded swivel chair, and became king.

There were other kings in the world, but he was the king of kings, and so perhaps the loneliest. The world he ruled over was home to almost 3 million people; still, at 10.30 most mornings, his throne room was empty. Each morning, the king usually strolled down to the castle gate: out of the throne room, along the stone corridors, down the carpeted stairs of the castle's great hall and out into the huge sloped floral courtyard. There were other castles in the world, but his was the Castle of the Kings: many times greater than anything else the world had seen. He walked down below the colossal battlements, among the royal flower gardens, and commanded the guards to open the gates. Except by force, only his royal court were allowed to enter the castle through these huge barred oak doors. Flanked by guards, he stood outside the gates and gazed out over the hills. The members of his court were out there somewhere, on a hunt – for sport, for furs, for honour – or at battle with the king's enemies.

Later, he would join in the hunt. For now, though, he had to go downstairs, fire up the oven, light the grill, and serve breakfast.

His subjects knew Kyu Nam Choi as Archirus. His kingdom, Lineage II, was thousands of square miles of mountains, desert, forest and sea. To walk across the Lineage II sub-continent would take days. When I met him, Archirus's kingdom, with its 3 million inhabitants, was the most popular virtual world on the planet – more densely populated than Brazil. All of the residents, like Mr Choi, led other lives: they were bankers, students, taxi drivers, housekeepers, hairdressers, and businessmen. All of them paid around $15 per month to enter Lineage II, a fantasy-themed virtual world where hunting parties gathered to venture into more dangerous parts to stalk monsters (from lowly wolves to near-invincible dragons). The more monsters they killed, the more powerful they became. And, as the most powerful inhabitant of this realm – the King of Kings – Mr Choi ruled over them all. He had the power to change laws, to raise taxes, to end their lives. When he walked by, they cheered. When he taxed them, they suffered. When he died – in the virtual world, not the real – they mourned.

I had travelled to South Korea to meet the king of kings, because there the mania for virtual worlds was at its most extreme. In part because of a mid-1990s government drive, South Korea is per capita the most Internet-connected nation on earth. (When I visited, in late 2004, 60 per cent of households had broadband, compared with just 14 per cent in the UK.)

In Korea, professional gamers can earn six-figure dollar-equivalent salaries, have three TV channels dedicated to them, and are recognised by screaming fans on the street. Pop songs are written about online games. The mania extends to massive online virtual worlds: almost all of Mr Choi's 3 million subjects are Korean. Of the 25–30 million people worldwide who play these games, a third are Korean, and nearly half – around 12 million – play Korean-made games. Each year, more than twice as many people around the world visit Korean-made virtual worlds as visit Korea. A week before my visit, the Chinese government – which had recently banned foreign animation from primetime TV – announced that Chinese companies should develop similar games, as too many Chinese people were spending their time in Korean-made virtual worlds, and too much virtual-world profit ($117.4 million in 2005) was leaking from China to Korea. To correct the balance, the government pledged $1.8 billion over the next five years, to develop 100 'domestically devout' virtual worlds, like the forthcoming 'Chinese Heroes', based on a Mao Zedong-era model soldier. According to the South Korean Culture Ministry's Game Development Institute, online games revenue in Korea was worth $1.5 billion in 2005.

Before my trip, I'd read up on the mania that encompassed South Korean online worlds. Apparently, gaming cafe owners had been convicted for putting amphetamines in the water coolers to keep kids playing their games. Runaways had reportedly supported themselves entirely through in-game fraud. In Asia, the scale of the phenomenon meant the retreat from life and body had reached its peak – to the point where some end up leaving their body entirely. (The same month that Kim Kyung-Jae died in his games cafe chair, 28-year-old boiler repairman Lee Sung Seop also died, from cardiac arrest, after 50 hours inside World of Warcraft. During 2005, in total, 10 South Koreans died in similar ways.)

The King and I met on the eighth floor of a Seoul office building owned by NCsoft, South Korea's most successful game developer (corporate motto: 'Create the Next Culture. Build the Next Game. Imagine the Next Life.'). In an NCSoft meeting room, Kyu – particularly weary from a long battle to recapture his castle the night before – brushed his fringe from his eyes, leant back, sipped a plum juice, and explained the double bind of his double life.

In the real world, on a good week, Kyu's restaurant served 200 customers; online, he was the ruler of 3 million subjects. In the real world, he had trouble paying his bills; online, he could always raise taxes. This was not always a trouble-free source of funds. When taxes rose too high, his people revolted. Each Monday morning, on the eighth floor of NCsoft's real-world offices, the Lineage II team met to monitor that other world's inflation rates. If Kyu was a king, these people who watched over the world they created should be gods. In fact, they said, they felt more like tax inspectors. To keep the economy in balance and stop in-game fraud, they audited the books of anyone who had acquired a suspiciously large amount of money or property.

Kyu sighed. He was, my translator relayed, particularly tired. Last night, he told me – with something of the calm self-deprecation of a movie star – had been the climactic battle of four months of struggle against a coup attempt. His most loyal subjects were a core of around a thousand people who effectively made up his government. They formed a chain of command, filtering the problems of his subjects up through the ranks. His court, his most loyal subjects, doubled as his defence force in case anyone tried to take the throne. They were so strong, he said, that no other group in the game had the power to conquer them in battle. They began to take for granted that the Castle of the Kings would remain theirs. Then, two weeks ago, he told me, his enemies had banded together to form a great temporary alliance, an axis of virtual evil. In a colossal battle, his cohorts were beaten – thousands were killed – and his enemies took the throne. Many of his court took the defeat personally. Hundreds left his service. He went from an entourage of 1,000 to fewer than 400 dedicated followers. Then, last night, he said, he and his subjects returned to lay siege to the castle. They conjured two huge stone golems to break down the castle doors. They fought their way up the sloped garden, under a hail of arrows from archers lined along the battlements. They fought up the stone staircase of the main hall, along the corridors, into the throne room. They were a smaller force than they had been when the castle was taken, he said, but his own bravery inspired his people. They reclaimed the seal of the king and took back the throne.

I asked him why his subjects had been so disappointed to be beaten. He explained it was because many of them died. 'Many gamers think the character is another me. So in fact when my character dies, I feel so sad. If somebody kills me, I feel like revenging the killer. It happens a lot.'

In most online worlds, player-on-player violence is common. Everywhere else in the real world, 'player-killing' stays within its virtual boundaries. People killed by other players are automatically reborn – no hard feelings, no loss. In Korea, though, players seem to take online deaths much more personally. There, the violence sometimes spills into revenge attacks in the real world.

As the most powerful player, Mr Choi was especially at risk of this 'offline player-killing'. Inside the world of Lineage II, Mr Choi could defend himself. His fighting skills were appropriate for an all-powerful warrior king: alone, using his bare hands, he could kill 10 players at a time. In the real world, those ratios didn't apply. When I asked if I could visit Mr Choi's restaurant to take photos, he smiled sadly and shook his head. 'There are unpleasant people in the game,' he said. 'Like any king, I have supporters and opponents. I can't risk my face being disclosed in case someone from the game used the photos to find me in real life.'

Instead, he logged on and showed me around his castle. I watched as Mr Choi transformed into the King of Kings. Archirus's eyes narrowed. On the screen, in a flash of blue light next to his throne, his character appeared: a silver hunter, with a curved sword, edged with jagged swirls, taller than him.

At this early hour, after such a huge battle, his subjects were likely still asleep. The throne room was empty, except for his trusted Royal Secretary Logan who, he explained, always attended the throne. Logan, a creature of habit, always greeted him in the same way. 'How are you, my highness? How may I help you?' Most mornings, the king explained, he handled his chores first. He asked Logan to check the castle gate was secure, and that no one had made an assault on the walls overnight. He checked the castle safe-deposit box, and asked after the castle's store of weapons, gold reserves, and general state of repair.

The upkeep of a castle was expensive. As king of kings, Archirus's assets – and bills – extended right across the world. Some mornings, when the castle defences were depleted or the coffers were low, he asked Logan to increase taxation rates. Logan put the word out, and across the whole kingdom, the tens or hundreds of thousands who bought or sold anything at all that day would pay a little extra into the pockets of the king.

Sometimes, when taxes approached 15 per cent, Kyu explained, they marched on the castle to protest outside the gates. He always made a point of going out on the battlements to explain the pressures he was under. They never understood. Only the king knows the true responsibility of being a king.

I asked the king whether he was tempted to cash in on his success. No one has ever sold a character as powerful as Kyu's. With the deed to his castle, with the account of the highest player in the game, with all his royal cash reserves, there would be millions of potential bidders. He could earn tens of thousands of dollars. When I asked him if he had ever considered making real-world money from the game, though, he looked hurt. No, he said, he never considered it. It would be dishonourable. His supporters had helped him attain his money, items and power. If he sold them, it would be a betrayal of their trust.

Mr Choi's virtual reign gave him real power: if he asked his followers to vote a certain way in real-world government elections, he said, they would. In fact, Choi compared his network of thousands of supporters – his royal court – with a political party. Much of his time as king was spent preparing his castle against attack, solving problems and mediating disputes between his subjects. Not just anyone could walk up to the king and petition for his help; the requests were passed up through his commanders. Enough problems filtered up to keep him more than busy. As an example, he told me, on hearing Mr Choi was visiting NCsoft that afternoon, one of his subjects, a level 75 player, asked Choi to see if he could persuade NCsoft to give him a virtual gift for his upcoming virtual wedding.

Mr Choi explained his dilemma. The more time he spent as king, the more his restaurant suffered; the more his restaurant suffered, the more he wanted to spend time as king. Until he discovered Lineage II, he said, his whole life had been the single-minded pursuit of success. He worked in restaurants, then managed them, then ran whole chains. His life, he told me, was nothing but work. He was successful, he made money, but he trusted no one. The people he met at work were usually looking to use him in some way. He had never had a close friend.

Then one afternoon, with two hours to kill after a cancelled appointment, he wandered into a branch of PC Bang – a 24-hour Internet cafe dedicated to online gaming – and saw rows of people playing Lineage. He played it, and liked it. That night, he bought his own copy of the game and installed it on his office PC. As his online life developed, he began to find the friendship he had missed all his life. Now he was making up for lost time. Kyu told me he had never had a girlfriend, but he hoped one day to meet someone online, get married and settle down. Until then, despite his struggling business, he wouldn't give up Lineage II for the world. He had tried every other pastime he could think of, but nothing soothed the pain of his struggles, helped him forget about his problems – the restaurant, being alone – as much as playing the game. Nothing else, Kyu said, gave him the same feeling of belonging.

Now, though, because of his second life, his first life was suffering. If it wasn't for his subjects, he said, he would have to quit. But he feels he can't; they depend on him.

He depended on them, too. 'People feel happiness and satis-faction through online communication, especially those who feel loneliness in real life,' Mr Choi told me. 'Because they can have attention from the communities in the game, while some people do not have that in real life.' In the games, he said, people talked to him, and he talked to people. In the streets of Seoul, he told me, nobody even said hello. It's funny, though, he said: he often met his online friends in the real world. Sometimes the most talkative characters turned out to be the most reticent.

'Some gamers are really shy in real life,' he said. Even so, Choi trusted the people he met through Lineage more than those he met through work. His work colleagues all seemed eager to use him in some way. The people he met through the game were interested in him as a person. 'We meet,' he said, 'with no conspiracy.'

This virtual community is real enough – and it has been known to save lives. In 2004, not long before my visit, the friend of one Lineage II player went into haemorrhage while giving birth. Her blood type, O negative, was shared by only one in 200 Koreans. The player logged on and advertised his friend's plight. Within the hour, an O negative Lineage player showed up at the hospital. Mother and baby survived.

The sense of community provided by virtual worlds seemed to resonate with a particularly Korean need to keep in touch. When I visited, communications technology was everywhere. On underground trains, people chatted on mobile phones, and at the Korean equivalents of 7–11 stores – LG-25 and Linko's ('A place for buying fun') – you could drop off your mobile battery and pick it up 40 minutes later, fully charged. Communications technology had a central role in the culture. As my translator explained, many Koreans thought 'cyber-electioneering' – website chat-room, text-message and email campaigning – had swung the 2002 election in the favour of the now-ruling liberal party. 'In war, families were separated,' my translator told me. 'Now Koreans like to be in contact.'

But the sense of community in virtual worlds had a downside, too. Gamers came to rely on the game to provide companionship. Virtual worlds offer the promise of paradise as well as the killing of time; and the Korean government had begun to recognise the addictive effect of these two powerful pulls on Korean youth. In 2004, a law was passed limiting online gaming to those over 18. The games companies now (reluctantly) enforce the law by linking online accounts to government ID numbers – but the kids find ways around the ban.

In 2002, the South Korean government established the Internet Addiction Counselling Centre, whose staff visit schools to measure Internet addiction, and offer advice and education for those who feel they are addicts.

I decided to visit the Internet Addiction Centre. Outside, as I left the taxi, the driver asked me for the Centre's telephone number, and asked which floor the Addiction Centre was on. He told me about his son, a high school student who never left his room. He used the Internet every day, from 10 a.m. to midnight, the driver said, mostly in chat rooms and inside Lineage II. His son wasn't alone: according to Lee Sujin, a clinical psychologist who greeted me at the Addiction Centre, more than two thirds of South Korean teenagers play online games. Over a quarter think of themselves as Internet-addicted.

Lee Sujin told me about a recent visit to a psychological conference on the subject, where, she said, her international colleagues viewed the Internet addiction problem in terms of chat rooms or online gambling (the US Centre for Online Addiction, founded in 1995, lists chat room and cyber-sex addiction above online gaming). In South Korea, she said, the main problem is online gaming. I suggested that, as well as distracting them from the world, online gaming also provides a sense of community that the children find lacking in the real world. She agreed, but pointed out that at the Addiction Centre they see only the ill-effects: depression, nervousness, absence from schools and cyber-crime – the theft of game accounts, for example. In South Korea in 2004, there were approximately 64,000 cyber-crimes; about half related to online gaming. There were nearly 10,000 arrests – around 30 a day – which resulted in some 5,000 convictions. (For comparison, the number of equivalent arrests in the UK in the same year was precisely none.) Most young

314

Koreans who commit cyber-crimes are sent to the Internet Addiction Centre rather than to prison. The Centre puts offenders through a re-education programme, then gives them community work – for example, renovating old computers for charity. They try to instil self-respect in the children, Lee Sujin told me, and to help them develop self-confidence in the real world, as well as to help define objectives that develop their real lives, rather than their lives in the game. 'It's not easy,' she said. 'It's so much easier to achieve things in the game. When these kids face problems in the real world, they give up.'

Lee Sujin showed me a handful of their questionnaires. Answers their young respondents had ticked again and again included: 'I have broken promises because of the Internet'; 'On the Internet, people acknowledge me more'; 'When I use the Internet, I feel confident and free.'

The word 'addiction' comes from the Latin word for a type of slave – an 'addict' – granted as a reward for brave performance in battle. When we become addicted, we become slaves: to a way of achieving our goals that makes us feel we have succeeded, but brings about no real change in our actual affairs. Eventually, though, the addict always finds their way back to the place they were trying to avoid. The heroin addict seeks peace, but ends up in anguish. The gambling addict seeks success, but ends up broke. The gamer seeks excitement and community, but ends up with an empty life.

Or do they?

I asked Kyu Nam Choi what kept him playing, even as his business slid towards bankruptcy. Was he addicted? Was he distracting himself from sorrow? He shook his head. It was the endless possibilities that most attracted him to live in a virtual world, he said. 'It's not addiction. It's a way to live a different life,' he said. 'Real life doesn't often live up to our expectations, but in the game, anything can happen. I have killed, I have been killed, I have been reborn. These are the things I can't do in real life. I don't own a car, but in the game, I can fly.'

Mr Choi turned to the laptop. Fingers rattled over the keyboard. On the screen, in his castle, his character began to yelp in strange magical tongues. Green and blue flame rose up to fill the throne room. The king of the world rose up in the air. NCsoft's Head of International PR gasped in what sounded like genuine admiration. 'Fabulous. I can't do that with my character,' she said.

Kyu logged off. As he unplugged his laptop and prepared to return to his hamburger restaurant, I asked him one last question. In order to play the game, you have to live in the real world. But what if that wasn't the case? If he could liberate himself from all the computer hardware, and become just one person, Kyu or Archirus, the real or the virtual, which life would he choose?

He leant back, folded his hands behind his head, and closed his eyes. 'In real life, even though I own my business, I am just an ordinary person. In the game life, I rule the world. Which would you choose?' He opened his eyes. 'I choose the game,' he said.

With that the king of the world had to leave, to congratulate his subjects and to celebrate their greatest victory. Also, he had to reopen his restaurant.

After Kyu Nam Choi and his NCsoft escort left the room, I asked my translator what she thought of the king of the world. Her eyes were bright. 'He's amazing,' she said, almost breathless. 'He had the feeling of a real master. Didn't you see his hands? They were artist's hands.'

Although Kyu has never had a girlfriend, it's not necessarily for the same reasons that a 32-year-old computer-obsessive from the UK might be single. Rather than being dismissed as nerds, in South Korea successful players become stars. In his book, *Game: the Revolutionary Power to Change the World,* the Korean critic Park Sang Woo argues that the difference between Korean and Western residents of virtual worlds is that Koreans identify much more with their virtual selves.

In a Starbucks in the huge underground warren of Coex Plaza – Asia's largest shopping mall – I met Park Sang Woo to talk about Lineage II. Park turned out to be a young Korean with a meticulous beard and an intense stare. When I arrived, his nose was deep in a Japanese book on postmodernism. (I was an hour late. As far as I could work out from the warnings in my guide-book about Korea's Confucian morals, I should prepare myself for a sharp rebuke; in fact, he threatened to leave, then talked about games for three hours.) In online worlds like Lineage, players can kill each other: a phenomenon known as 'player-killing', or PK-ing. 'In the West, death means nothing; you are instantly reborn,' Sang Woo told me. 'In Korea, players feel the death of their online player keenly. There is honour and repu-tation at stake,' he said.

'In other countries, alter egos are necessary for online games,' he told me. 'The focus is on building "another me", which is different to the "me" in real life. But in Korea, the real life and the game life are very much connected. The higher level our characters are, and the more splendid items we can get, the more praise we receive. In Korean society, people like to be noticed.'

I heard the same phrase again and again, from almost everyone I spoke with in Seoul: Koreans like to be noticed. In a country where the family name comes before the given name, and the middle floors of apartment blocks are the most desirable, every young person seemed to want to stand out from the crowd, but strong traditional Confucian pressures to conform made it very difficult to leave the pack. Online gaming has become a way for young South Koreans to remain conservative in their lives, but also stand out among their peers. (Megapass, South Korea's ultra-broadband Internet service, advertises with the English slogan 'I'm the champion, 100 per cent different.') One of the Games Masters of Lineage II told me she started playing the game because, in the street, she wasn't supposed to laugh. In the game, she could laugh wherever she liked.

Because virtual worlds have penetrated South East Asian culture so thoroughly, the attendant crime, too, has reached a peak there. Two days after I arrived in Seoul, I read a newspaper report about two policemen who attempted to arrest a suspected rapist, Hyuong Kim, and were stabbed to death. Kim became Seoul's public enemy number one. Police distributed 1,000 leaflets with his name, photo and Citizen ID. Two days later, they received a tip-off. Kim was accessing an online game from the Samsung apartment block in northern Seoul. Police barricaded the building and searched every apartment, scouring even the insides of washing machines. They found nothing – even though their computers showed Kim as still logged on. The next day, police discovered the culprit: a 14-year-old boy had seen Kim's ID number on the wanted posters, and used it to access an over-18 gaming site. Word spread. Soon, Hyuong Kim was logging on to play Lineage II from all over the city.

In South Korea, this kind of ID theft is widespread. An estimated 30 per cent of South Korea's ID cards are fraudulent; in June 2006, the ID numbers of President Roh Moo Hyun and Prime Minister Han Myeong Sook appeared on the Internet. The IDs were used to gain access to online games, and hundreds of pornographic websites. In another case, in July 2006, South Korea's National Police Agency began investigating 10 people, including a garage mechanic and an employee at a credit information firm, both of whom had access to databases of private information for their role in the sale of private ID numbers. The owners of seven gaming cafes allegedly bought the information, and set up 280,000 virtual-world accounts. They hired part-time gamers to work inside worlds like Lineage II, to earn virtual currency, which they sold for real won on Korean websites like ItemBay, for an estimated KRW 14.2 billion ($15 million). The Cyber Crimes Police also investigated a senior NCsoft executive, who allegedly knew about the false IDs, but – worried his company's revenues would go down (each of those 280,000 accounts paid a subscription fee) – he kept quiet.

NCsoft has 150 employees monitoring for 'bots' – automated characters designed to make virtual money without anyone having to sit at the actual keyboard. But the arms race was not in their favour. When I visited, NCsoft spent $10 million a year on cyber-security; less than the $15 million made by one virtual crime ring alone. South Korean police said they were investigating an additional 900,000 fraudulent accounts, which they believed were linked to organised operations in China making similar profits. (120,000 of these accounts were later closed.) In 2004, NCsoft accidentally leaked the account details of over 8,500 Lineage II customers (they failed to encrypt a single log file, which contained the customers' IDs and passwords). NCsoft was ordered to pay each affected customer KRW 500,000 (about $500) in compensation.

I met Inspector Kim Gi Bum, of the Cyber Terror Unit, in his Seoul headquarters. Bum, his ranks pinned on a black ribbon to his shirt pocket, led me to his desk. With a serious, bespectacled frown, he explained how his department had been established to handle criminal hacking attempts, in many cases North Korean attempts to disrupt South Korean business and government. Not long after, a Seoul politician had decided the unit's remit should include virtual crimes. Now, over half their workload was related to online games.

When I visited, Korean law did not yet recognise virtual items as assets with legal value. So, if you sold someone a virtual item but you didn't get paid, no crime would have been committed. You could bring a civil suit, but the game company would probably close your account before restitution could be made. If the tables were turned – if you paid someone and they didn't cough up the item – a crime would have occurred, and the seller who didn't deliver would be convicted of fraud. Another common crime, the Inspector explained, was hacking, where one user obtained access to another user's account and cleaned out their items. These cases were covered by existing Korean law about ID theft; the crime was punishable by up to three years in prison, but it still took a civil suit to get back your virtual sword. As Bum and I spoke, the matter of whether virtual items should have legal value was being debated by the South Korean parliament. The Inspector told me he and his colleagues hoped they wouldn't. In one stroke, their games-related workload would double. Also, such a ruling would criminalise all Korean online gambling sites, which were currently only valid for cyber-cash – gambling for real money was illegal. In a stroke, every one of the millions of virtual gamblers would become outlaws.

Inspector Bum confirmed the rumours I had heard, that Seoul cyber-cafe owners had been convicted of spiking water-coolers with amphetamines, to give their customers more energy to inhabit their virtual selves. He talked me through some other recent Cyber Police cases. In one, a 14-year-old runaway they recently arrested had slept in gaming cafes for an entire year. During that time he had made 128 fraudulent deals, where he promised items in return for money, but never delivered – to a profit of over US $10,000. In another case, a girl met in the flesh a friend she had made through Lineage II; she felt she knew him but, when they met, he raped her, and forced her into prostitution. Inspector Bum told me that other common cyber-crimes included violence against the families of games players, and hacking attempts to steal passwords and items – as well as many of the 'offline PK' attacks Mr Choi feared.

After meeting with Park Sang Woo, my translator led me through the depths of the Coex mall. South Korea has rebounded from the financial hardships of the mid-1990s to become a creditor nation. Around us, the coffee-and-sugar-fuelled, Gap-clothed business of modern capitalism seemed to be churning healthily on. Having shed their military dictatorship less than two decades before, squeezed between the two often hostile nations of North Korea and Japan ('As a peninsula, we feel like an island,' my translator told me), Korea came to modernisation late, and in a hurry. The Korean people seemed aimed like a rocket for the dream of capitalism: the primacy of the self. My translator wore Chanel shades, and her self-confessed role model was Audrey Hepburn. Nicholas Cage planned to marry a Korean woman he met while she was working as a waitress, my translator told me. 'See? It could happen to me,' she said.

She led me near the centre of Coex, to the largest PC Bang she knew. The proprietor gave us each a card, good for an hour's play, and we typed our numbers into two neighbouring PCs. Around us sat hundreds of young men, gazing through computer screens into their virtual worlds. Here they were in rows, their eyes bright, leaving the real world behind. In that moment, fazed as I was by jet lag, caffeine and crowds, they seemed not addicted but calm, a cool eye at the centre of Coex mall's hurricane of consumer abandon. I watched their fingers skitter across keyboards. I admired their skill. I wondered whether they were perhaps not escapees but misunderstood pioneers, beginners in the art of envisioning other worlds – determined to communicate with like-minded but distant souls, to share their visions of another kind of place.

Jung called alcoholism a low-level search for god. Virtual

321

worlds, even for those addicted to them, seemed like a low-level search for each other.

With my translator's help, I decided to log on and try Lineage II. I did my best to make my character, a wizard, look like me, but ended up with a pointy-eared, silver-skinned elf. It would do. Like everyone else, I was born fully clothed, in a windy castle with a stone-clad inner sanctum, where four wizards taught me how to move around and cast spells. Soon, bored of wizard school, I wandered out of the castle and down to the local village, to take my place among 30-odd players seated in loose groups around the village well. Compared to all the jet lag and stress of my journey, it was a moment of ease. With my translator's help, I struck up a conversation with another wizard who, he explained, had recently proposed inside Lineage II to his real-world girlfriend. He showed me the hills around the town. My internal river of self-doubt quietened, was calmed, ran dry.

After half an hour watching me watch the players watch their PC screens, my translator made her polite goodbyes. With nowhere else to go, I stayed. The conversation inside Lineage II was in Korean – still, I waved, and they waved back. I wandered outside the village, cast a few spells, killed some wolves, delivered some letters for other players. For a while, I sat by the edge of the sea, under a waterfall. When I looked up from my screen, four hours had passed. It was 2 a.m. I blinked. Around me, lit by the glow from the monitor screens, were all the same faces.

Now, at this early hour, their virtual adventures seemed to take on a darker edge. The landscape seemed to be a territory of nostalgia, not of optimism. Like fantasy fiction, the game seemed to declare a longing to regress. The players yearned for a return to simpler times, when people fought each other with swords instead of property.

Perhaps the players were pioneers, but they were stunted pioneers. In the game, you cannot die. When an orc slays you, for instance, you are reborn, fully clothed and fully formed. Without the possibility of failure, there is no growth. We remain as we are: entranced.

On my way back through Coex Plaza, searching among the stores for a late-night film, I passed the television station OnGameNet just as their offices were closing. The victorious games players – the people the fans projected their hopes onto – pushed their way through the crowd. Fans screamed and snapped their cameras.

'Life is pain,' wrote William Goldman. 'Anyone telling you different is selling something.' Through the electronic looking glass – inside the TV – the opposite seems true. Life is never what we expect; the games always deliver. The point of life is rarely certain; in the game, your goals are always clear. In life, we risk everything; in the games, we risk nothing at all.

I thought about what Kyu Nam Choi had said: real life doesn't often live up to our expectations, but in the game, anything can happen.

The power of this alchemical transformation, of awkward life transmuting into a coherent and plausible dream, has brought virtual worlds into the heart of modern Korean culture. In 2002, a Seoul primary school burned down with the kids inside. In response, a charity was formed. They commissioned a virtual world as a memorial. Grieving parents could wander in a small, peaceful city in memory of their kids. It was a tiny and particular heaven, devoid of crowds, traffic, and loss.

The mania for virtual worlds began in South Korea, but soon spread across South East Asia. In Thailand in 2004, a surge in subscriptions to another fantasy world, Ragnarok Online – then that country's second largest virtual world, with well over 2 million subscribers – led the Thai government to implement a temporary Internet cafe curfew. At the time of writing the same virtual world boasts 1.5 million residents in the Philippines alone. In June 2005, World of Warcraft launched in China. Timed with the launch, the game featured in a TV advert for Coca-Cola. Within a month, that virtual world had 1.5 million Chinese residents – then almost half of the total World of Warcraft population. That month, the first Chinese Internet addiction clinic opened, and a month later, the Chinese government introduced an 'anti-online game addiction system', to protect virtual residents against mental and physical harm from leaving their bodies behind for too long. Every local Internet company would have to sign up to a code of conduct to limit their customers' time inside virtual worlds – after three hours of consecutive play, a resident began to lose virtual experience; if they played for five hours straight, their virtual self was reset – they would have to wait five hours before they could continue. (A year later, one in seven Chinese gamers admitted to opening extra accounts to get around the limits.) Even with the limitations, the Chinese government estimates 24 million Chinese people log on to virtual worlds – as many as the rest of the world combined. If you include more basic, web-based online worlds, these numbers expand hugely. One such world, Westward Journey Online II, based on a famous Chinese novel, claims 83 million registered residents.

The inevitable crime, too, had begun to spread across Asia. In September 2005, a Chinese exchange student living in Kagawa prefecture, southern Japan, designed and programmed an automated virtual character, a criminal virtual robot, which logged onto Lineage II, and played for him. His robot self automatically attacked and robbed passers-by for the priciest of their virtual possessions – rare items like the Earring of Wisdom or the Shield of Nightmare, which conferred special virtual abilities on their owners – which the student then sold on a Japanese auction site for real yen. He was arrested by the Japanese police, although no virtual charges were brought against the virtual robot. In November 2006, 23-year-old Chinese student Wang Yue Si was arrested in Japan for selling virtual weapons and currency online since the previous April, earning real-world income in contravention of his student visa. (Police estimated his earnings at ¥150 million – about $1.3 million.)

In China, one player of a Chinese-made virtual world, Dahua Xiyou II – inspired by a traditional Chinese fairy tale – managed to obtain a temp job at the game's developer, NetEase. By faxing forged ID cards and resetting passwords, he obtained control of over 30 accounts, which he plundered for items and gold in exchange for real money – a total of around 4,000 yuan (£260). Yan Yifan, of Guangdong in southern China, was caught and convicted. He appealed, by arguing the items weren't real, and therefore weren't covered by law. In March 2006, the court found that the players he stole virtual items from had invested time, energy and money to gain them, and that Yan Yifan had profited in real terms, and therefore the virtual items did deserve legal protection. They upheld his fine of 5,000 yuan (about £360). In another case, two ex-employees of Shanda, the company which developed Legend of Mir II, were tried for copying and selling virtual items for a profit of 2 million yuan ($250,000).

In Asia, as I had discovered, the consequences of virtual crime weren't always only financial. In February 2005, Qiu Chengwei, a 41-year-old man from Shanghai, loaned his 26-year-old friend Zhu Caoyan a hard-won virtual sword, a dragon sabre from an online fantasy game called Legends of Mir III, where hundreds of thousands of Chinese players gathered to fight monsters and earn virtual booty. Instead of returning the sword, Zhu sold it on to another player for 7,200 yuan – about £470. Qui Chengwei approached the police, but because the sword existed only inside the game, no law had been broken. So one morning a month later, in the real world, Mr Qui broke into Zhu's house. Zhu barely had time to put on his underwear before Qui stabbed him to death.

When questioned by police, Qui Chengwei confessed, and in June 2005, he was sentenced to death. The sentence was suspended, and Qui will now spend at least 15 years behind bars.

But the tales of virtual mania tempting South East Asians into crime were only part of the story. In other ways, the facility of virtual worlds to connect us had also started to take root. I read reports of Chinese dissidents who had begun to congregate in far-flung corners of the Chinese World of Warcraft. There, among the more remote digital hills, where their conversations would be difficult for their government to monitor, gnomes, dwarves, and elves had begun to gather, to discuss democracy. It took the Chinese government two years to catch on, but in December 2006 it announced it would be monitoring virtual worlds more closely, after it discovered some worlds were carrying 'anti-government messages'.

On our last night in Seoul, to make up for the disappointment of the trip, I decided my girlfriend needed a treat. My translator told me Seoul's five-star Park Royal Hyatt hotel was running a half-price deal for local residents; to make sure we got the discount, she called to make the booking for me.

In the lobby, a grand cube of gold and indigo, a jazz singer sang 'Let's Stay Alive,' 'Brighter Days', and 'Breaking Up is Hard to Do'. At the check-in desk, though, they weren't happy with our reservation. They didn't believe we lived in Seoul, and it took half an hour to persuade them to give us the half-price rate. From then on, I was convinced, they tried their best to hustle back the difference. The staff served us snootily. The music was too loud. A small bottle of Perrier cost £4. On the next table, a spoilt British family nagged at one other incessantly. The place felt tacky, hassly and over-rich. I thought about logging on to play Lineage II, but Internet access – free in every other hotel – cost 50p per minute.

One way or another, we all find out. In life, Chinese sage Chuang Tzu wrote, we each have our hearts broken seven times. The Talmud said it differently: 'God is not nice. God is no uncle. He is an earthquake.' Virtual worlds, because they are a part of the real, must teach us that too. I found it out again, in an expensive Seoul hotel.

Life was hard, even at the Hyatt.

18

CONCLUSION
Back to life

When I began my journey, virtual worlds were largely ignored by the media. But Second Life, World of Warcraft and all the others soon took up their place in the global conversation about who we are and what we desire. 'Time gets compressed here,' Alayne Wartell had said, about how quickly her relationship progressed inside Second Life. In October 2002, I first set foot in EverQuest, the virtual world featured on Icons, a niche gaming show on the US gaming cable channel G4 TV – reported to be the least viewed cable channel in America. By October 2006, another virtual world, World of Warcraft, was the theme of an entire episode of a more popular TV show: the cartoon comedy South Park. The show, called Make Love Not Warcraft, was watched by 3.5 million viewers. The episode, inspired by cartoonist Trey Parker's observation that half his staff were World of Warcraft addicts, featured the series' cartoon cast becoming addicted to – and conquering – that virtual world. (In the show Blizzard, World of Warcraft's developers were flummoxed by how powerful – and how tragic – one South Park resident had become. 'How do you kill that which has no life?' one board member wondered.) The South Park trio of Stan, Kyle and

Cartman wandered among the world's huge population, which by that month had reached 7 million: twice their own viewership. ('I bet half these people are Korean,' Cartman says.) The addiction spread throughout South Park. Even normally strait-laced Kyle's dad succumbed. 'In the outside world, I am a simple geologist,' he said. 'But here, I am Falcor, Defender of the Alliance.' The cartoon even poked fun at the downsides of our new way to abandon our bodies. As the show's animated leads sat in front of their PCs and played World of Warcraft – their friends, mysteriously to them, still playing basketball outside in the sun – the trio trebled in weight.

Throughout 2006, a wave of press rose about virtual worlds, and especially Second Life. *Business Week* reported on Anshe Chung; the *Wall Street Journal* reported on the Tringo game's move to mobile phones. Driven partly by this wave of press, which focussed on the money to be made inside virtual worlds (consumption, after all, was a metaphor our society could easily grasp), businesses of all kinds – journalists, venture capitalist organisations, documentary makers and multinational entertainment corporations – rushed to dip their toes into our new virtual waters. The charities Fight Hunger and Comic Relief both planned to hold fund- and awareness-raising events in Second Life. Another charity, the World Development Movement, had built a house-sized billboard counting preventable child deaths since Second Life had opened, under the slogan, 'Don't forget the real world'. Harvard, the University of Texas and UC at Berkeley had constructed virtual lecture halls. In World of Warcraft, academics had begun to attend virtual symposia: whole gangs of trolls and night elves gathered in virtual wooden shacks to split hairs. In October 2006, Endemol, the production company behind the seminal reality TV show Big Brother, announced they planned to film a virtual Big Brother, with a virtual glass-walled house, inside Second Life. In the virtual version, as with the real show, residents would be forced to remain inside the confines of the Big Brother house, and face a weekly popular vote for eviction.

Across the board, the stakes were rising. As of October 2006, at IGE.com, you could still buy accounts on EverQuest, the first virtual world to capture our imagination, for over $2,000. (That much would buy you a level 75 Necromancer, 'from the original owner!') Economists revised their revenue projections: in 2006, virtual worlds were set to earn their creators over $5.2 billion. When I visited Linden Lab in March 2005, around 20 people made over $20,000 dollars a year from their virtual lives; by September 2006 there were around 500. But those making money were in the minority. That same month, just 10,267 Second Life residents made a virtual profit at all, and the majority of those earned less than $10 a month. Still, the promise of a virtual fortune – what looked to be easy money – continued to captivate new residents. After all, there was *some* money to be made. Second Life annual GDP was now $64 million. Everybody wanted a piece. Friends I assumed would never hear of these new places asked me how they could earn money inside Second Life. Back in August 2003, to protest in-world taxation, a group of Second Life residents had marched in-world, built replica tea crates, and set themselves on virtual fire. Next time, they might have to march on the real Capitol Hill: in October 2006, a US congressional committee began to investigate how virtual assets should be taxed. This was perhaps the first step to removing one of the main reasons to emigrate from the real into the virtual in the first place.

Mark Warner, once governor of Virginia and rumoured possible Democratic nomination for the 2008 US elections, appeared for a talk inside Second Life. (He later announced he wouldn't run for President.) In the eyes of big business, technology, communication and profit were already merging into one. The finance pages of newspapers were full of digital distractions: Sony's new PS3, the Nintendo Wii, Microsoft's iPod-competing Zune music player. For years, advertisers had taught us to seek comfort in machines, and now entertainment machines, designed to replace the real world with something more comforting, had become corporate battlegrounds, where money and power competed both for our cash and for our desires. I heard rumours IBM was considering buying Linden Lab. British newspapers like the *Guardian* published Second Life stories at the rate of sometimes two a day, and a Guardian technology editor, Vic Keegan – who had edited some of my own early journalism – published his new poetry collection, *Big Bang*, exclusively inside Second Life.

As I drew to the end of my journey into virtual worlds, the worlds themselves picked up pace. When I visited Linden Lab and Wilde, in March 2005, Second Life had 700 servers and 25,000 residents; in January 2006, it welcomed its 100,000th resident. When I first met Philip Rosdedale, he had told me, 'I don't know why we don't have a million residents in Second Life.' Then, on 18 October 2006 at 8:05:45 a.m. – around the same time the population of the US reached 300 million – the millionth resident entered Second Life. That was a tenfold increase since January – and the same day another 30,000 signed up. In a celebratory email, Linden Lab apologised for how crowded their Orientation Island had become. Within a week, another 100,000 had joined, and two weeks later, there were 1.2 million Second Life residents. That virtual world now had twice the population of Boston. Along with the huge numbers, there was renewed discussion of what those numbers meant. Of the total number, less than half had logged into Second Life in the last two months, and Philip Rosedale admitted as few as 10 per cent of first-time Second Life residents stayed to build a virtual life. There weren't a million real-world people playing Second

Life regularly, but the world was unarguably growing. There were now 2,006 privately owned islands, and 52,463 acres of rented virtual land; in total, the Second Life soil was now three times the size of Manhattan. In late November, Anshe Chung Studios issued a press release: Anshe's Second Life property and virtual cash holdings, not including her company's real-world assets – which she had parlayed from a $10 Second Life account – now had a total worth in excess of $1 million. Anshe was the first virtual millionaire.

Anshe called a virtual press conference. The venue had been built by the Anshe Chung Studios team in Wuhan, in the style of a traditional Chinese palace: silk partition screens, bamboo-print silk lampshades, a faded pink and yellow flowered rug, and virtual white china cups placed hospitably by every chair. At a long desk on the stage, complete with theatrical microphones, sat Anshe and her husband Guni, a pointy-eared elfin man with flowing brown hair.

Before Anshe spoke, I turned my head to look at the virtual crowd. There were many faces I recognised: the *Second Life Herald* owner Urizenus Sklar – who in real life, I knew, was Peter Ludlow, Professor of Philosophy and Linguistics at the University of Michigan, the man who had first exposed under-age The Sims Online escort Evangeline's exploits to the world. Also there, in a smart brown suit, was Adam Reuters, who mimed scribbling in a virtual notepad the whole time. There were a handful of residents with identical clothes and faces: reporters who had joined Second Life that day, to attend the conference, still in their default clothes. Catherine Smith was there too, as her virtual self, Catherine Linden, with a bright red bob and tortoiseshell glasses. Also in attendance, it seemed, was Wonder Woman, and for a while a humanised fox danced in the aisle.

Not long before, Anshe told us, she had ploughed back a large portion of her virtual profits to extend her empire. 'Before November 15th I used profits from this business and made one big investment of $250,000 US to expand Dreamland, our largest residential project. I think this might have been the largest investment in virtual real estate,' Anshe said. The million figure, she told us, 'is the net value of me, Anshe Chung, as resident of one virtual world. It is all assets that are inside Second Life. It is not money that my creator, Ailin, has put on her bank account.' (Throughout the conference, Anshe referred to Ailin as 'my creator', and in fact she requested those present focus their reporting on Anshe, the virtual self, rather than Ailin, the real person.) Anshe thought she had probably made more than a million dollars worth of virtual assets much earlier in the year, but she announced it now as her virtual land assets alone, at that day's market prices, were worth over a million. Also, she said, she thought someone soon would have announced the same, even if it wasn't true, just to get the press attention. 'I predict that in 12 months there will be at least 10, probably more, real-life millionaires in Second Life,' she said.

In a previous interview, Anshe had said her move to China had been a relief; she could work with a government that better understood the virtual economy. I asked her to elaborate. 'The situation is simple: in China there is a *huge* industry of companies that work in virtual worlds,' she said, 'usually game worlds. This of course makes the administration take this much more serious and have developed special laws and procedures. In Germany the administration is not so very used to this. They just treat you as whatever they classify you as. Basically, not being alone when it come to virtual profits helps.' Anshe paid real-world taxes on any virtual earnings she took out of Second Life. She wasn't averse to in-world taxation, either. 'I am more concerned about taxes being done wrong than about taxes in principle,' she said.

Anshe, too, had experienced a difficult virtual birth 'The hardest part was that when I started to become successful, I met one long established elite of business people who were here longer,' she said. 'This created some friction. I don't want to go into too many specifics. But at the time the business community transitioned from one very small community where people have arrangements and domains about who can serve which market, towards a more open cosmopolitan model. My philosophy was always centred on the customer and competitive: fair and open competition to create better and more affordable solutions.'

Despite the in-rush of corporate power into Second Life, Anshe believed there was room for new virtual entrepreneurs. 'There is still much opportunity for people who are innovative and creative,' she said. 'The nature of virtual economy is that it is hard to maintain margin when you do something that everybody does. You compete on global level. But when you are innovative you have even more opportunity than in real world.'

Like Linden Lab, Anshe hoped self-governance would emerge in virtual words. 'I hope we will soon see many governments in Second Life that people can choose from,' she said. She even believed those governments could act as examples for real-world countries. 'Ideologies could be tested in virtual worlds,' she said. 'Some might fail, some might work. I think it depends on the people who participate. Second Life has one very unique, very strong own culture and mentality. It is really like one foreign country.'

As the conference went on, people left their PCs, either out of boredom, or from the more mundane demands of their real bodies: a cup of coffee, a toilet-break. To indicate the real people behind them were away from their desks, their virtual selves – including Catherine Linden – slumped forward as if asleep. It was like a real press conference.

Prompted by this reminder of the real-world, I asked Anshe if she thought the exodus into virtual worlds reflected some rising difficulty – loneliness, dissatisfaction with the body, financial struggle – in the real world. 'Errol, imperfection in the real world always has existed,' she said. 'This is why people kept working hard to change the real world or to create things like literature or movies. I see virtual reality as one very powerful tool to enable people do things that they could never do in real life. For some of us this might mean flying or living in one villa. For IBM it might mean company meetings with people across the planet. For some it might mean just to lead one social life again, like some of my friends who are ill and cannot leave their bed.'

Anshe thought the exodus into virtual worlds might eventually attain legal status. 'People could be citizens of one virtual reality country and only tourists or visitors in RL [real-life] places,' she said. 'I mean, if you spend most time here, work here, earn your money here and so on and can move between real life countries at will, that might be theoretically possible. Of course, there are limits, because without reality, you die.

'I am still amazed that all this could happen,' Anshe said. 'I think Philip and the whole Linden team are big visionaries.'

Even Linden Lab, seemingly last in line for the virtual gold-rush, was nearly making money. After an investment of nearly $20 million, Philip Rosedale told me, they were heading for a profit. Second Life had been criticised for being opaque to virtual debutants. (One 'update message', shown to all residents when the Second Life software changed, included the unfathomable sentence, '* Added PARCEL_FLAG_RESTRICT_PUSH-OBJECT to llGetParcelFlags, and REGION_FLAG_RESTRICT_PUSHOBJECT to llGetRegionFlags()'. Another time I logged in and, because of a database error, my virtual self – along with thousands of others – had become a woman. Some days, it was difficult to log into the world at all.) Nonetheless, our need for a new place was strong enough to overcome these obstacles. By mid-November 2006, 1.5 million people had emigrated to Second Life. If the growth continued, the world would meet its 2 millionth resident sometime around New Year's Eve. (In fact, they reached that point two weeks early.)

In November 2006, a British man was jailed for a real-world assault after an online argument – on a web-page, but it didn't seem like it would be long before the UK saw its first real assault linked to virtual worlds. The drama among virtual residents hadn't faded, either. Each week, a new development inside the virtual world sent ripples through the community. Linden Lab had tightened its disciplinary procedure (they now held any accounts reported for abuse until they could verify that resident's real-world identity), but global attacks continued, including one with a series of self-copying gold rings which crashed the grid again. As of November 2006, the latest hot topic was an object called a 'CopyBot', effectively a copy gun that could duplicate any Second Life object. People armed with a CopyBot were strolling into virtual shops and taking copies of all the available merchandise for free. Nimrod Yaffle, the resident who had previously been banished to the cornfield, was spotted wandering the sandbox building area copying everything in sight. In an odd synchronicity, at the same time in the real world, Bath University's Adrian Bower announced a real-world CopyBot: a fridge-sized 'self-replicating rapid prototyper', which forged objects from downloadable designs. The machine had already made a belt buckle, an architectural model, and one of its own parts. Michael Hart, founder of the free online library Project Gutenberg, predicted a future where the virtual and the real drew closer together; when consumers would download objects – a pizza, a Ferrari – like they downloaded books from his website.

In the virtual world, the CopyBot could even copy virtual

selves; both Philip Linden (who told me he'd seen it coming) and Adam Reuters were hit, and found themselves face to face with their virtual doppelgängers. Across Second Life, virtual shop owners, faced with the threat of an end to virtual income, waged war. They built objects to block off CopyBot vending machines, and in some cases, they surrounded those still using the device with placards that read, 'Shame!'. Many shops closed down to weather the storm, until Linden Lab could figure out how to handle the problem. (Interestingly, its first recommendation was a reminder that residents could use the DMCA – a real-world US copyright law – to force other residents to stop using their intellectual property without permission.) Once again, Second Life residents – each one armed with an opinion – hit the bulletin boards.

I began my journey with a visit to the real-world Boston, to meet Wilde, a group for whom the enchantment of virtual worlds was unequivocally a good thing. For a year, though, I had hardly heard from Wilde. For a month or so, after I visited, their blog – a chart of their yearning – continued to mark their plans for the future. ('I want to write to my peers that they have hope, inspiration, and direction,' Scott had written. 'I want to write to the non-disabled world to give them insight and knowledge, and to provoke them to action.') They wrote up a guide for others with cerebral palsy to help encourage them to explore virtual worlds. Then, they went quiet. Wilde seemed to have disappeared from the virtual world, shipwrecked back from their virtual island into the real. In October 2006, as my journey drew to a close, Wilde sent me a message via Second Life, which bounced to my email and was forwarded to my phone. 'Hi Tim! How are you?' they wrote. 'We hope you are fine. We think about you a lot. Have you lost anything recently? Ha-ha.'

I logged back into Second Life, and sent Wilde an instant

message. They were offline, but I knew the message would be forwarded to their email inbox. The next day they replied, and I logged on to meet them, on the shore of their virtual island. I had caught them in their female phase: waiting on the shore of their virtual island was a tall, tanned beauty, with long, plaited blonde hair, a layered red south-sea-island dress and black heels. Above their head, their virtual title now read: 'I'm Greedy & On A Roll'.

'Wilde! How are you?' I said.

'We are well. We are trying to be on more. Doreen Beasley is our driver at Wilde now.'

'In Second Life they call me heartNsoul,' Doreen typed.

A year before, June-Marie had left Evergreen, which explained their absence. Without their 'mascot', they'd had trouble getting online – 'No one to be our hands that was into it like we were' – although they did manage a visit around Christmas, the same time I'd logged in to see their virtual carol-singing snowmen. Another time, during a visit by June-Marie, they'd built a virtual baseball pitch, with their own heads pasted over the players.

But now Wilde were back in Second Life, and they already had plans. In their absence, they had drifted off the virtual radar – but they were gunning for a comeback. To bring people back to their island, they planned to build some gambling tables, and host games on Tuesdays and Fridays. In the real world, too, their routine was being threatened; the Evergreen Center had faced closure, but the management had found money to keep it open until June 2007, at least.

I told Wilde how important it had been for me to meet them. 'We are glad you still have us on your mind; we think of your visit often,' Wilde said.

Wilde may have faltered a few steps in their journey online, but their example had inspired many others to follow behind. There was now a handful of similar support groups. John Palmer, a practising Buddhist from Dorset, in the UK, had built 'Support for Healing', a virtual island, a haven of Zen gardens and waterfalls, where those suffering from depression could visit and share their burdens. Simon Stevens, a real-life consultant and activist for disabled people – who also had cerebral palsy himself – had set up a nightclub called 'Wheelies', which, he said, 'aims to make guests feel comfortable about disability as well as dancing and just plain having a good time.' When, on Simon's invitation, I visited his chequered-floor dance club for 'Turbo Tuesday', his virtual self, Simon Walsh, had huge red dragon wings and waved blue and red rave-style light-sticks. His avatar wore a virtual version of his real-world head padding, and there was a wheelchair still attached to his behind, although he was dancing on his feet. Above his head, his title read 'Proud Spaz'. He had applied for the virtual Big Brother, he told me, although he'd yet to hear if he would appear in the house.

The next day, he sent me a message: he had been selected, and he was now a virtual Big Brother resident. He and 14 other virtual housemates had to log in for at least eight hours a day, and they couldn't leave a specially constructed glass-walled virtual house. There would be no TV coverage, but visitors could pass by, rap on the virtual glass, and greet or taunt residents as they pleased. Later in the week, I dropped by to say 'Hi'. The houses were glass boxes connected by see-through tubes. It looked like a pet house, and in one box there was even a man-sized virtual hamster wheel. Simon walked up to the glass, then sat down in his wheelchair. In the real world, news agencies would try to sneak messages into the Big Brother house; in the virtual world, Simon told me, people kept finding ways to sneak their virtual selves into the house. As we spoke, a woman called PrincessNina Prefect sidled up and pushed her virtual cleavage against the glass. Then, it was time for me to log off. A week later, before I could visit him again, Simon left the virtual Big Brother house. He sent me a note explaining why. 'Firstly, there has been no real publicity of the show and even two weeks into the show, there had been no reporting from any mainstream media,' Simon said. 'I have made Big Brother history and nobody knows about it!

'Secondly, Big Brother has not been able to control the show and have left the residents to themselves without supervision or support.' Some mischievous visitors had set residents on fire. Simon explained the show had begun to impact his health, and the glass rooms had even crept into his dreams. Also, the virtual Big Brother was more risqué than the TV show. 'While I am not a coward to sexuality I felt stupid and naïve being an honest clean gay disabled man in a house of whores,' Simon told me. So, nine days after he had entered the house, Simon left. It was 24 hours before any of the staff noticed. Still, he had no regrets. 'When I read George Orwell's 1984, where the whole Big Brother concept comes from, I never accepted the ending,' he told me. 'I always believed if I had been put in Room 101, I would have survived. And now I have had an opportunity to test out my belief, and I think I did survive. I beat Big Brother!'

When I first met Wilde online, I had wondered what might happen were the technology to exist to connect them more directly to virtual worlds, without the awkward obstacle of the keyboard. Wilde had already made a big impact among Second Life residents, I knew. I wondered how much more forceful their energy would be if it were completely unleashed, if they were to bypass June-Marie's cajoling and enabling self; if they were connected directly to their virtual selves. The group had enthused about the possibility of such 'enabling' technology. Mary said she would like to be able to use her eyes to drive Second Life; Scott said he would like 'an interface with hooks and wires to my head so I can play from inside.'

340

Real-world technology was fast catching up with their hopes. Back in 2004, at the University of Pittsburgh, scientists had demonstrated a robotic arm controlled by the brain signals of a monkey, monitored via electrodes. In March 2006, at the Centrum der Büro-und Informationstechnik (Centre for Office and Information Technology) exposition show in Hanover, Germany, researchers from the Fraunhofer Institute in Berlin and the medical school of Berlin Humboldt University, unveiled a more specific version of Scott's dream. The 'Berlin Brain-Computer Interface' was an electrode-dotted shower-cap that enabled humans to type with their mind. Then, in July 2006, researchers at University College, London, successfully tested a helmet which measured brain activity, and could control a virtual self. After a swimming accident on holiday in Greece, Tom Schweiger, a 31-year-old Austrian man, was made paraplegic. Using University College's helmet, he explored a simple virtual world (a simulated 'cave' room, with sound and projected images) through goggles, by imagining moving his arms and legs. An electrode cap measured the EEG readings from the motor areas of his brain associated with arm and leg movement. 'At first it all felt strange, having the cap on and being asked to think about moving my feet,' he told the *Observer* newspaper, 'but gradually I felt as if I was in that world. At one point I completely forgot it was a virtual world and that I was part of this experiment.' Robert Leeb, a researcher at Graz University of Technology in Austria, planned to develop this technology to allow disabled people to control their wheelchairs through thought – but I thought Wilde would be much more excited by the idea of controlling their virtual self without restrictions.

Wilde's dream to enable the disabled has progressed into a technology that could influence all our lives – and bring a return of the body into virtual worlds. In November 2006, Australian engineers at the Commonwealth Scientific and Industrial

Research Organisation built a T-shirt that turned air guitar into real sound, by sensing hand movements and feeding them to a synthesiser. In the arms race between the three main games console manufacturers, Nintendo was gambling they could beat Microsoft and Sony with their new console feature: a controller with movement sensors, in a small white stick which could stand in as a sword, a golf club or anything the games designers could imagine. A Korean company had developed a wearable 'personal digital assistant', which, through what it called the 'Body Area Network', let users touch computing devices to interact with them; you could touch a printer to make a document, or touch another person to transfer a file. Even the dead could now remain connected. One Second Life resident offered, for a fee, to continue your virtual self's life after your real death; and, in the real world, cemetery stones had been designed which, through a satellite connection, linked the departed's resting place with memorials in other worlds beyond our own (a website, an online photo book, a place inside Second Life). Our first forays into a virtual world seemed to involve abandoning the body; now, the body – alive or dead – was making a comeback.

Once, at a party, a man told me he was insane. Not long before I left, he leaned close and said: 'I'm psychotic, you know. Yeah. I'm schizophrenic. I'm on drugs. I'm basically OK, except – I believe the universe is man-made.'

My eyes had widened, and I'd moved away. After a year inhabiting virtual worlds, though, I found myself relaxing into a similar feeling. Sometimes, as I walked through a shopping mall or cycled down the road, I felt a strange, sideways motion, a fault-slide in my vision. I could almost see the constructed, perfect, other world – the smooth solids and cluttered polygonal curves – emerge here and there behind the real. The schizophrenic I met had spoken truth in his delusion. In our urban environments, almost everything – the roads, the buildings, the concrete slabs under our feet – is already man-made, a constructed buffer against the wild earth. Virtual worlds only extend the real world's already psychedelic quality – literally, from 'psyche' and 'delos': the capacity to make ourselves visible.

On the hoarding of a building site in Hackney, near my real-world home for most of my virtual journey, graffiti read: 'Write your MySpace name here.' Over some months, I watched the list of names stretch from two to over 30. At first, to me, and to others I pointed the graffiti out to, this seemed nothing special; but that lack of surprise only shows how we have already begun to take our virtual spaces, and how they interact with the real, for granted. MySpace names become a way to connect in the real world. We can start up Google Earth, gaze through our monitors – or even into the screens of our mobile phones – and look down onto our selves, or even our pasts. As I write this, Google has released its latest Google Earth software, with historical maps of places, including my home town, London. The cocoon of intimacy that mobile telephones extend around us has expanded to include more than just other people's voices. We can zoom down in a satellite view and look onto the topography of our past.

Virtual worlds are not other universes; they are new continents, extensions – like the past and the present – of now. And, like Roger Rabbit escaping from his cartoon, virtual worlds had begun to crop up in our real spaces too.

In August 2005, I attended an event that was an augury of the ways our virtual and real lives might begin to interconnect. As part of the Game Developers Conference in San Francisco, Linden Lab threw a party at the downtown Varnish Art Gallery. At the same time, they built a 'Virtual Varnish', a recreation of the real-world gallery; people partied simultaneously in the real and virtual worlds. Then – the first time this had ever happened

– the two worlds joined. On the wall of the virtual club was a video feed from the real-world celebration; on the wall of the real-world club, a projector showed the virtual party. Each world gazed into the other.

Philip Rosedale was inside the virtual version, in his incarnation as Philip Linden. 'Coming to you live!' he announced, then sat down on a virtual couch and said very little – perhaps busy enjoying the real party instead. Philip had told me about his plans for the event. 'It will have this whole *Alice in Wonderland* quality. You're in the virtual and you're looking through the window to the real, and you're in the real and you're looking through a window to the virtual.' The idea had been a wonder; the reality was a confusion. The dialogue around me was a mess of crossed wires: 'Hi Philip!'; 'Maxx is dandruffing!'; 'Stand up Marcos!'; 'Yay!'. For some, the video played off-centre; others saw only half the picture, or the whole image reversed – and yet it was a thrill. There we were, in a virtual world, watching the real, and the real was watching us back. I waved, in a jerky motion that was reduced to a crawl by the overloaded servers. I was sure someone in San Francisco – the real San Francisco, which we could see on our screens – waved back.

It seems that soon we may be able to step through the virtual looking glass both ways; not just from the real into the virtual, but also from the virtual to the real. We already have 'alternate reality' games, like PerplexCity: a subscription service which immerses subscribers in a story, through emails, websites, text messages and real-world events, to bring them a near-virtual experience. Theme-park environments like MagiQuest in Myrtle Beach, South Carolina, use a blend of low-frequency radio and infrared to create a real environment that works like a game: point your wand at real things and they spring to life; you can cast virtual spells at real things. Our journey into virtual worlds so far has been about conquering geography, replacing it with something that more closely fits our desires. The whole initial purpose of virtual worlds was to ensure that where you were in the real world didn't matter. The next phase in the early growth of virtual worlds will re-integrate the real, to bring the two more closely into line.

In 1991, John Ellenby and his son Thomas were sailing off the coast of Mexico. It was night, and they were lost, and John Ellenby had a terrible sense of direction. They decided that what they needed was a compass, a GPS device and a pair of binoculars, all tied together; then they could point it at any landmark, and their new device would tell them what they could see. Fifteen years later, their company, GeoVector, in partnership with three Japanese cell phone firms, launched a version of their dream. At the time of writing, in Tokyo, you can point a GPS cellphone at a building, and your phone will tell you what that building is. Ask your phone for a nearby hotel, and it will lead you there. It can't be long until the range of information linked to a particular real-world place expands; we'll have access to what the hotel wants us to know, but also what previous residents have said.

When we can define our identities online, it seems, we start to be able to redefine ourselves offline too. Philip Linden had told me about one virtual resident, who used the virtual versatility of his second self to reshape his real-world body. Over the course of a year – spending 75 hours a week inside Second Life – he customised his virtual self piece-by-piece (refining his face, buying a virtual earring or tattoo), until he realised he could do the same with his real-world self. He spent the next year remodelling his real body the same way – losing weight a pound at a time, remaking his style one garment at a time – until he was as happy with his real body as he was with his avatar.

My own experience was the reverse. My virtual life felt liberating, but my real self was suffering as a consequence. I was already inclined to neglect my body, but, as I spent more and more time online, my gym membership lapsed. (The gym, another monetised corner of the world, cost £80 a month – 10 times as much as my virtual office.) I gave up my real-world office, and set up my laptop in the spare room. My virtual strolls felt liberating, but in actual fact, I spent more and more time not moving. I wasn't going to die in my chair, but my body did seem to be resenting my regular absences online. Perhaps I had just come to virtual worlds too soon. For me, virtual activity meant real-world inertia, but perhaps that wouldn't remain true for long.

Kyle Machulis, the man who invented teledildonics for Second Life sex, had built a modified exercise bike, so that by pedalling in the real world, he could move forward in the virtual world. Another World of Warcraft fanatic set up a treadmill by his PC, and ran while he played. (In case you wanted to go the other way, too, you could use your virtual character in EverQuest II to order a real-world pizza without leaving your chair.) In 2004, 25 years after Pac-Man first appeared on our home TV screens, researchers at the University of Singapore constructed a version of Pac-Man that takes place in a university campus; wearable wireless-networked backpacks and virtual reality goggles put real people in place of Pac-Man and the ghosts, and university pathways in place of the haunted hallways. The players saw both the real and the unreal worlds; instead of collecting virtual yellow dots, they collected real sugar jars. These are the very early signs of a collision between our world and the virtual, and very soon they might leave us unsure about which is more important. Soon, as the technology improves, we may be able to choose whether to see people as they want to be seen, or as we want to see them – seeing them as they are in the physical world may be the least revealing way to look. (Which might not be a bad thing, given how many pizzas EverQuest players might end up eating.)

As well as changing ourselves, virtual worlds have the capacity to change our urban landscape. Our communication technologies already mean more people can work away from their colleagues than ever before. Virtual worlds may well extend that trend: transported by these software engines into another place, our relationship with self and distance will continue to change. Just as warehouses for physical distribution have moved toward redundancy, so offices – places where we travel simply to come together – may become redundant spaces. We may see people living in our office buildings, glass-walled monoliths to the motion of capital, in the same way warehouses have been transformed into urban living spaces. My time in virtual worlds had led me to imagine a future where, in the affluent West, office blocks would become as redundant as the warehouses in London's docklands already were. We would perhaps shift into a two-tone life, with a local, physical existence, and a global, virtual one. Tele-working would be replaced by a kind of astral commuting – we would travel to meet others without leaving our chairs.

In November 2006, I called Philip Rosedale, to see how he was coping with the runaway success of his world. He told me he shared this vision, of a real world shaped by our virtual lives. 'It's already happening,' he said, of our exodus into virtual worlds. 'There's no question that that's going to happen, by the way, to work. Very rapidly. Given that urban centres like London and New York are based on a confluence of people, directed toward doing specific types of work like finance – they're over. The writing's on the wall. What's interesting will be how many people choose to live in New York or London when they no longer have to.'

In fact, Philip believed our exodus into virtual connection would go further: the real world, he told me, would fade into the background. 'All of our creative energy will be directed there. The futurist in me says that the real world will become like a museum very soon. It doesn't mean we won't go to places like New York – it's just that they will be like museums, where we've carefully preserved the memories of what they were like before. So it'll be fantastically cool to go to New York, but in the same way that it's cool to go see the Mayan ruins. Because the big buildings will still be there, but they'll be covered in dust. Because no one will bother too much with them any more.'

Paradoxically, although virtual worlds seem to threaten a dead-end of physical isolation, this capacity to conquer distance without travel may help save us.

In most European languages, the words for time, work, and distance all share common roots. In virtual worlds, the software engine – so named because it does the work of calculating and displaying the 3D world – also transports us. (Young men still tinker with engines, but of a different kind: the car in the driveway has been replaced by the PC in the bedroom.) It is no surprise, then, that virtual worlds have the capacity to transform our ideas about travel. One of the first things people do when they enter Second Life is buy a new vehicle: an airplane, a parachute, a spaceship, a jetpack, a UFO. But then, they leave the vehicles behind and grow wings. In Second Life, I owned a Ferrari, but I kept it in my pocket. If I wanted to travel, flying was faster – and if I needed a mechanical boost, I would put on a jetpack. In most virtual worlds I visited, you could travel simply by tele-porting yourself; traditional modes of transport were redundant. That didn't stop our real-world car manufacturers from trying to persuade us otherwise. Toyota was the first car manufacturer to make a real-world model, their people carrier Scion B, inside

Second Life. They originally planned to give the car away but, afraid to alienate existing virtual car dealerships, they charged the equivalent of $2 per Scion. In September, Audi premiered a new TV spot inside Second Life, and in October 2006, General Motors, who 80 years earlier had bought up streetcar lines, bought 16 Second Life islands – 256 acres – to help extend their brands into cyberspace. A month later, Nissan built a four-car-high virtual car store, modelled on a soft-drink vending machine. Despite their efforts, and those of other car manufacturers, I saw no-one drive the virtual cars. In fact, as my life in virtual worlds developed, even my own real car began to seem outdated. As I made my way around the city, I carried along with me, in the shape of my car, a ton of glass and metal. It seemed a waste.

My virtual life reduced the time I spent in real-world travel. After overcoming their scoffing (and especially after reading about the money to be made) my real friends logged on; they came to hang out, watch virtual TV in my virtual apartment. Our virtual footprints reduced our real-world carbon footprint; by travelling to see them without moving, I was, in a small way, helping to reduce the strain on the lungs of the world.

James Lovelock, the environmental biologist who coined the term 'Gaia' for the earth's living ecosphere, has suggested virtual worlds might be part of the solution to global climate change. In his book, *The Revenge of Gaia*, Lovelock suggests virtual worlds may become an integral part of a more sustainable future, and an unconscious migration to low-energy activities. The figures are indisputable. A thousand-square-foot retail outlet in the real world uses around 280 kilowatt hours of electricity each week; the server technology behind an island-sized virtual outlet – set over 16 acres – uses the same amount of energy in a year. When I travelled to Boston to visit Wilde, my air flight produced nearly a million grams of carbon pollution for my seat alone – equivalent to running a car for two and a half years. When I travelled to meet Wilde in Second Life, I produced almost no carbon pollution – equivalent to leaving my fridge open for five minutes. If, as it seems, we face a new global challenge, the worldwide analogue to the challenge of managing our own unhappiness – the management of the health of the earth – then perhaps virtual worlds can help. As well as the possibility of continued neglect of the real, they also contain the hope that we can save ourselves. If we do end up in a future where oil is scarce we may have already discovered a different, more efficient means to conquer distance: to project our selves, but leave our bodies behind.

All this thought about bodies reminded me of Second Life's mafia boss, Jeremy Chase. I had emailed Tommy Fitzsimmons, the target of my 'hit', to come clean about the job, and to see if we could arrange a set-up for Marsellus in turn – who, it now seemed, had taken my money and run. I'd found out more about Fatal1ty, the player who Jeremy Chase claimed to be as famous as: he was the world's most successful Quake player, Jonathan Wendel, who made his name in international video games tournaments. Wendel had earned over $1 million in cash and prizes, plus sponsorship money, and had his own line in PC equipment. Well . . . Chase had at least earned a hundred bucks off me. I emailed Marsellus a few times to set up the double-cross. Each time, I was convinced he knew about the set-up. I emailed Tommy Fitzsimmons, who now believed I was working with him. I considered a double-cross, or a triple-cross, or something. Either way, they would both have to trust me. I had continued my mafia homework; now I felt like Donnie Brasco, undercover, infiltrating the family. Any badly told lie could break the whole story. In fact, Marsellus only half took the bait. After congratulating me for taking the initiative, his emails tailed off again. The meet never took place. Still, Tommy didn't think I'd given

350

anything away; I forwarded the emails I had sent Marsellus, and Tommy paid me the ultimate mafia accolade: I could have been a made man. 'You'd make it pretty good doing this type of stuff,' he told me.

Although Marsellus was evasive, I did finally catch up with Raymond Polonsky, Chase's more legitimate virtual self. He was branching out into designer jewellery, he told me. He'd kicked out almost every member of his virtual crime family. Plus, he said, Linden Lab had started clamping down on his virtual mafia. 'I got suspended for the first time ever,' Polonsky told me. 'No appeal. They wouldn't even return my emails asking for specifics.' Even some of Polonsky's friends turned their backs. 'I started getting the cold shoulder from regular associates of mine that are Linden Lab employees.'

Chase was still contorting to keep his legitimate characters separate from his mafia selves. I was asked to help set up a short interview about Second Life for NBC's *The Today Show*, and the presenter wanted to be a pirate. I scoured the virtual world, but couldn't find a parrot for his shoulder. I mentioned my dilemma to Polonsky, who sent me a parrot immediately. 'Handy knowing a mafia don,' I wrote back. 'What? Who do you mean?' Polonsky replied.

Noah Burn, the EverQuest forger, was also getting out of the life. For a while, he had come up with another virtual business also on the edge of the law. An EverQuest II resident, who had heard about his previous forgery exploits, had approached him with a new business idea. He'd found a small spot on a cliff-side in EverQuest II, where they could attack monsters, but the monsters couldn't reach to fight back. They could stand there all day, and earn experience at a far higher rate than normal. They began to charge other residents for earning experience for them; those residents would lend their account passwords to Noah and his business partners – like handing over their car keys for their virtual selves. Noah and his partners would stand on the ledge and fight all day, earning in three days the experience points most people would manage in a year. By working with three borrowed characters at a time, they earned about $1,000 a day, split between three of them. It worked, until one of Noah's partners – who he'd met only inside the virtual world of EverQuest II – gave in to temptation, and looted all the items from one of their borrowed virtual selves. 'There's no loyalty in virtual scams,' Noah told me. Sony customer service got involved, the thief spilled the beans, and the plan came to an end. Now, Noah said, he spent hardly any time in virtual worlds. 'The joy of killing a monster that takes 20 minutes to beat for the off-chance that you may get a few gold pieces has really lost its lustre once you've been on the other side,' he told me. He now ran a vinyl business, making car signs and stickers with a friend, and hoped to return to school for a creative writing degree.

Each individual I met had found something new in virtual worlds, something they lacked in the real world. It reminded me of Philip Rosedale, with his Star Trek sliding doors: frustrated by the limitations of the real, he'd headed off into virtual worlds of his own creation, confident he would find a better, easier, more flexible place.

Still, Second Life a remained awkward and obtuse. 'What's so great about Second Life, is that with all this attention, it still doesn't really work all that well yet,' Philip told me. 'And as we improve the technology, things like search, frame-rates, crash rates, and all that stuff – and as we improve that, good grief. You think it's growing now!' As the visual realism improved, as physical interfaces allowed us to bring our bodies, as well as our minds, into virtual worlds, how would things develop? What will happen when the technology catches up with our eyes and sense of motion? What will happen when virtual worlds were hard to distinguish from the real? How will we find our way home? I might meet you, and choose to see you as you are, or as you want to be seen, or as I want to see you. At that point, the only criteria for finding our way back to what we think of as reality would be: which of these worlds didn't we make? How healthy would that future be? Would we be in danger of forgetting our bodies completely?

For some, this abandonment was a hope, not a fear. 'Without reality, you die,' Anshe had said, but Philip Rosedale didn't quite agree. When we spoke in November 2006, after he talked excitedly of the next big Second Life audio innovation – residents would be able to talk to one another with their real voices, and the volume would rise and fall as you passed by – the conversation turned philosophical. Philip shared some of his science fiction inspired dreams. 'I think – and science backs this up – that Second Life has as much computational power as a human brain,' he said. He told me he envisioned a future, perhaps not too far away, where people could upload their entire minds into a global, networked machine.

Rosedale wasn't the only one to feel this way: that the mind can, in some circuitous way, conquer itself. For some people, the temptations of an entirely virtual life remain seductive. Towards the end of his life, the late LSD guru Timothy Leary began to dream about a new kind of digital immortality: he would upload his mind onto the Internet, conquer death through electronic storage. This movement, known as 'transhumanism', which has taken root through the work of Californian critics like Ray Kurzweil, seems a particularly American dream. The Americans, in whose time we all live, have the right to happiness enshrined in their constitution. And if you can't find happiness in this world, why not send yourself entirely into the next?

Philip explained he shared this belief, that we might eventually leave our bodies behind. 'There's a reasonable argument that we'll be able to,' he said. 'As you could probably imagine, we think a lot about the nature of the brain, and whether computational substrates can be dense enough to enable thinking within them. I can tell you that I'm quite sure the answer to that is yes. I know exactly how that's going to go down, I think. We're not there yet, obviously. The computational density of Second Life is not enough to support thinking. Although I should note at a side-point that the combined computational capacity of the aggregate Second Life grid, running 24 hours a day as it does now, is in excess, by almost any measure, of at least one human brain at this point. Second Life is dreaming. It could be looked at as one collective dream. In an almost neurological sense.'

To Philip, even the most powerful emotion, love, was a product of the mind. 'I mean, people kill themselves over love, all the time. And that is purely an artefact of the interaction between two minds.'

I put it to Philip that life and feeling had their roots, not in the mind, but in the body. He slipped the question with science-talk. 'As many modern thinkers would assert, and I would assert it at a neurological level, we are not localisable,' he said. 'Your body is a part of your memories as well. It is mutable, like a synapse; it's actually changeable. If, out of pleasure, I decide to work out, my body is changed – so your body is an extended aspect of your mind.'

I didn't agree. No one confuses the photograph with the camera, but some people confuse the mind with the self. Wilde's wisdom had come not from their minds, but from the struggles of their bodies. The dream of a digital mind seemed a particularly Californian kind of hubris. In Silicon Valley, where Philip Rosedale called home, a whole generation had grown to associate technology with money and power. To them, there was nothing technology could not conquer. Just as the Western world, brought to its success by the powers of the mind, has raised the mind above the body, so these technologically inspired Californians are susceptible to raising the machine over the self. The appeal was clear: a new kind of heaven, the promised perfection of virtual worlds taken to its logical extreme. Without a body at all, our minds would have nothing to hold them down: risen in a pure plane of computation, they would be solely under our control, outside the reach of even the gods. Then, everything will be easy, and there will be *no more death*. Although, if we did somehow make it, so would the W-Hats, and Marsellus Wallace. Trouble will follow us there too. We'd have to build a fourth life, to escape our third one. In either case, you can leave me out.

The dream of uploading our minds is yet another manifestation of the desire to leave our bodies, with their messy births and deaths, behind. If anything, our early experience in virtual worlds stresses the importance of the body; except for death, there is no way to leave the body permanently behind. But why were the people I met so afraid of death? Our end is shrouded in mystery. How can we answer that mystery without directly experiencing it for ourselves? What if Walt Whitman was right, and 'To die is different to what any one supposed, and luckier'?

'Soul is only the name of something in the body,' Nietzsche wrote; in *Also Sprach Zarathustra*. Nietzsche saw those who desired to leave their body behind as those who were 'angry with life and with the earth'; to him, the urge to transcend the body was the urge for death. 'Even in your folly and despising, you each serve your Self, you despisers of the body. I tell you, your very Self wants to die, and turn away from life.' It seemed to me that our new virtual journey, although led by the urge to leave ourselves behind, might hold lessons which, if we stood firm, might serve the cause of life.

On my visit to Linden Lab, I had given Philip a copy of my previous book, and, when we spoke again in November 2006,

I remarked on the similarities between the disciples of my mother's guru, and his employees – two groups of people out to make a better world; the new names, the logo pendants. (Except in Linden Lab's case the seventies mantra, 'Be here now', had been replaced with a new kind of remote presence: 'Be there now'.) To my surprise, Philip laughed. Before they settled on Second Life, he told me, Linden Lab had considered giving their new world a Hindu name. Inside Second Life, near their first Linden HQ, there was even a shrine to their ideals: a temple, with an inner sanctum of a slowly turning Second Life logo. In 2003, Rosedale first met James Currier, a dot-com entre-preneur who later became a Linden Lab investor. 'When he met me – this was in 2003, when we had 500 people inside Second Life – he said, "You know what? You know what you have to decide?" I said, "What's that, James?" and he said, "What colour are the robes going to be?"

'That was always his thing. That was what he said when he first saw it. He said, "This is a religion."'

I liked Philip. He'd forged a world I'd dwelled within. His world had given me a new name, and his dream was a good one – he wasn't preparing to poison hundreds with salmonella, like a small group of my mother's guru's disciples had done. Still, like all messiahs, he couldn't see the dark side of his dream. 'We always joke that it's like the *good* cult,' he told me.

'Take it from me – that's what they all think,' I said.

The scale of our virtual emigration is hard to gauge precisely. In 2004, when I began this book, our best estimates ranged from 25 to 30 million virtual residents worldwide. By the end of 2005, the Chinese government estimated there were 24 million virtual world residents in China alone. It's not hard to imagine that there may now be more than double that figure across the globe: greater than 50 million souls seeking a new kind of place. It seemed too early to precisely chart how this mass movement would influence our lives, but my instinct was that, as with literature and cinema, we would integrate virtual worlds into our culture. These new places would become another string to our bow, another sun against the cold, another way to connect. Mindful that, if anyone had the capacity to integrate virtual worlds healthily into our culture, it was the young, I called Todd, to catch up with his online life, and to arrange a visit to his home brew universe.

'Ah. Well, I have some news,' he said. A week before, he and his friends had heard about an FBI raid on the homes of the founding members of L2Extreme, the most popular private Lineage II server. NCsoft had apparently been monitoring the servers for over a year. Computers had been seized, and one member had been taken into custody.

At first, Todd and his friends had thought it was a scam, a way for the creators of L2Extreme to cut and run with their donated profits, but in November, NCsoft made an official announcement: 'FBI and NCsoft Close Down Computer Game Operation'.

'FBI Agents working in conjunction with officials from NCsoft's North American business successfully closed down a computer game operation alleged to be reaping profits by providing a fraudulent service to its players,' the announcement read. 'The operation was closed down after multiple raids and interviews were conducted in various cities from California to Virginia. NCsoft estimates that monetary losses and damages from the operation are costing NCsoft millions of dollars per year.'

Once again, real-world law enforcement had moved in on virtual worlds. I logged on to the L2Extreme website. The page had been redirected to show an FBI warning. 'This site has been seized by the Federal Bureau of Investigation. The unauthorized reproduction or distribution of copyrighted work is illegal. Criminal copyright infringement, including infringement without monetary gain, is investigated by the FBI and is punishable by up to five years in federal prison and a fine of $250,000.'

Todd and his friends' joy at their new-found freedom had turned into a fear of imprisonment. The night before I called, they had taken their virtual world offline.

In some ways, Todd told me, he was glad. Recent trouble with his exams had awakened him to the pressures of the real world. He had school to finish, and running a whole world had been taking up too much time. They'd divvied up their small earnings from donations, and a friend had bought Todd a legitimate Lineage II account, but Todd wasn't sure he would ever log on. In real life, he said, he was busy enough.

The more time, effort and money people invest in virtual worlds, the more they have to lose; but in the end, sometimes after many years of play, people do leave virtual worlds behind. Some, like Plastic Duck, are ejected; others simply choose to leave. They sell their virtual property for what they can get, sometimes sell their characters too – 'Good reputation, many friends', the advert for one Star Wars Galaxies character read – and they move back to their first lives. Sometimes these people feel empty; but sometimes people in this, real world, at the end of their lives, feel that way too.

When I began my journey into virtual worlds, the people addicted to them were stereotyped as loners. But the loneliest world, I discovered, is the real one. In June 2006, a study at the University of Arizona linked use of the Internet to a decline in close friendships. Between 1984 and 2004, the number of people who said they had no one to talk to about close matters had doubled, and the average number of close friends had fallen from three to two. 'I think behaviour online is more supportive than in real life,' Philip Rosedale has said; and in other ways, the figures backed him up too. A 2002 study showed the reverse:

that using the Internet had positive effects on communication, social involvement and well-being.

I would leave virtual worlds behind too – or at least, spend less time in them, use them as a place to meet, not as a place to live. Perhaps I would take a keepsake back with me: for $75, plus $8 shipping, a Second Life resident called 'Hal9k Andalso' would craft a five-inch-high real statuette of your virtual self. On the website, I noticed, John Lester had ordered one.

In virtual worlds you can do anything; nothing puts up too much of a fight. Virtual worlds expand our sense of what is possible, but the ease with which they give up their secrets does not always build the strength we need to put those possibilities into motion. This ease is so seductive, I had found, that it had led some kids to push themselves out of their bodies: some had unpeeled themselves, stepped out of their skin, and died in their attempt to enter the perfect world on the other side of the screen. The French culture ministry has designated video games as art; not everyone agrees. To critics like the *New Yorker*'s John Lahr, virtual worlds are 'a sign of the nihilistic times' – a demonstration of modern society's preference for motion over thought. But the story I found had other sides too.

Virtual worlds seemed to me simply an extension of the human gift and curse. We can imagine the world to be different, which is our strength – we can begin to journey from the imperfect present to a more perfect future – but it is also our weakness. The world we live in never measures up to our idea of heaven, which instils in us an insoluble yearning, what Tennessee Williams called 'that long-delayed but always expected something that we live for'. Virtual worlds are a new chart of an old affliction, the basic human wound: whatever it was that drove humanity away from the real world, and into our imagination.

*　　*　　*

On my journey, I had met a whole range of people who had travelled through the monitor screen into a looking glass world. There, for a time, they had found what they sought. For a while, in virtual worlds, the rocks under the surface disappeared. We had plain sailing. For the short while we played, our way was clear. I'd travelled with them to a temporary land of plenty, and I had discovered my own dream, too, which was that there's a way to hold trouble at bay. Well, it was nice while it lasted. In virtual worlds, as with all dreams, we can inhabit ease only for so long. Inevitably, our struggles re-emerge.

My troubles began to re-emerge, too. I was out of shape, unhealthy from too much time through the screen. I would renew my gym membership, I decided. I would give up smoking, too, and find a new, non-chemical way to manage my anxiety.

Dreams give us hope, to inform our waking life: but we have to be awake to make use of them.

Like our dreams – like all our stories – our new virtual worlds have something to teach us. And, like our dreams, we can only begin to put those lessons to use when we wake up and leave our dreams behind. When we go to sleep, and entrance ourselves with other possibilities, we escape momentarily from gravity and from friction. The people I had met had found a new way to dream, and some had tried to lose themselves in fantasy worlds completely. But, as in all fairy tales, only the disenchanted are free.

Walking is controlled falling. Without the pull of the Earth, and without the resistance of the ground, we would remain still. That's why, in our dreams, we can fly; and that's why, in our dreams, we find it hard to run. We need gravity, and friction, to move forward.

Finally, I received a reply from June-Marie, from a different email address. She had left Boston for California. She and Rob, her boyfriend, had broken up, and she had moved to LA, leaving her beloved posse behind. 'It was hard as hell to move away from Wilde,' she said, 'but we've managed to stay in pretty good touch, and I even flew out to see them the end of June. They still get to play at least twice a week, thanks to heartNsoul, my best friend in Boston. These days, rather than build stuff, they play games in-world and chat with friends. They can only do the things their "driver" is able to do – but at least she gets them in, which is really all that matters to them.'

June-Marie was now working with the mentally ill, at a social rehabilitation centre for people with schizophrenia and other severe mental disorders, to help them back into society. June-Marie already seemed as bonded in with their plight as she had been with Wilde's. 'I think one of the saddest things for me to see is the volume of abuse these folks have endured. I think if I had to endure what they have, then I'd be mentally ill too. But then, I've come to the conclusion that everyone is mentally ill from time to time.'

June-Marie and I tried to meet up again inside Second Life, but we never seemed to overlap. June-Marie had moved on, both in Second Life (the profile of her Second Life self, Lilone Sandgrain, now declared she was 'a member of RTG society of submissives and slaves') and in the real world. She had a new pet, a guinea pig called Sunflower, and a new name. June-Marie was now 'Sunshine'. 'I am called that more than my real name anymore,' she wrote. 'I guess it works, it at least gives me some-thing to aspire to be.' She shared her California home, close to the ocean, with a group of friends who had all met inside Second Life – a small-scale, virtually inspired commune. 'We are a family of sorts,' she wrote me, 'and very close.'

She signed off her email urging me to appreciate my own life. 'Enjoy your life, Tim. It's always shorter than we want!'

* * *

When I was nine years old, eager to leave the confines and struggles of the communal world I found myself in, my favourite thing to do – when I wasn't at the arcades with my father – was read Nicholas Fisk's *On the Flip Side*. The book's basic premise was that one day, out of the blue, people started to disappear. They packed their bags, closed their affairs, and then blinked out of existence. Animals, too, started to vanish – pet tortoises, squirrels, lions at the zoo; they all left, and made a discreet 'pop' as they went. As it became clear what was happening, people in the book started to discuss their departure plans: 'Are you ready to go?'; 'I'm thinking of leaving myself.' It was something like the Christian Rapture, except the decision to leave was entirely each person's own. And no one knew what lay on the other side. The idea gripped me. I too wanted to leave behind the heartache of this world, to abandon my troubles and vanish into some other, easier place. I willed it to happen to me. I blinked my eyes, frowned and concentrated furiously, but I couldn't seem to find the right thought or secret word that would send me through to the other side. I recently re-read *On the Flip Side*, and found the story just as powerful. The book seemed to me to tap into a basic human longing for some other, better place, where what we lack is suddenly plentiful.

In one way or another we all have this hope. The yearning to transcend, to reach up, to let go of our skins and find a new place without sorrow and loss. Virtual worlds have the capacity to promise that redemption, to entrance us, to make us forget ourselves until it's too late. They could encourage us to neglect the real, in favour of the virtual, until our lives – like Kyu Nam Choi's restaurant – slide into ruin. On the other hand, virtual worlds could provide something which is missing, a balm to our wound: a place to take our sad hearts other than the supermarket.